KIM PHILBY

KIM PHILBY

THE UNKNOWN STORY OF THE
KGB'S MASTER SPY

TIM MILNE
IAN INNES MILNE CMG OBE

WITH A FOREWORD BY PHILLIP KNIGHTLEY

Biteback Publishing

First published in Great Britain in 2014 by
Biteback Publishing Ltd
Westminster Tower
3 Albert Embankment
London SE1 7SP
Copyright © Ian Innes Milne 2014

ISBN 978-1-84954-699-7

10 9 8 7 6 5 4 3 2 1

A CIP catalogue record for this book is available from the British Library.

Set in Baskerville

Printed and bound in Great Britain by
CPI Group (UK) Ltd, Croydon CR0 4YY

MIX
Paper from
responsible sources
FSC
www.fsc.org   FSC® C020471

CONTENTS

Foreword by Phillip Knightley   vii

Acknowledgements   xi

List of Illustrations   xiii

Introduction   xv

1. The Public Schoolboy   1
2. New Frontiers   13
3. Change of Life   41
4. Own Trumpet   57
5. Section V   65
6. On the Map   93
7. Ryder Street and Broadway   123
8. Decline and Fall   159
9. Over and Out   181
10. 'The KGB Officer'   197
11. The Elite Force   223
12. Retrospect   239

Epilogue   249

Appendices   253

Source Notes   267

Index   279

'If in the end he still remains something of a mystery, we should not be surprised: for every human being is a mystery and nobody knows the truth about anybody else.' – *A. A. Milne*

FOREWORD

This memoir is the previously unknown story of the long friendship between Kim Philby and Ian Innes 'Tim' Milne,[1] an association which lasted for thirty-seven years, from the time they first met at Westminster School in September 1925 until Philby's defection to Moscow in January 1963. It is the only first-hand account of the Philby affair ever written from the inside by someone who served in the Secret Intelligence Service (SIS) and worked alongside the so-called KGB master spy. Philby's own book was of course written in Moscow under KGB supervision and is therefore suspect.

From Westminster Milne and Philby proceeded to different universities – Philby to Trinity, Cambridge and Milne to Christ Church, Oxford – but they travelled together in central Europe during university holidays and remained close.

Philby joined SIS in September 1941. Milne followed him some weeks later, recruited by Philby as his deputy and serving alongside him in Section V for most of the war years. Like Philby, Milne stayed on in SIS after the war and they remained professional colleagues as well as friends until Philby's dismissal from the service in 1951. Their friendship continued for a dozen years after this until Philby's flight from Beirut.

When the Philby story first broke and became a hot news item in 1967, largely as a result of a series of articles in the *Sunday Times* written by me and two colleagues which subsequently became a bestselling book,[2] Tim Milne was identified in print as being a close friend of Kim Philby, and although Milne was then still a serving officer in SIS, press interest in him became intense. I was working on the Insight team at the *Sunday Times* and the editor asked me to find Milne and try to persuade him to talk about his long association with Philby, particularly the holidays they had spent in Europe together. Was there a clue to be found there that explained Philby's treachery? Milne politely sent me on my way, pleading the restrictions of the Official Secrets Act. He retired from SIS in October 1968, continuing in government service for another seven years, but he never spoke publicly on the subject of his friendship with Philby, although in later years he was invariably courteous to the various authors who approached him for information.

Tim Milne died at the age of ninety-seven in 2010 and his obituary in *The Times*[3] stated in part that his 'feelings on learning of his old friend's sustained betrayal of his colleagues and his country can only be a matter of conjecture: he himself maintained great discretion on the subject for the rest of his life'. It was not widely known, outside his family and former service, that he had in fact written a very full and frank account of his association with Philby, nor that his memoir had been accepted for intended publication in 1979. However, before any such publication could happen, Milne was required to submit the manuscript to SIS and obtain their permission to publish, in view of the confidentiality obligations incumbent on him. In the event, permission was denied and Milne reluctantly had to abandon the project.

Free of these obligations today, Milne's daughter has now given permission for her father's memoir to be published, and this account of a friendship which lasted almost forty years and included a professional relationship for ten of those can now be related in full. Over the past forty-seven years, since the first articles on Philby were written, a considerable number of other articles, TV documentaries and drama treatments, as well as countless books, have appeared: none, however, have been written by someone who knew him as well, or for as long a period, as Tim Milne.

It comes as little surprise that this memoir is so elegantly and well written, given that Tim's father, Kenneth John Milne, was a contributor to *Punch* magazine and a close literary collaborator with his brother (Tim's uncle), Alan Alexander Milne, the author of the Winnie-the-Pooh books among others.[4] Tim's own inherited and natural writing excellence was also in demand after he left Oxford, as he worked for five years as a copywriter for a leading London advertising agency before war intervened.

Although Kim Philby's treachery was to cause Milne personal distress and considerable professional difficulties, he writes about his long association with Philby without any hint of rancour or bitterness. When I interviewed Philby in Moscow in 1988, he told me, 'I have always operated at two levels, a personal level and a political one. When the two have come into conflict I have had to put politics first. This conflict can be very painful. I don't like deceiving people, especially friends, and contrary to what others think, I feel very badly about it.'[5] Philby's widow said in an interview in 2003, 'To the end of his days he openly talked about how the hardest and most painful thing for him had been the fact that he had lied to his friends. Until the very end it is what tortured him most.'[6]

It is not known whether Milne knew of these statements, as undoubtedly he was one of the friends to whom Philby was referring. When the news came that Philby had died, in Moscow on 11 May 1988, Tim's daughter asked, 'I suppose you have mixed feelings?' Milne replied, 'No, for me he died many years ago.'

One recent author on the subject of Philby wrote, 'Many individuals exert a fascination over the public, but rarely has one individual held such a fascination for so many years for a country that they betrayed.'[7] The year 2013 marked the fiftieth anniversary of Philby's defection to Russia and twenty-five years since his death in Moscow: following these anniversaries, the publication of Tim Milne's full account of his close friendship and association with this most unusual man may now provide readers and historians alike with the closing chapter on the story of Kim Philby.

Phillip Knightley
January 2014

ACKNOWLEDGEMENTS

This book is dedicated to the memory of my parents. My father wrote his account in longhand, and my mother typed and retyped the manuscript many times. Though it is ostensibly my father's book, in reality it was a joint project which involved them both for several years. I know how very pleased they would have been to see the publication of this memoir, even so long afterwards.

Most, if not all, of my father's colleagues and contemporaries in SIS have now died, and Kim Philby himself died more than twenty-five years ago. However, this is one story which never seems to lose its fascination for many, despite the half-century which has passed since Philby's defection to Russia.

The final version of my father's manuscript was accepted for publication both in Britain and in America in 1979. I remember how disappointed and discouraged my father was when he was denied permission to publish. The manuscript was subsequently abandoned, and during his lifetime my father never revisited the possibility of publication.

Considerable thanks must now go to my collaborator, Richard Frost, who first encouraged me to proceed with this project, and then worked tirelessly on the editing and the source notes, before acting as intermediary between me and Biteback Publishing. Without Richard, it is certain that the typescript of this book would still be languishing in a ring binder, unseen.

I should also like to thank Phillip Knightley, who contacted me after my father's death to enquire whether a manuscript still existed, and if so whether he could read it to express an opinion on its suitability for publication today. I am very pleased that he has contributed the foreword to the book.

Finally, I must warmly thank my editor, Michael Smith, for all his advice and friendly help, Hayden Peake for his expert guidance, and the excellent team at Biteback, not least the copy-editor Jonathan Wadman, who is himself an 'Old Westminster'.

Catherine Milne
February 2014

LIST OF ILLUSTRATIONS

Images in the plate section are reproduced with kind permission of the following:

Page 1 top and bottom, page 2 bottom left and right, page 8 bottom left and right © Catherine Milne

Page 1 middle © Adelphi – The Latin Play, 1928. Reproduced with kind assistance of the Governing Body of Westminster School.

Page 6 top and page 7 top © Press Association

All other images are supplied from a private collection.

INTRODUCTION

Many books have appeared on Kim Philby, including the chief character's own account.[1] Much of the story has been laid bare. But from my long friendship with him I believed that, although I had no startling revelations to make, I could fill a few gaps in the published record and perhaps correct one or two misconceptions, as I saw them, and having now retired from government service I would like to contribute my recollections.

This is not a researched book. I have no documents or letters, and no access to unpublished material. It is many years since I had anything to do with intelligence work. I write from memory, jogged here and there by books and articles already published, though there must be many I have not read. On several points of wartime detail where my recollection differed from existing accounts I consulted former intelligence colleagues, long retired.

The original *Sunday Times* articles of 1967 published for the first time many of the basic facts about Philby's career. Although these articles caused some publicity difficulties for me at the time, I thought the *Sunday Times* helped to establish a valuable point of principle, which I fully support: provided its current and future work is not seriously handicapped, a secret service has no right to permanent immunity from public scrutiny and criticism; it cannot expect that faults and errors should be hushed up indefinitely.

In my own book, the first nine chapters (excluding Chapter 4, which is largely autobiographical) describe chronologically my acquaintance with Kim Philby from our first meeting in 1925 to our last in 1961. I have tried as far as possible not to duplicate what others have written, but to rely on my personal recollections. However, there were several periods of his life of which I knew little at first hand, notably Cambridge, the Spanish Civil War, Washington and Beirut; to the small extent I have touched on these I have usually drawn on other accounts. But for the most part I have described things as I saw them at the time, with occasional passages of hindsight. The period 1941–45 and the Iberian subsection of Section V of the Secret Service, in which he and I worked, are treated in some detail. I have freely discussed wartime intelligence matters, as have many others; but post-war intelligence, for the most part, is mentioned only in passing. Chapter 12, without pretending to be a deep analysis of Kim Philby, man and spy, offers some thoughts on his motives and personality.

I do not agree with several writers who have stated that Philby was essentially an ordinary man in an extraordinary situation; rather, I would say, he was an unusual man who sought and found an unusual situation. Nor, from what I saw of Kim and St John Philby, do I believe the theory of the domineering or dominant father.

I have tried to avoid either condemning or condoning what Kim did. This is not because I have no strong views, but because I am trying to write a factual account of what I knew of him. It would only confuse things if I were to hold a moral indignation meeting every few paragraphs. If the personal picture I have presented is friendlier than several others that have appeared, well, that is how I saw him.

Tim Milne

Author's note

The Soviet organisation which Philby joined in the 1930s had many titles before settling down in 1954 as the KGB. I have not attempted to follow these changes, which would merely confuse the reader, not to mention the author. Where the context requires, the term KGB should be considered to include its predecessors, and the term NKVD its successors; the intervening titles have not been used.

I have referred throughout to SIS, not MI6; and to MI5, not the Security Service.

THE PUBLIC SCHOOLBOY

September, 1925. A very small boy is happily trying to squash a bigger boy behind a cupboard door. Another small boy, me, is watching with some alarm.

That is my first memory of Kim Philby. An hour earlier I had been deposited at 3 Little Dean's Yard, one of the new batch of King's Scholars at Westminster School. Kim, although only six months older than me and still diminutive in his Etons,[1] was beginning his second year. The forty resident King's Scholars formed a separate house, called College, which in some ways was a kind of school within a school, with its own traditions, rules, clothes and vocabulary. The juniors, as scholars in their first year were called, had a fortnight to master these mysteries. During this time each junior was assigned to the care of a second-year scholar, who not only would be his mentor but would take the rap for any sins committed by his protégé. My own mentor was now ignominiously pinned behind the cupboard door, and I wondered – unjustly as it turned out – what good he would be to me if he could not manage this small pugnacious fellow with a stammer.

Kim was the only person in College, and almost in the entire school, that I had heard of before. Over a period of about a decade at the turn of the century, my father and his brother Alan, and Kim's father, St John Philby,[2] and his father's brother, had all been at Westminster, the first three in College. St John Philby had earlier been a pupil in the 1890s at a preparatory school of which my grandfather J. V. Milne was founder and headmaster. (In his autobiography,[3] he says, 'I cannot but feel that in J. V. Milne we enjoyed the guidance of one of the greatest educators of the period – certainly the greatest of all who crossed my path.') The two families had been acquainted, but had drifted apart. I had never previously met any of the Philbys but my father had told me to look out for Jack Philby's son.

Books and articles on Kim have made much of his public school background. Some accounts have implied that he was very much a product of the system and, that when suspicions of him arose, the system closed ranks and succeeded in protecting him for several years. In fact Westminster at this time, and particularly College, were not very typical of public school life, and Kim himself was highly untypical even of Westminster.

The school was not just in London, but in the very centre of London, closely linked with Westminster Abbey, which was our school chapel. (I must have attended between 1,200 and 1,500 services there in my time.) Two-thirds of the rather small complement of 360 pupils were day boys, and of the boarders (who included all the resident King's Scholars) most lived in or near London; Kim's house was in Acol Road, in West Hampstead. I myself, living in Somerset at the time, was one of the few boarders who could not go home at weekends. This was not a self-centred school, divorced from the outside world. It was also not one of the most successful schools, by the usual criteria of the time. We did not get many university scholarships, apart from our closed scholarships and exhibitions to Christ Church, Oxford and Trinity College, Cambridge. Unsurprisingly, with our small numbers and relative lack of playing fields on our doorstep, we were not too good at games. And socially we were not quite on a level with Eton, Harrow and one or two others.

But Westminster was an unusually humane and civilised place. There was room for a hundred flowers, if not to bloom, at least not to be trampled on. Eccentrics were prized, particularly if they made you laugh. In College, and perhaps in other houses, there was little or no bullying; the small boys tended to take advantage of this by taunting and tormenting the larger or older ones, as a puppy might an Alsatian. It was not a sin to be a dud at games, and there was in any case the alternative of the river; you can't be a dud at rowing. In College, administration and discipline were mainly in the hands of the monitors, who had the power to cane juniors and second-year boys – usually for trivial offences. The fear of being caned was real enough in my first two years, but I was caned only once, and I'm not sure that it happened to Kim at all. There were many rules and restrictions, but once you reached your third year most of them ceased to apply.

Some accounts have suggested that Kim had a bad time at school. I would say he had a rather easy life, particularly in his later years. He was never a popular figure, but neither was he unpopular. People accepted that he was something of a loner, who had erected barriers around himself, and were not disposed to ill-treat him or try to knock him into a different shape. There was little hint at this time of the convivial and gregarious Kim of the 1940s. He had something untouchable about him, a kind of inner strength and self-reliance that made others respect him. Nobody ever mocked him for his stammer. But between Kim and perhaps half a dozen people there was a strong mutual antipathy. This was notably true in the case of our housemaster, the Reverend Kenneth Luce. He did not have a lot to do with our daily routine – he came more into my life as a form master for two terms than as housemaster at any time – but he made a strong impression on us; whether it was of Christian dedication and moral fervour or of sanctimonious self-righteousness depended on your outlook. Once from my nearby cubicle I heard him trying to persuade Kim that he ought to be confirmed. Kim let him carry on for several minutes before revealing that he had never even been baptised. Luce, recovering, tried to shrug it off by saying that that could easily be arranged, but thereafter it seemed that he never pursued the subject with the same drive; perhaps he reckoned that he would have to convert the parents as well as the boy.

One account I have read describes the battle for Kim's soul in much more dramatic terms. Kim was 'badly mauled in the struggle' and later allegedly claimed to have suffered something like a nervous breakdown. I find this hard to accept. He seemed to have little difficulty in holding his position as one who was prepared (because he had no choice) to attend services, but not to go further than that. He certainly did not change his beliefs: he allowed that the prayer book had some value as a 'handbook of morality' but nothing more. Luce himself was a so-called Modern Churchman (he had been chaplain to Bishop Barnes of Birmingham), which in some people's eyes was halfway to agnosticism, and was perhaps inclined to take a less dogmatic view than other headmasters in Orders might have been.

Kim was not brilliant at school. No doubt he was handicapped at the start by his youth – he was only twelve and three-quarters when he entered in 1924 and might have done better to have waited another twelve months – and by ill health in his first year. Scholars were expected to pass School Certificate at the end of their first year, or their second at the latest, but Kim took three years to get over this hurdle. I have a school list from Lent term 1927 – his eighth – which shows him still in the Shell (the School Certificate form); he is placed fifteenth out of twenty-three boys, a little below a later Regius Professor of Medicine at Oxford but above a later Bishop of London. He had only two years left after School Certificate, but in those two years caught up rapidly.

College, although the smallest house and consisting entirely of King's Scholars, was rather good at games. Kim, while far from outstanding, was by no means a rabbit. If he had not abandoned games in his final year – an option available to a senior – he might have made a reasonable mark at soccer and cricket. He was a fair goalkeeper. At cricket he played in the school 2nd XI – I recall especially his bowling action: front facing, round arm, head and chin raised high as if he were peering over a wall, and with a distant air of meditation even at the moment of releasing the ball. He used to field on the offside. I wish I could report that his regular position there was third man, but I think he was more usually to be found at deep extra cover – itself appropriate in its way. Like many of us King's Scholars, he played a lot of Eton fives. The gymnastic prowess ascribed to him in one account has vanished entirely from my memory, but he was a keen boxer. I have documentary evidence – rare in this narrative – to show that he was in the team that boxed against Tonbridge School in March 1928, and was beaten. 'Philby got off with a thick ear, against Campbell, who was at least half a foot taller than himself. He was handicapped by a shorter reach than that of his opponent, and was on the defensive most of the time.' Kim was not often on the defensive, then or later.

Unlike practically everyone else in College, and indeed in the school, Kim never joined the Officers' Training Corps. Thereby he saved himself not only a good deal of trouble, but also the appalling discomfort of the uniform of those days, invariably known as 'the million' for some facetious reason to do with fleas. I am not sure why Kim stayed out of it. He can hardly have taken up a pacifist attitude at the age of twelve. Perhaps it was simply an offshoot of St John Philby's non-conformist philosophy. I, with one or two others, left the corps at the end of my third year for pacifist reasons, but I will not deny that a secondary motive was the alternative it gave me of playing fives on the two corps afternoons, Wednesday and Friday. Probably it was on those afternoons that Kim was to be found in the gymnasium.

He was prankishly inclined. One evening, in his 'box' or small partitioned-off study, he had the idea of baring the wires of his reading lamp, connecting them to drawing pins and inviting several of us to give ourselves mild shocks; why we were not electrocuted I do not understand. Later, during prep, there was an enormous blue flash from Kim's box. The lights went out all over College, and, or so we believed, over a large part of the City of Westminster as well. By the time the candles arrived, Kim had managed to conceal all evidence of his misdeeds, and the cause was duly diagnosed as a faulty reading lamp.

Kim had a considerable sense of humour, but in some ways a peculiar one. Much that others found funny he did not. He displayed more than a hint of *schadenfreude*, a characteristic that remained with him all the time I knew him. He derived a fairly harmless enjoyment from the discomfiture of others, and had a mocking tongue; but he was never one to bully the smaller or weaker – his targets were usually larger than himself.

Kim and I were not particularly close friends at school, until perhaps his last year. I do not know what drew us together. Neither of us was homosexual and there was never, now or later, the remotest sexual or physical attraction or even romantic attachment between us. We seemed to agree on few things. There was always considerable reserve, and one that persisted into afterlife. We did not even use Christian names until after he had married Lizy.[4] Surnames were more commonly used then than now among schoolboys and undergraduates, but even so, with everyone else I knew well it was first names.

Two things, however, formed an early meeting ground – an interest in professional soccer and cricket, and music. It was with Kim that I saw my first professional soccer match – Chelsea against Clapton Orient at Stamford Bridge. He was an Arsenal supporter, I a Chelsea one. At cricket we were both Surrey fans. Naturally we had our idols – mine was Gloucestershire's Wally Hammond, whom as early as 1924 I had seen make a superlative 174 on a bad wicket, an innings that remains with me yet – but for Kim, always individualist and unpredictable in his likes and dislikes, it was the Surrey professional Andrew Sandham, a highly solid and dependable batsman but hardly glamorous. By contrast, Kim also nursed a passion for Tallulah Bankhead, surpassed only by my infatuation for Janet Gaynor.

My musical education at Westminster (I was never a performer) came largely from Kim and another friend of mine, Jock Engleheart. Their tastes were almost diametrically opposed. Jock was a fine musician with such absolute pitch that if a choral piece were transposed a semitone to make it easier for the first tenors or second basses he found it quite difficult while singing from a score to check himself from reverting to the original key. He had two gods: Bach and Delius. Kim liked neither of these – Bach, he said, never developed, you couldn't tell early works from late – but it was from Kim's records that I first heard most of the standard classical symphonies, concertos, sonatas and chamber music, though little or no opera or choral or vocal works. In his last year he bought one of the best gramophones that those days could offer, with a huge specially designed horn, and spent his games-free afternoons buying, or more usually borrowing on approval, records from shops in the Charing Cross Road. His favourite work at the time was the César Franck symphony, and his favourite composer, then as later, Beethoven.

I said earlier that Kim was not a homosexual. I was amazed to read that, after leaving school, he apparently claimed that at Westminster he had 'buggered and been buggered'. I find it difficult to believe either that such incidents took place, or, even more, that he would ever have spoken of them in this way, or at all – Kim, who was so private that one never observed him using the lavatories, the doors of which had to be kept open; it was a lasting mystery how he performed his bodily functions at all. He was never at any time given to sexual boasting, confession or fantasy. Even in later life he seldom discussed his ordinary heterosexual relationships. Nor can I imagine who could have been the other party, or parties. There were plenty of romantic friendships at Westminster, but Kim appeared aloof from all such diversions. Moreover we had remarkably little privacy in College. Although in the dormitory we each slept in a separate cubicle, the curtain that formed the door ended two or three feet from the ground, and there were strict rules about not entering someone else's cubicle. There was nowhere to go for country walks, no haystack to retreat behind. It is true that anything could have happened at weekends, when boys who lived in London could go home. But homosexual relationships and romantic friendships at public schools are seldom totally secret for long, if at all; and Kim's name never came up in this connection. Perhaps I was simply naïve, and all sorts of things went on under my eyes that I never knew about. But unless strong evidence is produced, I shall continue to disbelieve the story.

Kim grew up very quickly in his last two years. By the final year he had become bored with everything the school had to offer, though he must have continued to work hard to get his close exhibition to Trinity, Cambridge. He was not made monitor – an honour, or chore, imposed annually on four out of the eight or nine seniors, i.e. scholars in their last year. Luce, who was responsible for making the selection, was notorious for excluding anyone of a strongly independent turn of mind. Forceful characters like John Winnifrith,[5] with a good academic and athletic record, were passed over. But to be fair I think any housemaster would by then have regarded Kim as too little concerned in College life to be eligible.

Kim's career at school does not bear out the theory sometimes put forward of a son under pressure to live up to the standards of an overdominant father. St John Philby had been captain of the school and for two years a member of the cricket XI. Kim was uninterested in trying to emulate either of these successes, nor did he give the impression of having turned his back on them because he know he would fall short of his father's achievement: it was merely that he thought he had better things to do. Kim's stammer has also been attributed to early fear of his father. But since thousands of children with a dominant parent *don't* stammer, it could hardly be the cause. In any case I do not believe that St John Philby did 'dominate' his son, certainly not by the time he reached Westminster. Kim at school was tough, self-reliant and self-confident. His father was abroad most of the time, and must have seen relatively little of his son.

St John Philby at this period was widely known as an Arabist of unorthodox views, though he had not yet made his celebrated crossing of the Rub' al Khali, the 'Empty Quarter' of Arabia. Kim showed no great interest in the Middle East, but admired his father's expert knowledge of Arabia and the Arabs, by comparison with what he saw as T. E. Lawrence's romanticism. I had chosen *Revolt in the Desert* (the shorter version of *Seven Pillars of Wisdom*, which had not yet been published) as a school prize and asked Kim what he thought of it. 'Well,' he said, 'I found the first sentence so magnificent that I never really managed to read the rest.' One small service rendered by Kim to his father during his schooldays is acknowledged in the introduction, dated August 1928, to one of St John Philby's best-known books, *Arabia of the Wahhabis*, later republished. Kim was responsible for a number of small line drawings – architectural elevations and the like – that appear in the book. Like everything he did on paper, they are neat and accurate.

What brought us together? I think it was partly the attraction of opposites – Kim the quiet rebel, me the rather conventional boy enthusiastically involved in school life. I began to be intrigued by someone who seemed to reject many of the things I automatically accepted, but who was not in the least a dropout. What he on his side saw in me I don't really know. Perhaps he found in me a useful sounding board for his developing views. Perhaps he simply liked me. Though he was not my closest friend at school, he was undoubtedly different from the others. I would have been surprised to learn that the friendship would last another third of a century; and astonished that one day I would be writing a book about it.

2

NEW FRONTIERS

Kim went to Trinity College, Cambridge, in the autumn of 1929, while I returned to Westminster for my final year. My father had died in May, after a long illness, and my family had left Somerset to return to the London area, though we did not have a proper home for another two years. Kim, unlike most of his school contemporaries, was not in the habit of revisiting Westminster once he had left it, but we met during the Christmas holidays of 1929–30 and made a tentative plan to travel on the Continent after the summer term was over. We did not meet in the Easter vacation of 1930 (he went to Hungary), and must have made the subsequent arrangements by letter, because the next time I saw him was at our rendezvous at Nancy in eastern France at the beginning of August. I recall, however, that before Kim left England my uncle, A. A. Milne, who had taken my family under his wing since my father's death, invited him to lunch so that he could vet his nephew's friend. Kim evidently passed the test.

This was the first of three Continental trips I made with Kim between August 1930 and April 1933. It has been suggested that his recruitment by the Soviet secret service might have taken place on one of these occasions, or at least preliminary contact made, which is why I am describing our travels in some detail.

I had not been abroad before and was extremely green. My mother, who never set foot outside Britain in all her long life and distrusted foreigners, thought to provide some measure of insulation for at least the first day by buying me a first-class ticket from Victoria to Nancy (the only time I can remember travelling first class by rail, sea or air, except at public expense). Thus I arrived in style, to the amusement of an unshaven Kim, who met me at the station.

The Cambridge term had of course ended some weeks earlier. Kim had bought an old motorcycle and sidecar and gone off to Budapest with a Trinity friend, Michael Stewart. Whether he distrusted my ability to get to Budapest under my own steam, or else thought I might like to see rather more of the Continent than the view from a train, I cannot remember, but he elected to leave Michael behind in Budapest and drive all the way back to France to fetch me. The bike broke down in the Black Forest and was left to be repaired while Kim came on to Nancy by train. He had been robbed of a camera and money by a German youth to whom he had given a lift, but was in good heart and we talked till long after midnight in the station restaurant before taking a train into Germany: hard class of course. There we picked up the bike and set off on our five-day journey eastwards, Kim driving and me in the sidecar.

It has been said that Kim first learnt to ride a motorcycle in Spain before going up to Cambridge, and boasted later to friends that he had reached speeds of eighty miles an hour. I don't believe this story, and it certainly could not have been on this machine. I think our highest speed on the entire trip was about thirty-five miles an hour, going downhill slightly out of control. People don't travel on motorcycles with sidecars nowadays, and fond though I became of the bike, I can see why. On the second day we had heavy rain which soaked not only ourselves but also our luggage. Most of Kim's stuff was probably in Budapest but I had on the pillion a suitcase which was henceforth a sorry thing, as were many of its contents. The further east we travelled the worse the roads became. According to the Baedeker guide of 1905, 'the roads of Austria-Hungary, on the whole, fall considerably short of the English standard, for the steamroller is unknown in that country'. By 1930 the steamroller had made its entry but it still had a lot to do. Somewhere in Austria our bike and sidecar began to lean ominously inwards towards one another. An Austrian garage did a rough patch-up job, and we managed to push on into Hungary and spend an exotic evening at Magyaróvár, all gypsy music and heavy red wine. But the next day the inward leaning was more pronounced than ever, and getting worse. After further attempts at garages, we decided to try a blacksmith. In the small town of Kisbér we found one who within an hour or two had hammered out and fitted a number of strong metal struts and bolts which not only restored each of us to a vertical position but were to last all the way back to England. We rattled into Budapest in fine style.

This first of my three journeys with Kim was a light-hearted juvenile affair. Kim and I were eighteen, Michael nineteen. The other two had found a luxurious (by our standards) room in Károly király utca,[1] complete with running water, almost unique in our various journeys. From this base we explored the city, walking the splendidly baroque Andrássy út, watching the fireworks rise above the ramparts of Buda, bathing in a swimming pool constructed in the flowing yellow Danube, lunching at a ridiculously cheap island restaurant where an orchestra most appropriately played the Franck symphony, buying hot Wiener schnitzel or goulash or *kukuruz* for a few pence from automatic machines, seeing Marlene Dietrich in *A kék angyal,* otherwise *The Blue Angel,* and meeting Hungarian friends whom Kim had got to know on his visit to Budapest in April. After several days of this we had to quit our room, which was booked for someone else. Our money was running low but we had no wish to leave Budapest. Fortunately among Kim's friends were two brothers named Szegedi-Szűts. The elder, István, was a film cartoonist (some of whose work I saw later at the Oxford Film Society). The younger, György, among other things owned a garage where a number of cars were kept; he suggested we should stay there for nothing, sleeping in whatever cars appeared the most comfortable. We followed this excellent plan for five days, living mainly on chocolate and crisp white rolls.

It was a good time. I am sure that Kim and Michael, with a year of Cambridge behind them, must have found me irritatingly schoolboyish, but they were generally tolerant. The only sinister character we met was a smooth rich Hungarian who got into conversation with us at the Danube pool. He took us out to a sumptuous dinner under the stars, followed by a trip on the river in his speedboat. His intentions turned out to be strictly dishonourable, but I fear he had no return at all for his outlay.

The time came for our journey back to England. Since the bike and sidecar seated only two, and since only Kim drove, Michael and I had to take it in turns to go by rail. It fell to Michael to take the train to Vienna, where we were to meet him at the Westbahnhof. Our rendezvous arrangements never made proper allowance for delay or mishap. As far as I can recall, Michael simply had to hang about the station until we turned up.

Kim and I had progressed only fifty miles from Budapest when, in the village of Bábolna, we broke down: a large nail through one of the tyres, and other troubles now forgotten. There was no hope of any help that day: the entire village was drunk, celebrating some unidentified occasion. We joined wholeheartedly in the celebrations, but afterwards had nowhere to sleep. A kindly and still fairly sober farmer or horse breeder offered us room in his stables; passing between the backsides of two long rows of horses, we sank gratefully into the straw of a small windowless barn at the end of the building, happily unaware of the rats. In the morning heads were clear, the sun shining and the bike soon repaired. Reasoning that as Michael had waited so long he would not mind waiting longer, we made a detour to Bratislava in Czechoslovakia, largely to buy *The Times* and find out what was happening in the final Test. It was late in the day when we reached Vienna.

From there we continued to Salzburg, Munich, Cologne, Liège, Brussels and finally Wissant, between Boulogne and Calais. We were not, I think, complete philistines. I remember our standing in Vienna in almost shocked silence before a Raphael Madonna, and listening in a Salzburg courtyard to Mozart. But generally the journey was uneventful. Somewhere in Austria we thought we would sleep in the open to save money, but were driven indoors by thick mist and dew. In the Rhineland, Kim had a letter from home saying that St John Philby had turned Moslem. Kim made light of it, but I suspect that he was a little distressed that – whether for political reasons or not – his father had renounced atheism or agnosticism or whatever had been his exact brand of scepticism.

We finished up at Wissant because Kim's mother, Dora, his

three young sisters, Diana, Patricia and Helena, aged about ten, eight and six, and a male cousin of Kim's age were staying there in what we regarded as a truly palatial hotel. Dora Philby, with her red hair and husky voice, was very attractive; much the best looking, I thought, of the mothers of my various friends. Kim moved into the hotel with the others, while Michael and I found a modest pension which gave us full board and lodging for five bob. We spent much of our time at the hotel, taking illicit baths and playing auction bridge with the Philby family. After four days I had to return to London to take part in a family celebration. There was no room inside the bus to Boulogne, so I sat on the roof rack with the luggage: a suitable finale to the whole enterprise.

So ended my first look at the outside world, and it enormously whetted my appetite for more – preferably in the company of Kim if possible. He was a marvellous travelling companion, intensely interested in everything and impervious to discomforts and setbacks. Also, although I think he never formally studied languages after doing School Certificate French, he was an excellent linguist. His German was already more than adequate and he had some Hungarian.

Kim's politics at this time, September 1930, were still somewhat vague – certainly left wing, but he had not yet acquired the knowledge of or interest in Marxism that marked his third and fourth year at Cambridge. Michael Stewart was seemingly more interested in art than politics. In later years I met him once or twice at Acol Road, but he was never an intimate of the Kim–Lizy or Kim–Aileen homes. After the war he had a distinguished career in the diplomatic service, became British ambassador in Athens and received a knighthood.

In October 1930 I went up to Christ Church, Oxford. It was

nearly two years before I managed to get abroad again with Kim. I saw relatively little of him during this period, but from time to time we watched cricket or football together. Occasionally we met at Lord's. Indeed a kind of coterie, including some Oxford friends of mine, would gather in the upper tier of seats by the sight-screen at the Nursery End. At times Kim's father turned up, sometimes in the company of Harold Hardy the Cambridge mathematician. On one memorable occasion St John Philby found himself sitting next to Bertram Thomas, who – to St John's intense disappointment – had beaten him by a year or two to the first crossing of the Rub' al Khali. I expected fireworks but instead the two conversed gravely and politely, like two old Arabs over a hubble-bubble.

I have no real recollection of Kim's father before the early 1930s. I never got to know him well but always liked him. In spite of his quarrelsome reputation he was invariably pleasant to me – perhaps more because he had known my grandfather, father and uncle than because I was a friend of Kim; unlike Kim, he looked back on his school and university days with great affection. He was small and stocky, with a beard – unusual for his generation – which gave him an air of distinction and made it easy to imagine him in Arab costume. Dora Philby has sometimes been pictured as a meek character whom St John treated as a doormat. No one who knew her could have thought of her in this way; and Elizabeth Monroe's very well-informed and documented study, *Philby of Arabia*,[2] makes clear what a resourceful and courageous woman she was and how much her husband depended on her. Kim was often rather contemptuous of his mother, but when he was in trouble in 1955, he turned to her rather than anyone else; nor did she let him down.

On such occasions as I saw father and son together, the relationship always seemed friendly, relaxed and adult. While Kim can have agreed with few of St John's political views, he respected his realism and outspokenness. He quoted to me something his father had said about India. One of the arguments then currently used against home rule was that only 10 per cent of Indians were literate. St John pointed out that 10 per cent of 400 million was forty million, about the same as the then population of Britain: why use forty million literate British to govern India instead of forty million literate Indians? For the life of me I could not see a flaw in this argument, as far as it went, and I'm not sure that I can today. Another of his father's remarks quoted by Kim was 'The Times has a profound distrust of the expert'. St John believed strongly in experts; he was one himself, and for all his pugnacity he recognised expertise in others. I think Kim inherited something of the same attitude.

In the long vacation of 1931, for family reasons, I stayed in England. Kim went off to Yugoslavia, in particular Bosnia. He had a strong attachment to the former Austro-Hungarian Empire – not of course its political system, but its lands and peoples. The most beautiful parts of Europe, he thought, were to be found within those old boundaries, and whenever he had the opportunity to travel he went there: in 1930 (twice), 1931 and 1932, not to mention his long stay in Vienna in 1933–34.

In the summer of 1932 we made our second trip. This was the most ambitious of the three. We planned to visit Yugoslavia, Albania and, if possible, Bulgaria. Kim had already left England, and I visited the Albanian consulate in London to seek a visa. The consulate turned out to be a small British solicitor's office in the City. Visas were no doubt filed somewhere between Torts and Wills. The Bulgarian visas had not yet reached London, but we had hopes of picking them up at the Bulgarian legation in Tirana. I left London in mid-July, and met Kim in Paris; where he had been in France, I cannot remember. We were going to have to do a lot of walking in the Balkans, as means of transport from one place to the next, and decided to get ourselves into condition in the Black Forest. We walked there in hilly country for three or four days, gradually lengthening the day's stint to something over twenty miles. Our plan was to go on to Munich for a day or two and then take the train to Venice. But a crucial general election was going on in Germany, and Kim, who was by now extremely interested in German politics, felt impelled to make a diversion to Berlin; he had a strong journalistic urge to be wherever things were happening, or might happen. We had already attended a rally in Stuttgart, where Alfred Hugenberg (of the far right) spoke. So we separated for a week: Kim to Berlin, I to Munich, where I spent the time trying to learn a little German and walking endlessly until I knew almost every street in the city. When I felt bored or lonely, I would go to Munich Hauptbahnhof and watch the expresses leave for exotic parts of Europe. Kim duly rejoined me. He was keeping a diary on this trip, but though I read the Berlin entries I do not recall anything of them. I do recall that he wrote, 'Milne has found lodgings that boast the prettiest housemaid in Munich.' This was news to me; but his views and mine on female attraction seldom agreed. Certainly she was a charming and friendly girl.

On the eve of the election we attended a vast Nazi torchlight rally at which Hitler spoke. Unlike Kim, I could not follow much of what was said, but that mattered little; he had said it all before, many times. What impressed and alarmed us was the totally uncritical attitude of so many perfectly ordinary German men and women. Our predominant feeling was contempt for the whole circus – the showmanship, the schoolchildren prancing round in gymnastic displays, the stupid petit-bourgeois citizens swallowing it all. Politically I think that at this stage we were more concerned over the threat to the left, even the moderate left, than to world peace. A day or two later we sat in a workers' café listening to the ominous election results on the radio: Nazi gains everywhere. The main left-wing parties had held their ground, but most of the small parties had been almost annihilated. Just how far Kim had moved towards communism or Marxism at this time I find it difficult to judge: my political education had a long way to go. According to his own story, his final conversion came in the early summer of 1933. Sitting in the Munich café, we applauded both Social Democrat and Communist victories.

Our fortnight in Germany, intended primarily as a loosener before we tackled the Balkans, must have left a deep impression on Kim, as it did on me. The Nazis were not yet in power, there were no concentration camps, Germany was still a free country; but we felt we had seen into the future.

We took a night train over the Brenner Pass, spent two or three hours in Verona, and reached Venice in the afternoon. This was not a Baedeker tour and we did no justice at all to Venice: our boat was leaving for Dubrovnik at 6.30 the next morning. We asked the proprietress of the *albergo* to call us at five. She forgot, but at five past five, for no discoverable reason, a brass band struck up outside our window and woke us: I have never been able to think entirely ill of Italy since.

So here we were in the Adriatic, two healthy undergraduates in good physical training, on a sunny August day of 1932. We had nothing with us but rucksacks. At least half the weight in mine consisted of books I was reading for greats – Plato, Aristotle, the Greek and Roman historians – and a heavy raincoat which I never wore. I had but two shirts – one on, one off – and no spare shoes: when my shoes wore out, as they did twice, we had to wait while they were repaired. No spare trousers, no medicines. I think Kim's outfit was much the same, except that he had a camera. For money each of us had merely a bank letter of credit, a single sheet of paper. With this I could walk into any bank in the Balkans, even in Albania, and draw two or three pounds' worth of local currency with no trouble at all. Optimistically we thought we might be able to use it on the boat during our thirty-six hours' voyage, and had come aboard with only a few lire. The pleasures of Adriatic travel began to pall when we found that the boat was not a bank, and we went to bed that evening – that is, dossed down on a wooden bench – extremely hungry.

Up at six the next morning, the day already hot, we were looking wistfully over the ship's rail at Diocletian's palace in Split, and wondering how to raise a meal, when we became aware that we were being watched with curiosity by two people, apparently Englishmen, who had just come aboard and like us were travelling third class. One of them looked familiar to me, and after a minute I placed him: Maurice Bowra,[3] already a celebrated Oxford figure, who had been one of the moderators when I took honours mods a few months earlier and had invigilated some of the papers. We all got into conversation, and before long Bowra and his companion, Adrian Bishop, were standing us the most delicious omelettes I have ever tasted. The rest of the voyage was highly entertaining. This was Bowra off duty: not the Oxford don of brilliant and malicious epigram, but the relaxed holiday acquaintance in whose company we all sparkled. Everything that happened was funny, or could be made funny: the world suddenly seemed a much more interesting place. Bowra had had a fascinating early life: three times as a boy before the Great War he had travelled to China by the Trans-Siberian Railway. When we arrived at Dubrovnik, he and Bishop – who for some reason had been living at Metković, a small malaria-ridden town lying between Split and Dubrovnik – forsook their third-class status and went off to a good hotel, while we sought a cheap but adequate place which sported twin adjacent thunder-boxes. During the next two days we continued to see Bowra and Bishop until they left for the Greek islands. It was a highly civilised interlude.

From Dubrovnik we took ship southward to Kotor, at the head of a superb fjord, and trudged up the mountains towards Cetinje, the capital of the former kingdom of Montenegro. Kim had been at prep school with the sons of the Montenegrin royal family, and we visited the decaying so-called palace, part of which was known locally as 'Biljarda' because it had once boasted a billiards table. We spent three or four days walking in Montenegro, and finally took an ancient bus down to Bar, a small port not far from the Albanian frontier.

Our boat was due to leave at six the next morning for Durrës in Albania. This time, taking no chances, we kept awake in turns. I spent my hours trying to learn Albanian by candle-light from Archibald Lyall's splendid little volume *Twenty-Five European Languages*. Lyall was obviously a humorist. In addition to a vocabulary of 800 words, there were some thirty conversa-tional sentences, the same for each of the twenty-five languages. These included 'Where is the water closet? On the fourth floor.'

In Albania, we found later, there appeared to be, as far as one could judge, neither fourth floors nor water closets. Albanian was clearly a primitive language, borrowing widely from others to deal with any invention or concept later than the Stone Age. But there was something endearing about a language which took seventeen words to say 'Have you a cheap single room?'

Not many Englishmen have been to Albania – for lack of facilities and attractions before the war, and political reasons since (at least until about 1991). I liked it so much that I went again in 1938, not with Kim but with my wife, and got to know a few Albanians with whom we corresponded until Mussolini invaded the country in 1939.

Arriving in Durrës in the evening, Kim and I began our Albanian interlude in highly uncharacteristic fashion, knocking up the British consul to complain that we had been overcharged by the boatman who brought us from the ship. The poor consul, in dressing gown and slippers and suffering from malaria, could do nothing for us. Later we got into conversation with two British engineers staying in our so-called hotel, and listened with amused superiority to their ultra-conservative political views. Theirs were the last English voices we were to hear on our Balkan journey.

One of the likeable things about the Albania of the 1930s was its air of self-deprecating inefficiency and absence of nationalist self-importance. But there could be efficiency, too. In Durrës my shoes, which had been badly repaired in Montenegro, began to disintegrate. We found a little cobbler in an open-fronted shop, and within an hour they were not just repaired but stronger than when new. (I was truly sorry when later my mother gave them away to the Boy Scouts.) From Durrës we took a bus to Tirana, the capital, but there was no transport eastward to Elbasan, our

next objective. We would have to walk the thirty miles in a single
day, which meant getting on the road by 4.30 in the morning. As
we had to share our room in Tirana with four Albanians, and the
beds were too dirty even to get into, we slept little and were glad
to leave. Our plan was to divide the day into three: five hours
on the road or track leading to the top of a 2,000-foot pass, five
hours resting there in the heat of the day and five hours walking
the remaining fifteen miles down to Elbasan. The map, which
owed as much to imagination as to research, showed a spring
at the top of the pass. Parched with thirst, we struggled up the
rocky bed of a waterless stream, but no spring was to be found.
It was some time before we came across a local inhabitant. Here
was a chance to try my Albanian, and I pulled Lyall out of my
rucksack. Splendid fellow, he actually gave the word for spring!
'*Ku asht prendvera?*' I asked eagerly. The man looked completely
blank: two foreigners, plainly unhinged by some experience,
had just asked him 'Where is the springtime?' Eventually all was
explained and we were guided to a bubbling ice-cold spring in a
green glade. When we finally reached Elbasan it was nearly dark.
By the time we had eaten, we had had enough. I was attacked
all night by mosquitoes and later counted seventy bites. The
next morning, after buying a Flit-gun, we spent our time resting,
washing our clothes in the river Shkumbin and walking around
a town as oriental as anything in Asiatic Turkey.

There was a road of sorts eastwards from there to the Yugoslav
frontier, a distance of some fifty miles. We managed to get a lift
on a truck nearly full of merchandise; the small remaining space
held six Albanians, two gundogs and ourselves. The journey,
with many stops and minor breakdowns, took ten hours, and it
was getting dark when they dropped us a mile or two from the

frontier. Knowing that it would be closed and the guards liable to shoot on sight, we had to call out continuously as we walked, '*Granica! Granica!*' (It was the Serbian word for frontier, but we hoped it would do.) At last torches flashed on us from an Albanian frontier post, where, after identification, the commandant gave us a fine welcome. Soldiers were turned out of a small room and put in with the goats, straw palliasses and a meal provided, money refused. In the morning we crossed into Yugoslavia and walked down to Ohrid, at the head of the beautiful lake of that name. Here we spent three relaxing days. The insects still bit, but we took encouragement from a theory – probably false – that malarious mosquitoes were not found above 1,000 feet.

Things had changed somewhat from our previous journey. Kim was now even more of an ascetic, more serious without being pompous, determined not to make the slightest concession to tourism or even normal comfort. Wherever we went we automatically sought out the cheapest place to sleep; by train we always went third or 'hard' class, and would have gone fourth if it had existed (as it did in Bosnia, where Kim the previous year had travelled around in what amounted to cattle trucks). But he was as interesting a companion as ever. As usual he had taken the trouble to read up the history of the area. This knowledge was all the more valuable because we had no guidebooks (a French *Guide Bleu* to Yugoslavia was published later). So I came to know something of the conflict of Turk and Serb over the centuries, a subject we found more interesting than the sterile contemporary politics of Yugoslavia. But most of our thoughts, energies and discussions were devoted to the simple business of living: finding somewhere to sleep, food to eat, good water to drink, getting from one place to another. Alcohol we drank sparingly in the Balkans: occasional beer when we could find it, a little local wine, the odd *slivovitz*. The whole trip, like the other two, was completely sexless. Asceticism was not the only reason for all this. We had little money – I was living entirely on my Oxford scholarship income, and Kim was certainly not well off. I kept careful accounts in a tiny notebook. It may all sound very joyless, but in truth it was a very full and satisfying time: to this day I can reconstruct practically the entire journey from memory. The greatest deprivation I suffered from was the absence of English newspapers.

For language we relied very largely on Kim's Serbo-Croat, which was more than adequate for the minor traffic of life. I managed to learn a few of the essentials myself. *Ima li voda ovde?* Is there water here? *Imate li grozhdje / hleb / sobu?* Have you grapes/ bread/ a room? *Gde je nuzhnik?* Where is the loo? (This last question was usually unnecessary. The *nuzhnik*, if indoors, was a noisome little den that proclaimed itself at a distance; if outdoors it was a sort of solitary sentry box, easily identified.) Very frequently, when we arrived in a village, the local 'English speaker' would be trotted out. This invariably proved to be someone no longer young who had emigrated to America in about 1910 and had returned some time after the war, leaving behind him most of the English he had acquired. We got used to being greeted in friendly but ancient American slang – 'Hi, you son-of-a-bitch.' Kim's Serbo-Croat was really much more useful: he was able to make conversation.

The 'hotels' of the Balkans at that time were not those of today. Their names were in the highest traditions – Ritz, Bristol, Carlton – but they were, frankly, hovels. I think one or two had enough electricity for the occasional light bulb, but most did not.

There would be nothing like running water, and the so-called lavatories were too awful to describe. The beds were not too bad, although one was not always sure of the last occupant. But the food was surprisingly good, though perhaps more because of our hunger than anything else. I do not recall any bathrooms – indeed, I doubt whether I had a bath throughout the journey, certainly not after leaving Germany.

Primitive and lacking in amenities though the Balkans were, they were a friendly enough place. We never had any fears for our safety or that of our few possessions. Except for Dubrovnik and Kotor there was virtually no tourist trade in any of the places we visited. Often we were assumed at first to be Germans – I expect many people had never seen an Englishman before. Once or twice we were taken for brothers: there may have been a slight physical resemblance at that time, but it probably appeared more pronounced to people unused to English faces. We were thrown together so much for these few weeks, with so little company and so few other diversions, that we might have become seriously irritated with one another; but personal relations held up well, though I do remember one occasion when for reasons now forgotten we strode along for several miles, one slightly ahead of the other, not on speaking terms; each with his own cloud of flies and thoughts.

While in Albania we had had to abandon hope of getting Bulgarian visas and had settled instead for a short foray into northern Greece. The Greek legation in Tirana gave us visas on the spot (unusual in the Balkans in those days). Our plan was to walk the forty-odd miles from Ohrid through Resan to Bitolj, in the very south of Yugoslavia, whence we could get a train into Greece. The road was not well provided with villages and we had done some twenty-seven miles before we found what appeared to be an inn, but turned out to be a brothel. Refreshed by a beer, and repelling all advances, we pushed on and even entertained thoughts of reaching Bitolj that night. This would have been overdoing things. We had been humping our rucksacks all day over rough roads and hill tracks, with the temperature in the nineties, and it was getting late. Fortunately after a couple of miles, and tiring rapidly, we found somewhere to stay. We made Bitolj the next morning, after three more hours of walking.

Two days later we were on our way by train to a village called Arnissa in Greek and Ostrovo in Macedonian, about halfway along the railway to Salonica. We had chosen it from the map because of its situation on a large lake, under the great massif of Mount Kaimakchalan. The scenery turned out to be as good as we had hoped, but I doubt if Arnissa had ever had much in the way of visitors before (it is now said to be an up-and-coming summer resort). There was not even what passed in those parts for an inn. Nor were there any roads; to get down to the lake, we had to walk along the railway line. At the little station restaurant we came across a peasant who offered us a room in his house. There we stayed four nights, paying the equivalent of about three (old) pence a night each. The room did not actually have any beds but there were two hard wooden chests covered with quilts of a sort. We slept on these, although I suppose we might have been just as comfortable on the floor. The lavatory was magnificent in its architectural simplicity. A small part of the first floor which jutted out beyond the ground floor was screened off; two floorboards had been prised apart so as to leave a small triangular hole, through which one could see the sunlit ground below. That was all. For meals we ate excellently at the station restaurant. The local population was Slavonic, speaking Macedonian – a mixture of Serb and Bulgarian, close enough to Serb for our purposes – but there were a number of Greek soldiers with whom we talked mainly in French. It was a confusing area linguistically. The Greek for 'yes' and the Macedonian word for 'no' were both pronounced 'nay'. Heads were nodded upwards for 'no' and from side to side for 'yes', again misleading for an Englishman. It was very easy to find yourself misdirected. There was nothing to do but sit peacefully by the lake, bathe in its medicinal-tasting waters, read Plato and Thucydides, eat at the restaurant and talk to the villagers and soldiers. My total expenditure in the four days was six shillings.

We took the train back to Bitolj. From now on we would do no further walking as a means of transport, but would make our way slowly up to Belgrade by rail. The first day took us from Bitolj to Skopje, or Skoplje as it was then spelt. Though only 120 miles, the journey took fully twelve hours. At that time a stretch of eighty miles lay over a superb narrow-gauge mountain railway, the kind which has a turning radius of about a hundred yards; one could – and did – get out of the train on one of those 180-degree turns, cut across a field and jump in on the other side. It was intensely hot. We ate grapes and bread and sweated. On the other side of the little wooden carriage a woman was coughing blood on the floor.

But we were about to rejoin civilisation, in a sense. Through Veles ran a main line connecting Salonica, Skopje and Belgrade. So from Veles to Skopje we enjoyed the experience of travelling at speed – perhaps forty miles an hour. A tremendous thunderstorm cooled the air and turned all to mud.

At Skopje my inside decided to rebel for the first time against

its unaccustomed dietary and physical regime. The last straw
was a meal consisting of a whole melon and a glass of sour
cream. Balkan peasants are supposed to live to 120 on this kind
of diet, but I lay on the bed feeling terrible, while Kim, who
seldom suffered from internal upsets, gaily called attention to
what was happening in the street below. Only when a perform-
ing bear walked past did I manage to drag myself to the window.
Next day things were better and we explored the town. Much
of the attraction of Yugoslavia lay in the Turkish legacy – the
mosques, the buildings, the little eating places where many varie-
ties of food were kept hot in tureens displayed in the window.
There were still a number of older people of Turkish descent to
be seen, gravely courteous, writing Turkish in the Arabic script,
which was now forbidden in Turkey itself. By comparison the
Serbs seemed brash and unpolished.

We continued our way to Belgrade by slow stages. The last
leg was by night train, so full that we had to stand on the open
platform between the coaches, where we choked every time
we went through a tunnel. Arriving sleepless at 5 a.m., we had
to tramp the streets for an hour before we found somewhere
cheap enough.

By now I was beginning to feel the need for home comforts
and company, and decided it was time to head for London. Kim
preferred to visit Belgrade yet again before returning home.
Before he did so, he probably made a side trip down the Danube
to the Iron Gates, about a hundred miles east of Belgrade: he
claims in his book to have gone there before the war, and this
seems the most likely occasion. For my part, after travelling
thirty-two hours hard class, I broke the journey at Frankfurt.
Not to be outdone by Kim I searched for some time before I

found a cheap enough bed, to discover in the small hours that I was sharing it with at least a dozen bedbugs. Next day, having no German money left, and not wishing to draw more from a bank, I visited the British consulate, outside their official opening hours, to ask if they would kindly give me a mark in exchange for a shilling. The consul justifiably regarded me with loathing, thrust a mark angrily into my hand and told me to beat it. Kim and I at this time seem to have expected an unusual range of services from His Majesty's consular representatives. Finally, after a day in Rotterdam, I came back to the family flat in the Old Brompton Road. The first thing I did was to have a bath; the second, immediately after, was to have another.

Kim still had a year to go at Cambridge. This was because after managing only a third in Part I of the history tripos he had switched to economics. (In this subject he was eventually to achieve a II:I, which – since firsts in economics were rarely awarded – was probably equivalent to a first in most other subjects.) I never had anything to do with his Cambridge life, nor he with mine at Oxford. Of his friends at Cambridge, to the best of my memory, I met only Michael Stewart, (briefly) John Midgley, mentioned below, and later Guy Burgess. I saw Kim once at Cambridge, when I was on a visit to other Westminster friends. He came once to Oxford, in the autumn of 1932, and we lunched with Maurice Bowra at Wadham. It was a long way from the Adriatic; others were present, the conversation was rather portentous, no one sparkled.

At Cambridge Kim seems to have had few relaxations. He did not play games or take part in social life. But his time must have been fully occupied by his work and by his very deep involvement in the University Socialist Society. I did not hear much about his Cambridge political activities, now well documented, but it was clear enough then, and is even clearer now, that there was nothing secret about them. I recall his mentioning that he had even begun making political speeches, in spite of his stammer. I saw him little if at all in the Christmas vacation of 1932–33 because he had gone to stay in Nottingham as part of his political education.

In January 1933 Hitler became Chancellor of Germany. Kim suggested we should go to Berlin in the Easter vacation and see what was happening. I had vague ideas at the time of trying to get into journalism after I had finished at Oxford, and agreed at once. So it was that we arrived in Berlin on 21 March, *der Tag von Potsdam*.[†] A huge torchlight street parade was held that evening, ostensibly in celebration of the reopening of the Reichstag in the Garrison Church at Potsdam, but primarily it was a Nazi propaganda exercise. We watched from a balcony in the Potsdamer Straße, where we had taken a room. Somebody in the next house was feeding out a roll of toilet paper high above the heads of the marching storm troopers. It was hard to say whether this represented enthusiasm, crude German humour or, as I hoped, disrespect.

We were staying in the house where Kim had stayed on his previous visit in July. It was not a left-wing place, rather the opposite. One of the tenants was a storm trooper, and he and we used to meet in the landlady's room to argue politics. Kim and I were

---

† *Editor's note:* 'The Day of Potsdam' was the ceremony celebrating the opening of the Reichstag after Adolf Hitler came to power. Hitler chose 21 March for the ceremony because it was on that date, sixty-two years earlier, that Otto von Bismarck had convened the Reichstag of the 'Second Reich'. The date in 1933 signifies the start of the 'Third Reich'.

quite open about our anti-Nazism – or rather Kim was, since my German was not good enough to sustain a discussion. As far as I remember he argued that Nazism was not a revolutionary movement, but merely a reactionary means of preserving capitalism against the advance of socialism; and that the form it was taking in Germany was likely to lead to war. We made fun in a small way about the military exercises the storm trooper took part in at weekends in the nearby countryside; small, middle aged, slightly pot bellied, he was an unimpressive physical specimen of Aryan manhood. On his side he would riposte strongly but good-humouredly – he was really quite a nice little man – while the landlady, who had a soft spot for Kim, would listen nervously in case anyone overheard. The *Gleichschaltung*[†] of Germany into totalitarianism was by no means complete at this time. Kim, who had brought one or two Marxist books with him, added to these by buying a twelve-volume set of Lenin, in German, from a street barrow. As he pointed out, this was the time and place to buy that sort of book cheap. But outwardly Berlin was now a sea of Nazi flags and anti-Jewish notices: even Wedding, formerly a communist district, was no exception.

Kim's politics had developed a good deal in the six months since our Balkan trip. It was not so much a shift of view as a wider knowledge of and especially a greater interest in Marxism. I am said to have described him at this time as a communist,[4] and I probably did, for want of a better label, though I am not

---

†   *Editor's note:* Broadly translated as 'forcible coordination' or 'bringing into line', this was the Nazi term for the process by which the regime successively sought to establish a system of totalitarian control and coordination over all aspects of German life and society. Among the goals of this policy was bringing about adherence to the regime's specific Nazi doctrine.

sure precisely what, at the age of twenty, I would have meant by 'communist'. If it meant someone who slavishly accepted an imposed party line – or sudden change of line – then, I would have said, that could not be Kim. I always thought of him as the most independent-minded person I had ever met. Talking to him, I realised that most of my views were received views; Kim seemed to have thought out all of his for himself. But at the time he must have seen in Marx a golden key to the interpretation of history and of political and economic struggle. He admired Lenin as a practical revolutionary who had simultaneously put it all down in writing. But he did not seem greatly interested in Russia; the Communist Party of Germany, which had been capable of polling several million votes in a general election, had been of much more concern to him. The German Communists had been unable to prevent Hitler's advance and were now in eclipse. Possibly this helped to turn Kim, always a believer in the realities of power, away from international communism and towards the Soviet Union as the mainspring of resistance to fascism.

Our three weeks in Berlin were very different from our previous trips abroad. Each of us had brought work and spent a good part of the day on this. Sometimes we went out together but often each would wander off on his own. One day Kim ran into a Cambridge acquaintance, John Midgley, whom we met thereafter once or twice. I think he was with us when we attended a political rally which has been mentioned in one or two books or articles on Kim. It has been said that when the Nazi salute was given Kim heroically braved hostility by refusing to raise his arm. It is true that we didn't salute; but heroism was unnecessary since those standing near us either realised we were foreign or were not the kind to make a fuss. At the same time, it is also likely that we would have gone to some lengths to avoid giving the salute or saying 'Heil Hitler'.

To return to the question I mentioned at the beginning of this chapter, did these three journeys involve any direct or indirect contact between Kim and the Soviet intelligence service? Alternatively, was he brought to their notice as a result of them? I cannot of course speak for those periods when I was not in his company, for instance immediately before and after the 1932 journey, or during his Berlin side trip, or for that matter the many occasions on our Berlin visit of 1933 when we were separated. All I can vouch for is that while we were together nothing happened to suggest even remotely to me a Soviet or other clandestine contact, presence or interest, direct or indirect.

In June 1933 Kim came down from Cambridge for good. I think he must have gone off to Vienna almost immediately (in his book he says that his underground work began in central Europe in June 1933), and I doubt if I saw him before he left. According to Elizabeth Monroe,[5] Kim's stated intention was to improve his German with a view to getting into the Foreign Service. He seems not to have publicised this intention very widely: I myself had a hazy but erroneous impression that he was doing a postgraduate year at Vienna University. (His German was already good; if he had been thinking only of the Foreign Service it would have made much more sense to go to France for a year. Good French was more or less obligatory.) Perhaps his chief reason for going to Austria was to get into the thick of European politics. If so, he chose well: the winter of 1933–34 saw Viennese socialism crushed by Chancellor Dollfuss, and the huge socialist-built blocks of workers' flats blasted by government artillery. Kim, as is now known, threw himself into the task of aiding left-wingers in danger from the police, including refugees from Nazi Germany, and helping to organise assistance and escape.

I heard nothing of this activity at the time, and little later. Kim scarcely ever wrote to me, and in any case could not have written freely in the circumstances. But in February 1934 I had a letter to say he was about to be married to a girl with whom he had been sharing a charming flat for some weeks. The flat was described, the girl was not. I wrote back to congratulate him, adding regretfully that I supposed this meant the end of our travels. I had had hopes that after the Oxford summer term was over it might be possible to make one more journey abroad with Kim before we each got down to the business of earning our livings.

Lizy (for so she spelt it, not Litzi) was Jewish, of part-Hungarian origin, a communist or communist sympathiser, and a year or two older than Kim.[6] She had already been married and divorced. Kim had met her soon after arriving in Vienna and for a time had lodged in her parents' house. They arrived in London in May 1934, but it was several weeks before I saw them. Up to mid-June I was totally preoccupied with greats, and thereafter equally preoccupied with a German girl I had met. It was not until July that I first met the couple, at Dora Philby's house in Acol Road. Lizy was quite different from what I had expected: a *jolie laide*, more *laide* perhaps than *jolie*, very feminine, not obviously 'intellectual', but full of animation; her attraction lay in her liveliness and sense of fun. She can hardly have been the kind of wife Kim's family had expected him to marry; but since his middle teens he had been accustomed to make his own decisions.

By now I was at a loose end. The German girl was about to return to Frankfurt, and it was not the best time of year to start looking for a job. At that moment Dollfuss was assassinated. Vienna seemed clearly the place to be, as Berlin had been sixteen months earlier. Vienna had the added attraction that Frankfurt lay en route. Kim and Lizy supplied me with names and addresses of Viennese friends. I left for Vienna – stopping over in Frankfurt – in early August.

It may be that Vienna was the place where Kim was recruited or spotted by the Russians, but I am sorry to say that I can report little of interest from my own visit. First, nothing of the smallest political importance happened: Vienna was completely quiet again. Second, although I duly contacted nearly all the friends named on my list, I learnt little or nothing of the exciting underground political life that Kim and Lizy must have been leading. Probably their friends were cautious over what they said to a newcomer, but an equally important reason was that scarcely any of them spoke any English and my German was halting. If I had been able to meet the only Englishman on my list, the *Daily Telegraph* correspondent Eric Gedye,[7] I would probably have learnt more, but he was out of Vienna all that month. One friend I remember was the daughter of an imprisoned Austrian Socialist deputy. She was acting as a guide to British tourists from the Workers' Travel Association, and I joined in one of her conducted tours. As tourists they were like most others – Schönbrunn was not as good as Leeds, and where could they get a cup of tea? – but they were also fervent socialists to a man, or woman, and keen to discuss what was happening in Austria. Our guide thought it safest to wait until we had reached the Vienna woods and left the bus. At her instruction we became quite conspiratorial, huddling together, lowering our voices and keeping a lookout for strangers. There is a similarity here to the story recounted in Patrick Seale's book[8] of a conspiratorial socialist meeting in the Vienna forest arranged by Kim through an Austrian girl for Gedye. Perhaps it was the same girl. Another on my list was a refugee from Berlin, living under an assumed name. But while all these friends appeared to be left wing, and in some apprehension of what the future might bring for them, none seems a likely candidate for a Soviet intelligence role in relation to Kim.

After a two-day visit to Budapest by river, and a final week in Frankfurt, I was back in England. Jobs were hard to come by in September 1934. Before I had made any progress, I went down with severe tonsillitis. For convalescence Dora Philby offered the use of a cottage she rented in north Wales, fronting directly on to the scenic narrow-gauge railway between Blaenau Ffestiniog and Portmadoc. Here my mother and I spent a week or two. The trains, which went by gravity alone in the westward direction, had ceased to run now that the summer was over, and the nearest road of any kind was a mile and a half away. It was a delightful place.

I finally landed a job on the last day of 1934 as a copywriter at S. H. Benson Ltd,[9] one of the largest advertising agencies in England. Kim had meanwhile made his entry into journalism with a job on the *Review of Reviews*. We both began at £4 a week. I went up to £5 after two months; I never heard whether or when Kim got a rise.

But by this time, it seems, he had more important things on his mind.

CHANGE OF LIFE

For the next few years, up to October 1941, I was somewhat less involved with Kim than I had been before or was to become later. My job, marriage, the war and many other interests dominated my life. Kim for his part was out of England for much of the time from early 1937 onwards. The period has been covered in detail in the Philby literature, and I do not intend to go over the same ground at second hand. All I can contribute on this obviously crucial stage in Kim's life is how it seemed to me at the time.

The accepted historical theory is that, at some point after recruitment by the Russians, Kim was instructed by them to break away from leftism and create a new persona with some sympathy for Nazism and fascism; he joined the Anglo-German Fellowship, attended official German functions and visited Berlin. So much evidence has been published for the metamorphosis that I assume the theory to have some truth, and Kim himself gives support to it in the introduction to his book. Kim, however, seems to say there that the main reason was not so much the long-term one of 'laundering' him of the taint of leftism as the shorter-term one of establishing him as an informant on 'overt and covert links between Britain and Germany'.

Either way, the new persona must have made very little impression on me at the time. For example, until I read about them in the *Sunday Times* articles of October 1967 I had completely forgotten about Kim's activities in the Anglo-German Fellowship or his abortive efforts to start a German-financed trade journal. This is all the odder since, as I am now reminded, my own sister Angela actually assisted Kim for a time on the trade journal. She says that once they had prepared the material for the first number, which never appeared, there was little office work to be done; she and Kim spent much of their day doing crosswords and the like.

Kim's political standpoint certainly seemed to be undergoing some change. He no longer expressed strong leftist views and was now more often on the fence. I assumed he was beginning to come to terms with the real world. I could understand this as I was working in a citadel of private enterprise myself, and greatly enjoying the experience. But I never thought of him as turning even slightly pro-Nazi or pro-fascist. He was strongly anti-Mussolini at the time of the Abyssinian invasion of autumn 1935 and strongly against the subsequent Hoare–Laval pact. I cannot remember what he may have said about Hitler's remilitarisation of the Rhineland in March 1936, but if there had been a word in favour it would have made a strong impression. I recall that he was anti-Baldwin and pro-Edward at the time of the Abdication, but this was clearly from hostility to the Baldwin government and the Establishment attitude, and nothing to do with Edward VIII's alleged pro-Nazi leanings.

It has been suggested that Kim had to tone down his prescribed change of views when speaking to old friends. No doubt he realised that I would have found it very unconvincing. On the other hand, on the occasions I saw him in 1935 and 1936 there were often other people around; if he had taken one line with me when alone and another in wider company I would certainly have noticed. I do recall his saying at this time – not in company – that, although Marx had been remarkably successful in analysing economic and political forces, he had altogether failed to foresee, or provide an explanation for, the rise of nationalism. I took this as evidence that his views on Marxism were undergoing a significant change: but perhaps it was all part of his cover plan.

One point may be worth making. There was a possibility, gradually increasing to probability as time went on, that Britain and Germany would soon be involved in a war with each other. The Russians would have been very unwise to allow Kim to become too publicly identified with German interests. Although there was no likelihood that after the outbreak of war he would, like his father, actually find himself interned, his ability to penetrate British intelligence or government might have been seriously handicapped. It obviously made sense that he should gradually obliterate his communist or Marxist past, but there was no need to go very far the other way. A measure of disillusionment with the left, and perhaps a cynicism about politics in general, would have been much more convincing, and indeed he sometimes gave this impression. If the Russians really did urge upon him a positively pro-German line, with little need for caution, is this possibly an indication that they thought the future would see Britain and Germany fighting on the same side, against the Soviet Union? My own belief is that the accounts of his ostensible switch to a pro-German position have been exaggerated.

There have been several theories about the Kim–Lizy marriage. Some say it was a marriage of convenience from the start, either to suit the Russians or to get her out of Austria.

Others say it was genuine to begin with, but was later broken up at Soviet insistence. Seeing them together, one had no reason to doubt that their marriage was as real as any other. The arrival of Lizy probably changed Kim's lifestyle even more than a marriage usually does. He had been very much a bachelor before; as far as I know he had never even had a girlfriend. Now the atmosphere was cosy, domesticated and rather Bohemian.

Sometime in 1935 they took a flat in Kilburn, not far from his parents' house in Acol Road. It was there that I first met Guy Burgess. He made an immediate impact – as he did, I imagine, on everyone who met him. I once nourished a theory that Evelyn Waugh's Basil Seal was partly based on Guy, if one ignores Guy's homosexuality, but the dates do not fit well. Kim and Lizy's scruffy little dog was called Guy after him, when it wasn't called Menelek after the later ruler of Abyssinia; the two names were used indiscriminately. An even more outrageous character who turned up once or twice at the Kilburn flat was Tom Wyllie, another homosexual and a brilliant classicist who had been at Westminster and Christ Church. He was now chiefly occupied in turning the War Office, where he lived as a resident clerk, into a centre of alcoholic orgy. When after years of patient endurance the War Office could take no more, he was transferred to the Office of Works, where the requisitions and invoices that passed across his desk provided a rich field for creating havoc among Whitehall office supplies. Like Burgess, he flaunted his homosexuality. Although Kim had known Wyllie at Westminster, I think it was probably Burgess who brought him along. Kim was amused by the stories of Wyllie's exploits and drunkenness, but did not like him much.

Most of Kim's and Lizy's friends were normal and well-behaved. Lizy was a very sociable person and Kim was becoming more and more sociable himself; the Kilburn flat was a lively place. Here I first encountered the 'Mitteleuropa lot'. These were a number of Austrians, Czechs and Hungarians – some were recent Jewish refugees, others longer established in London – whom Lizy was gathering around her. Most if not all were left wing. They were presumably just the sort of people whose company Kim was now supposed to eschew, but at this time he certainly did not.

In February 1937, having so far made little progress in journalism, Kim went off on his freelance visit to Spain. We are now told that this was an assignment for the Soviet intelligence service, which provided the money. It seems surprising that Kim, with all his experience and that of his Soviet employers, was nearly floored by the question Dick White[1] of MI5 put to him in 1951: who paid for the trip? One would have expected the provision of a good financial cover story to be one of the first points in the briefing given by the Russians. But at the time his decision to try his hand in Spain seemed perfectly natural. If I had thought about the financial side at all, I would have assumed that he had managed to save a little or had borrowed from or been helped by his parents. He had made plenty of previous journeys to Europe at his own expense. Travelling and living in most European countries was extremely cheap. The theory has also been advanced that it was, in the long run, a serious flaw in Kim's 'front' that he did not have proper newspaper accreditation for this first Spanish visit. I cannot agree. I am sure that if he had not turned out to be a Russian spy no one would have seen anything at all unusual in his seeking his journalistic fortune in Spain. After all, the freelance trip was abundantly justified by the result: within three months he had landed a plum job with *The Times*.

This was in May 1937. Lizy and I gave a farewell party for him at my mother's house in St Leonard's Terrace, Chelsea, where I was living. We each asked about fifteen to twenty guests. Lizy's included some of the 'Mitteleuropas'; mine included friends in advertising. Fairly early in the evening a friendly policeman turned up to say that there had been complaints about the noise, but he agreed the law could do nothing about it as long as we stayed indoors. Well after midnight he knocked again, with the same message. This time we hauled him in, gave him a drink, put on his helmet and were photographed with him. The party went on till after dawn.

I mention these trivia because life – Kim's life no less than anyone else's – consists mostly of trivia. One gets the impression from many books on Kim – including to some extent his own – that he was always serious, always immersed in his lone silent thirty years' war. The TV film *Philby, Burgess and Maclean*[2] made him out to be dull, the one thing Kim never was. You could not imagine from this film that he could be great fun, and had a personal magnetism for many people. I don't know whether he enjoyed the farewell part – probably not, he seemed a little subdued – but he usually had a very positive attitude towards life and the enjoyment of it.

Now followed a period of some four and a half years when I saw Kim comparatively rarely. When I joined SIS in October 1941 my wife Marie, whom I had known since early in 1937 and in whose company I usually was from that time, had met Kim only three or four times. I saw him not much more often than this.

Soon after Kim left for Spain as a *Times* correspondent, I made an abortive attempt to join him there for a few days during my annual fortnight's holiday from Benson's. This was in August

1937. I still nursed hopes of breaking into journalism, and Kim had told me that if I had some sort of journalistic pretext he could probably fix my entry with the Spanish Nationalists. I see from my old passport that on 23 August the British vice-consul in Bayonne endorsed it as valid for a single journey to Spain: 'Holder is proceeding there as correspondent of the London General Press.' It was from this agency, according to the *Sunday Times*, that Kim had a letter of accreditation when he visited Spain in February, so I assume he must have organised my own letter. Having applied to the Spanish Nationalist Office in, I think, Biarritz, I went on to St Jean-de-Luz. There, according to Kim, I would be sure to pick up at the Bar Basque all that could be learnt in France of the movements of himself and other journalists in Franco's Spain. I did indeed meet many journalists there, some of whom had seen Kim very recently. Unfortunately, Franco's troops were engaged at that moment in a drive on Santander in north-west Spain, and Kim, who was with them (indeed he entered the town ahead of them), was incommunicado. None of the journalists was on the point of going back into Spain, and whatever messages I was able to send off to Kim were unlikely to reach him in time. After a few days of sunning and bathing in the Atlantic surf, I gave it up and spent my second week walking in the French Pyrenees; I could not risk getting back to the office late. Sometime after my return to London my Nationalist permit came through, but of course could not be used.

One small incident occurred during the Spanish war which might conceivably have given a slight clue that Kim had other interests and stresses in his life besides those of being a *Times* correspondent. In 1937 a young friend of mine and Marie's at Benson's, Buz Brackenbury, who was then a romantic leftist, had walked out of his job and was next heard of driving a truck on the Spanish Republican side. After about a year of this, and disenchanted with what he had seen, he conceived the idea of visiting Nationalist Spain as a freelance journalist. He entered from France under his original surname, Klein, but had not got very far before he was arrested. Accused of being a Republican spy and faced with threats of a firing squad, he claimed friendship with the *Times* correspondent, H. A. R. Philby. (I think he had probably met Kim only at the farewell party. He may also have said that they were at school together, although in fact his career at Westminster began after Kim had left.) Kim told the Nationalists that he hardly knew him but believed him to be merely young and irresponsible. In the event Buz was simply taken to the frontier and thrown out. When I next saw Kim, he was still extremely incensed by the whole affair: he said he had been put in serious danger. At the time I thought he was making unusually heavy weather of it. I can see now that it was very awkward for him, but would it have been quite so awkward if he had been simply the impeccable *Times* correspondent? After all, anybody in a jam might claim anybody as an acquaintance on the basis of one meeting. Buz obviously behaved unwisely but he needs no apologia: he joined the RAF at the outbreak of the war, and was later killed.

I followed Kim's career from *The Times*, to the extent that its then rather impersonal reporting traditions allowed, and read with great relief of his remarkable escape from death in the Teruel region on the last day of 1937. A Republican shell – Russian made – blew up the car in which Kim and three other correspondents were sitting; Kim was the sole survivor. I remember only one letter from Kim in Spain, and one sentence in it: 'Frances Doble is here and very nice.'[3] He said no more about this quite well-known London actress of the 1920s and early 1930s, whom I had seen on stage or screen; it could have been just a chatty news item. It was not until I read the books on Kim that I learnt of their prolonged affair in Spain. Whatever role Kim and I played in each other's lives, it was never that of confidant about personal matters.

Kim was *The Times*'s correspondent in Nationalist Spain, attached to Franco's headquarters, for more than two years. Some writers seem to have interpreted this as almost equivalent to fighting on Franco's side, and as something which his former left-wing friends found shocking in itself. This puzzles me; newspaper correspondents posted to Soviet-era Moscow, for example, were not thereby branded as communists. It is true that Kim's despatches from Spain often tended to give a favourable picture of the Nationalists. But in those days a foreign journalist's report on a totalitarian country or regime was allowed very little freedom – far less than now; and on top of that Kim was working for a newspaper which under Geoffrey Dawson went out of its way not to upset relations with Hitler's Germany. I never felt that Kim's reporting reflected his true feelings, but did not find this remarkable; caught between Franco and Geoffrey Dawson, he seemed to have little choice. Was I not myself writing ecstatically about products in which I had not the smallest interest? Yet I and some of my colleagues drew the line at (and were excused from) writing advertisements for the Conservative Party, one of the Benson accounts. I sometimes thought that Kim went further than he needed in presenting the Nationalists in a good light, but concluded that he was not his own master; and that, of course, was truer than I knew.

From recent accounts it appears that some of Kim's fellow journalists in Spain regarded him as slightly out of the ordinary: unusually well informed, unusually interested in military information of a kind too detailed for press despatches. No one seems to have suspected the truth, or even to have surmised that he might secretly be reporting to, say, the Spanish Republicans. One or two journalists concluded that he was working for British intelligence. Kim himself says that 'to the best of his knowledge' – and I am sure this is true – his first contact with the British secret services took place in the summer of 1940. But he admits that in both Germany and Spain he had half-expected an approach. He must have been hoping for one; it would have made him even more interesting to the Russians. He told me that on one occasion while travelling southwards through Spain to Gibraltar – probably during his freelance visit – he had found his progress continually coinciding with that of a Spanish Nationalist military unit of especial interest, and on arrival in Gibraltar he had reported what he saw to British authorities. But if he hoped thereby to attract the attention of the Secret Service, it evidently had no effect.

Though I was not in close enough touch to be aware of it, his and Lizy's marriage had probably been coming apart for some time before he first went to Spain in early 1937. This may have been a factor in his decision to go abroad (I am sure it is a mistake to see every move in his life as entirely dictated by the needs of Soviet intelligence). He and Lizy never shared a home and life together after February 1937, although they were no doubt under the same roof when he came back in May of that year and perhaps occasionally later. In about 1938 she took an apartment in Paris, but sometimes appeared in London; in fact,

I connect the 'Mitteleuropas' more with 1938–39 than earlier. I last saw them, and Lizy, in the early days of the war.

One final comment on Kim and Lizy's marriage. The Scarlet Pimpernel theory makes little sense to me. Although Lizy was subject to some kind of police supervision, she could probably have got out of Austria without much difficulty, at least up to March 1938 when Hitler invaded the country. The theory that the Russians were behind the marriage also holds little water. Why should they prescribe a marriage which, almost immediately, it was apparently in their interests to see undone? It may be that Lizy had some direct or indirect contact with Soviet intelligence in Vienna and it may be that Kim had been introduced to them by the time of his marriage, but I doubt whether the Russians were then – if ever – in a position to dictate to him what he should do about so private and personal an affair as marriage.

During this last year or two of peace I saw a little more of Kim's mother and sisters than I had previously. Diana, the eldest, was put through the gruesome process of 'coming out': presentation at Court, debs' parties, large formal dances. Kim of course was in Spain and his father was usually in the Middle East, so Dora Philby had to do most of the organising. She joined forces with some of the Sassoon family, whose daughter was also coming out, and a party for both girls was held in the grand Sassoon house at Albert Gate. I was roped in for this as for one or two other expensive junketings. The two younger sisters, Pat and Helena, had plenty of the family intelligence and charm. Pat went to Cambridge, became a civil servant and married someone named Milne (not related to me), but her marriage broke up and she eventually died tragically. Helena appears later in these pages. I also met from time to time their grandmother – St

John's mother – a splendid old battleaxe and matriarchal figure who was treated with great respect and affection by all members of the family.

I must have seen Kim three or four times on his return visits from Spain, but it was not until about the summer of 1939 that I realised what a change had come over him. It was not just that he had grown fatter – too fat for a young man – but he seemed to have discarded all his previous asceticism and idealism, which I had admired without much wishing to follow. Now the talk was about the fleshpots of Spain, the booze, the marvellous seafood, the nightly fish train which ran, with priority over guns and soldiers, from Vigo to the Nationalist-held north-west area of Madrid. He did not go so far as to suggest he had moved over to support of the Nationalists: on the contrary, he avoided ideological judgements altogether. Perhaps I was now, belatedly, getting a taste of the cover plan: but I think also that there was a real change of attitude in Kim. He was more cynical, more worldly wise, more interested in material comforts, more gregarious. Indeed, he had become a rather Falstaffian figure, and seemed to enjoy it: with some glee he said that a doctor had told him that he – then twenty-seven – had the arteries of a man of fifty. I was intrigued by the change, but at the same time disappointed. It was more than two years before I found myself once again *en rapport.*

Those two years were, approximately, the first two years of the war. I have no idea what Kim's reaction, genuine or assumed, may have been to the Nazi–Soviet pact and the carve-up of Poland: if I saw him at all at this moment it has left no impression. But very soon he was off to France as a *Times* correspondent with the British forces. I for my part got married at Christmas, and joined the Royal Engineers in June 1940. The fall of France and my arrival at Fort Widley near Portsmouth, where I was to join the Royal Engineers Survey Training Centre as a cadet, are forever interlocked in my memories. The next four months, spent partly in basic military training but much more in learning every aspect of map-making, were among the fullest and most fascinating of my working life, even though my total Army pay in all that time came to no more than eight pounds. But in November 1940 I was commissioned, and spent the next eleven months in the training and administration of others – tasks which had little attraction for me. For most of this time Marie and I were living at Ruabon, in Denbighshire. I heard almost nothing of Kim, but Marie ran into him in the winter of 1940–41 in Shaftesbury. He was with a woman whom later we were to know so well – Aileen, who eventually became his second wife.

In April 1941 Kim wrote to me to say that there was a job going in his outfit (I had no idea what this was) for which I might possibly be suited, and if I was interested he could arrange lunch in London with the people concerned. Keen to get away from north Wales, I accepted at once. Over lunch at the Normandie I was told a little – very little – about the proposed job, which as far as I recall involved training people in covert propaganda, producing leaflets and so on. Kim, I learnt, was working at Beaulieu for SOE, the Special Operations Executive, but my ignorance of secret organisations at this time was total. He had thought my knowledge of advertising might be useful, as no doubt it would have been. However, the job went to an older and more experienced advertising man who was present at the same lunch.

The year 1941 wore on. Germany invaded Russia, making the

Russians our allies and, presumably, life rather less of a strain for
Kim. At the Survey Training Centre in Ruabon, I moved from
training raw recruits in square-bashing and the rudiments of
warfare, of which I knew little, to being assistant adjutant. This
was a nine-to-five sort of job, with much paperwork, and deadly
dull. In September I was about to be promoted to captain and
adjutant when a telegram arrived from Kim to say that a new
possibility had arisen in another quarter and he had arranged a
London interview for me through the War Office. A summons
duly arrived and I travelled to London. The interview turned
out to be with a Major Felix Cowgill; Kim was present. Again
I learnt little from this of the nature of the work, but later that
afternoon Kim gave me an outline. It seemed the job was in
Section V of the Secret Service – the counter-espionage section,
which Kim had joined a month earlier. The pay would work out
at a little more that I had been getting as a second lieutenant, a
little less that I would earn as a captain. But the work sounded
a hundred times more interesting. The office was in St Albans.
It was not London, the only place at that time of my life where I
wished to live, but it was only a Green Line journey away. I had
no hesitation in saying I wanted the job.

That evening I went to an impromptu party in Kim's flat in
South Kensington, or more precisely in Aileen's bedroom; a week
or two earlier she had given birth to their first child, Josephine.
I had met Aileen briefly at the time of my Easter interview for
the SOE job. Once again I was struck by the change in Kim, or
rather in his company and surroundings. Central Europeans, of
course, were out; MI5, it seemed, were in, though I did not yet
know them as MI5. Among those I met for the first time I can
recall with certainty only Tommy and Hilda Harris. The sole

relic from the past, apart from me, was Guy Burgess. After many months in north Wales, among worthy sobersided RE officers and Welsh farmers, I found myself in a different world: everyone seemed enormously intelligent, sophisticated and well informed, and given to mildly malicious gossip. It was a fascinating but, as it turned out, scarcely typical introduction to life in the Secret Service. Kim and Aileen were not only celebrating the arrival of their first-born but also saying goodbye to London, while St Albans did not lend itself to parties of this kind.

I returned to Ruabon, where Marie and I made preparations to leave the remote and now increasingly uninviting farm on the river Dee where we were living. A few days later my posting order arrived, assigning me to 'Special Duties without pay and allowances' from Army funds. On 8 October we drove down in our small second-hand Ford 10 and spent the night in Chelsea. The next day I presented myself at the War Office, and was told to report to Broadway Buildings, opposite St James's Park Underground station. I can remember only two of the interviews that followed. One was with the office doctor, who asked me if I was going abroad. Nobody had said anything about going abroad, and I wondered, wrongly, if I was being gradually introduced to some quite different kind of job. Then I was passed along to the security officer. 'You'll need some kind of cover story,' he said. He thought a moment. 'There are still a lot of refugees coming over from the Continent. You'd better tell your friends you've been seconded to the Passport Control Department of the Foreign Office to help in their interrogation.' It was difficult to imagine anything less likely than that a supposedly trained RE officer, aged twenty-nine, graded A.1 in health and with indifferent languages, would be pulled out of the Army for this purpose. I ignored his advice, or instruction (it wasn't clear which), and told everyone as occasion arose that I had been posted to War Office intelligence. People readily accepted this and I was seldom bothered over cover problems for the rest of the war.

On the afternoon of the following day I drove to St Albans and turned through an unguarded gateway into the drive of a large late-Victorian house: Glenalmond. A job that was to last twenty-seven years had begun.

4

OWN TRUMPET

This is a book about Kim as I knew him and the interaction of his life and mine. But now I must digress to say a little more about myself. The reader may well have been asking: who is this man? What did Kim Philby see in him? Why did Philby try to get him to join first SOE and then SIS? Was there some ulterior motive? The *Sunday Times* articles from 1967 suggested that I might have played a part, conscious or unconscious, in one particular stage of Kim's Secret Service ambitions. That it might strike people in this way had not really occurred to me before I read the articles, but I can see there could be points to answer.

Necessarily some of this must turn on the question of my own education, qualification, ability and mental make-up. This means I shall have to talk about myself, even blow my own trumpet a little. I promise this trumpet involuntary will not be a long one.

My father taught all his four children to read at an early age – I read fluently and avidly by the time I was four. How he – a busy and successful civil servant (he had a CBE before he was forty), but handicapped by poor health – found time and energy to do this, I cannot imagine. He was a marvellous teacher; the secret was, I think, that he seemed to be learning with you rather than teaching. By the time I reached my kindergarten, just six years of age, I had, among many other books – and for no reason that I can remember – read Kingsley's *The Water Babies* ten times. I was put into a class that could read – and our book for the term was *The Water Babies*. My education proceeded through kindergarten, first prep school, second prep school, but also through my father. He, like his brother Alan, had been a mathematical scholar at Westminster, though unlike Alan he had not gone to university. I was never to be a mathematician myself, but he gave me a lasting feeling for arithmetic and algebra. His greatest love was books, and we children grew up in a house lined with English classics.

I began to acquire a capacity for mental arithmetic and for absorbing statistics, dates and names. Along with other useless but agreeable information, I became a walking Wisden's. The scores and players of the early 1920s are still vivid in my mind. I tested this statement the other day, and found that of the first hundred players in the batting averages of 1922 I could name the teams of ninety-eight. We were, needless to say, a crossword family; Sunday was Torquemada day from the moment he first appeared in *The Observer*, in the middle or late 1920s.

At my second prep school – the one which my grandfather had founded and which St John Philby had attended – I was groomed for a scholarship in my last four terms, working on my own. The school spent a lot of effort on this, although they had not had a success for some years. Most of my time was given to Latin and Greek. The mathematics master, a man of wisdom, simply handed me a thick volume of Hall and Knight's *Algebra*, with answers at the end, and left me to get on by myself. A year later I had reached the binomial theorem, though it was true I had slightly neglected things I found less interesting, like geometry.

On my thirteenth birthday I sat for the Westminster scholarship examination and came out top. At the end of my first year at Westminster I and several other juniors in College took the School Certificate, something like today's GCSEs. I had to get five credits to pass. Four I knew were in the bag – Latin, Greek, French and mathematics – but I also needed history or English or divinity, to none of which had I devoted enough attention. Numbers and dates came to my rescue. A few hours before the history exam, I was feverishly trying to 'revise' – i.e. learn things I ought to have learnt earlier – when I came across an account of John Wesley, full of dates of journeys and statistics of conversions in various towns and counties. That afternoon I was delighted to find in the history paper a question about Wesley. The examiners must have been surprised to receive a whole page of accurate dates and statistics: perhaps they thought I was an ardent Methodist. Anyway, with Wesley's help I got my credit in history.

In the same summer term of 1926 my arithmetical turn of mind came in handy in another way, and one which may have made an impression on Kim. The Cheyne Arithmetic Prize (it actually involved algebra rather than arithmetic) was open to the whole school. The paper was compulsory for those who had not yet taken the School Certificate and voluntary for others, but the prize was usually won by someone in the top mathematical form. To my astonishment, when the marks list was published, I was first, although as I was barely fourteen, I was only allowed to receive the junior prize. (In my last year I sat for it again and was again top, so I got the senior prize in the end.)

After the School Certificate one had to choose between classics, science, history, mathematics and so on: I decided to stick with classics. I turned out to be a reasonable solid classicist but not a brilliant one. Possibly I might have done slightly better in science or mathematics; I cannot say. I continued to do a little mathematics on the side and learnt the elements of calculus, trigonometry, statics and dynamics. At the end of my third year I took Higher Certificate in Latin and Greek, with mathematics as a voluntary subsidiary. When the results were published it appeared that I was the only person in the entire country that year to have got both a distinction in a classical subject (Latin) and a pass in the mathematics subsidiary. I know this sounds a little like being the only left-handed red-headed person to have ridden a bicycle from Wapping to Wigan on a Thursday, but I suppose it does indicate a slightly unusual mental combination, and one that could come in useful in certain types of job.

At Oxford, where I had a close scholarship to Christ Church, I read honour moderations (classics) for five terms, and greats (philosophy and Greek and Roman history) for seven. I got a sound but uninspired double second, the thing one is always advised to avoid – the only classes worth getting, people said, were a first or a fourth. But my double second did well enough for me, and no doubt helped me to get into advertising.

Everyone knew Benson's advertising in those days. Our star client was Guinness, but we also had Kodak, Bovril, Johnnie Walker, Austin, Colman's, Wills's, and many other names famous in the 1920s and 1930s. Dorothy Sayers's *Murder Must Advertise* was written about Benson's, a year or two before I got there, and conveys extremely well the atmosphere of moderately gifted amateurism. Advertising ideas never came easily to me, but I had some family facility for writing verses and parodies, which occasionally came in useful for Guinness and others. Most of the work was hard slogging; I was especially concerned with one of our most interesting clients, Kodak. There were only about nine or ten of us in the

Benson copywriting department, which was responsible for planning the campaigns, thinking up the ideas, writing all the words,
doing much of the contact with various clients and a great deal
besides. Mortality, in those competitive days of the Depression,
was high; I think that in my five and a half years, Michael Barsley
and I were the only two completely new boys in the copy department to survive infancy. By the outbreak of war, still a bachelor, I
was probably better off in real terms, that is, net purchasing power
after tax, than I was to be again for at least twenty years.

I continued to work in Benson's for a few months after the war
began, in an increasingly unreal atmosphere, until the time came
to join the Army. A friend of my sister's, Peter Shortt, was a
major in the Royal Engineers (though at that time he was acting
as personal assistant to General Gort, the Commander-in-Chief
of the British Expeditionary Force). Knowing my predilection for
maps and travel, and that I had a grounding in mathematics, he
suggested I might try to get into the Survey Service of the Royal
Engineers. So it was that I became one of twenty-four officer
cadets at Fort Widley in June 1940. About half the twenty-four
were master printers and others from the printing profession,
while the other half were supposed to be, or have been, mathematical specialists. I was neither, but it turned out that what
was needed, apart from basic trigonometry, was the ability to
handle figures quickly and accurately. At the end of the course
we were marked on mathematics, knowledge of instruments
and astronomy. I came second, missing 100 per cent through a
single elementary slip. On the practical map-making side in the
field, which took three weeks, I had 96 per cent for accuracy but
only 40 per cent for speed. Probably I was more cut out for the
Ordnance Survey than an RE map-making unit in battle.

The *Sunday Times* book says, 'We know nothing about the political stance of [Kim's] admiring former school-friend "Ian" [i.e. me].'[1] Let me try briefly to fill this gap. In my twenties I was, of course, left wing. I say 'of course' not because everyone of my age had those views – a number of my friends did not – but because most young men who took any interest in politics, particularly European politics and the rise of fascism, were left wing. I never joined any political party, except that in my first term at Oxford I was persuaded by an old school friend to part with half a crown as subscription to the Oxford University Labour Party or Labour Club – I have forgotten the exact title. I attended no meetings and my membership soon lapsed. In my undergraduate days and for a time afterwards I regarded myself as belonging to the left of the Labour spectrum. My guiding light was the *New Statesman and Nation*, which I devoured weekly as soon as it came out. Though I never managed to read more than a page or two of Marx or Lenin, I recall that when I was studying Roman history at Oxford and had to write an essay on 'The Year of the Four Emperors' (those who followed Nero in rapid succession in AD 68–69), I tried to interpret the whole complicated story in what I conceived to be Marxist terms of class struggle. The attempt went rather well, and maybe had an element of truth, but I realise now that the available facts could probably have been made to support any other historical theory with equal effectiveness.

Kim certainly had some influence on my politics up to the time I was twenty or so, but in the eight and a half years between April 1933, when our Berlin visit ended, and October 1941 I suppose I saw him no more than a couple of dozen times, nearly always in general company. In any case, as I have recounted above, he became less and less communicative about politics from 1935–36 onwards. I went my own way. My views in the second half of the 1930s were largely conditioned by the Italian invasion of Abyssinia, the Spanish war and the rise of Hitler. Domestic problems interested me less, and I do not think I felt much involvement with the Jarrow marchers and the millions of unemployed. Russia I regarded as a country that could be relied upon for hostility to Hitler. The Nazi–Soviet pact came as a tremendous shock, partly for this reason but even more because it clearly meant that war was inevitable. For the few months of the phony war I floundered in political confusion, and it almost came as a relief when the Germans began attacking in the west; it certainly did so to join the Army in June 1940 and become immersed in a new world. There was little time to think or read about politics, which anyway seemed to have simplified wonderfully. By the time the war ended I had outgrown a great deal of my rather woolly left-wing idealism. I voted Labour for the last time in 1945. As far as I recall, I did not vote in 1950 or 1951 owing to absence abroad, and since then I have voted Conservative.

I have no doubt that Kim's primary reason for proposing my entry into Section V was that he had a particular and unusual job to offer which, as I hope to show, was right up my street. Politics did not come into it, nor did he ask what my current politics were. No doubt he was glad to have an old friend joining, but it must be remembered that the usual method of recruiting into the Secret Service was by personal recommendation of this kind. He told me later that he had known after four days that he had picked the right man for the job.

It seems quite likely that before long I would have got into one of the clandestine organisations anyway. No fewer than six of my relatives and connections got jobs during the war in one or more of the 'funnies'. My wife was in SOE for a time, and later the London office of OSS, the American equivalent of our Secret Service. My brother joined SOE in the Middle East.[†] My sister Angela was in the famous Government Code and Cypher School at Bletchley. So was my father's cousin, Janet Milne – indeed she had joined it before the war. I had a cousin in MI5, and my brother-in-law's wife was in SOE. Each obtained his or her post independently of me and independently of the others. I myself was approached by a friend in December 1941 and asked if I would like to be considered for an SOE covert propaganda job in Turkey, but by then I was firmly entrenched in Section V.

And it is there we must now return.

[†] *Editor's note:* The four children of Kenneth and Maud Milne were Marjorie, Angela, Tim and Tony, who was three years younger than Tim. Tony was also a scholar at Westminster School before going up to Christ Church, Oxford. He travelled in Europe as a freelance writer between 1937 and 1939 and during the war worked in the SOE in north Africa and Greece. He joined SIS in 1944 and remained with them for the next twenty-five years.

5

SECTION V

As I walked through the front door of Glenalmond that afternoon, there was little to tell me I was entering a highly secret office. I recall no security guards or showing of passes. Somebody – probably a passing secretary – directed me to a door on the right of the hall, which opened into a large room with unbarred windows on two sides and a view over the garden. Two or three people of about my own age were working there. Kim, they told me, was upstairs with Felix Cowgill. He came in a few minutes later and began to give me a rundown of the section I had joined.

Section V, the counter-espionage department of SIS (as I now learnt to call the Secret Service), was responsible for counter-espionage operations and intelligence outside British territory; within British territory, this field was covered by MI5, otherwise known as the Security Service. Section V not only directed the collection of counter-espionage intelligence by SIS stations abroad, but also collated and appraised all such overseas counter-espionage intelligence whatever the source: it was largely its own customer. It was for us in Glenalmond to build up as complete a picture as possible of enemy intelligence organisations in foreign countries: their staffs, agents, premises, operations, communications, plans and so on. It was also for us to keep MI5 abreast of this general picture, and more specifically to give them advance information if possible of any hostile espionage operations and plans against British territory, or of the arrival in Britain of an enemy agent, and to carry out enquiries abroad arising from MI5's work at home. A third potential task for the section, scarcely as yet embarked upon, was to initiate or encourage whatever steps could be taken abroad to stifle enemy espionage organisations and activities on the spot, through diplomatic or other means.

Section V was organised into a number of subsections, some geographical, some functional. The geographical ones included at this time Va, dealing with the Americas; Vb, occupied with western Europe; and Ve, covering eastern Europe and the Middle East. The room I was sitting in was the home of the Iberian subsection, called Vd (the name was liable to be a subject of ribaldry, but after five minutes you got used to it). The 'symbol' Vd was also used for Kim himself, head of the subsection: names were not used in communications within SIS. The other officers in Vd had the symbols Vd 1, 2, 3 and so on. I was to be Vd 1; three others had already joined the subsection, and one arrived shortly after. Thus the total officer establishment, including Kim, was six. Until a few weeks earlier it had been no more than one. The suicide of one officer, the nervous breakdown through overwork of another, and complaints from MI5 of inadequate service, had together precipitated the sudden increase. The total officer strength of Section V as a whole at this date was probably only about twenty. In addition there were perhaps twenty to twenty-five secretaries and cardists. The term 'officer' did not necessarily mean an officer in the armed forces. Some, including

Kim, were civilians, as were all the girls. Everyone was allowed to wear civilian clothes, and I did so for the next two years or more.

Kim gave me an outline of the job I was now beginning. I was to be the 'ISOS' officer in Vd. ISOS was the code-name for German intelligence service wireless messages which the British had been able to intercept and decipher. The deciphering was done by the Government Code and Cypher School (GC&CS) at Bletchley, which by October 1941 had broken a number of hand cyphers used locally by German intelligence in Spain, Portugal, Tangier and elsewhere but had not yet cracked the machine cypher used for the main links such as those between Berlin and Madrid, Berlin and Lisbon, and (very importantly) Madrid and Algeciras, overlooking Gibraltar. The number of such intercepts that would appear on my desk each day averaged about twenty, and there was lively expectation that before long the machine cyphers would also be broken, which would bring a vast increase in the work. Meanwhile, Kim showed me samples of what I would be dealing with. The daily batch from Bletchley was cut up by the secretaries into its individual messages, which were then pasted into files according to the terminals: Madrid–Barcelona, Madrid–Bilbao and so on. Madrid to Barcelona would be on the left-hand page, Barcelona to Madrid on the right, and all in date order.

I am not sure how much of this Kim was able to explain to me that evening before we reckoned it was time to go home. Most of the officers and secretaries were billeted in private houses scattered all over St Albans, but one or two married officers rented their own houses. Kim and Aileen had acquired one on the northern outskirts of the town – The Spinney, in Marshalswick Lane – and had invited me to join their household, consisting of themselves, the infant Josephine and Nannie Tucker. This was to make an enormous difference to life. Later I had an interval of three miserable months in a billet because Aileen was ill, and I was able to appreciate the contrast. For the remainder of my twenty-one months in St Albans I was living at The Spinney, except that for two nights and a day each week I would join Marie in Chelsea.

On that first evening, I was a little apprehensive how it would work out. It was many years since I had seen much of Kim, and I knew he had changed, as I had myself. I reckoned that the sheer interest and pressure of the work would make it easy enough for the two of us to find a *modus vivendi*, but Aileen was an unknown quantity and with a new baby in the house I might well feel in the way. It was a week or two before we all got to know one another, and it might have been longer if there had not been a very minor contretemps. The dining room had been made over to me as my bedroom, but it was also being used, increasingly, as a dump for anything for which no other home could be found. Finally, when I discovered one evening that I could not get into my bed except by climbing over a bicycle, a sewing machine and a pram, I launched into a rather pompous protest. Aileen laughed so much that the situation was immediately deflated, and thereafter we were all on very easy terms. They even moved the bicycle out.

Aileen had little in common with Lizy, except that the attraction of each lay in personality rather than looks, and both liked to laugh. She was slight in build, pale, almost fragile, but with plenty of toughness. In spite or because of coming from a 'good' family, she appeared to lack formal education. But she was intelligent, gossipy, human; she loved company, reminiscing, dropping names in a harmless way. She was the very opposite of either a bluestocking or a dedicated political woman, two possible types that a few years earlier one might have expected Kim to marry. Her spelling was rather capricious: Kim and I would come home to find a partly solved *Times* crossword with a word falling short of its allotted space or spilling over the boundary of the puzzle. Kim maintained that her second name, Armanda, was really Amanda but had been misspelt by Aileen from the start. (I half-believed this until recently I read that her father's second name had been Armand.) The two of them shared a liking, which they could do little about in wartime St Albans, for good food and drink. The first time Kim had taken her out he had suggested oysters, and between them they had downed several dozen, Aileen matching Kim plateful for plateful; after that the affair never looked back. In those days, before pressures had begun to show, their life together seemed easy and casual. I don't remember any real quarrel or tiff between them at The Spinney.

In subsection Vd we were all very new. There was no training of any kind: we picked things up as we went along, by asking other people. I am sure that this was by far the best and quickest way of getting the work going. There was little danger of serious mistakes, since everything was discussed and if necessary put up for approval. In any case there was no one available or competent to do the training. In doubt, we turned to Kim. Although he had been in Section V only since August he already seemed to have a mastery of the complicated procedures. While the rest of us were floundering about and wondering what the various 'symbols' meant and whether a letter or a minute was the correct way of writing to this or that department or person, Kim never appeared in difficulties. He knew not only the procedures, but the people as well. One of us, needing to telephone MI5 on some matter which appeared to cut across their various compartments, consulted Kim. 'Get on to ——,' he said. 'He'll tell you it's nothing to do with him, but he'll give you the right answer.' And so it proved. Kim says in his book that when he first joined SIS in 1940 (of which SOE, or rather its predecessor, was then a part), he thought that 'somewhere, lurking in deep shadow, there must be another service, really secret and really powerful'. Although he adds that it was his Soviet contact who put this idea in his head, I think that many on joining SIS had something of the same feeling. We even disputed among ourselves what SIS stood for. IS was presumably Intelligence Service, but what of the first S? Most thought it meant Secret, but some said it was Special, and one or two even held that it was like the M in Ethel M. Dell, for ever unknowable. The press have now settled for Secret, but I am still not quite sure (The other popular name, MI6, was not much used among us.)

Within a few days I knew rather more about the German intelligence service – or rather services, for there were two, the *Abwehr* and the *Sicherheitsdienst* or SD – than I did about SIS. The *Abwehr* was in some ways the equivalent of SIS and SOE combined, but differed in being a constituent part of the German High Command. It was divided into three main sections: I, for collecting military, economic, technical and to some extent political intelligence about the Allies; II, for organising sabotage and subversion (the counterpart, though with many differences, of SOE); III, for counter-espionage. The SD, much less important to us at this time than the *Abwehr*, was a Nazi Party organisation. It was largely concerned with broad questions of internal security in Germany and German-occupied territory, where it functioned alongside the Gestapo, but it also had an important overseas function, particularly in political intelligence.

Over the next few weeks, I began to learn a little more about the service I had joined. The headquarters sections of SIS, apart from Section V, were mostly located in Broadway Buildings; we used the term 'Broadway' to mean 'SIS apart from Section V'. In pre-war days, Section V, as its symbol indicates, had been more or less on the same footing as the Broadway Sections I, II, III, IV and VI, whose job was to circulate intelligence obtained from SIS stations abroad to various Whitehall departments, and to relay the requirements of those departments to the stations; Section V's particular customer was MI5. The circulation sections were not purely postboxes, since they were supposed to know what was worth circulating to Whitehall, how to grade the source, and how to interpret Whitehall's demands in terms of what it was practicable to put to the station. But few staff were necessary, and even to the end of the war the other five circulating sections never consisted of more than a handful of officers each; whereas Section V, as I have said, already numbered about twenty officers, and by 1945 must have had well over a hundred at home and abroad.

The reason for the difference lay in the nature of counter-espionage intelligence. In the study of enemy intelligence and sabotage activities, there was no clear division between foreign and British territory. Most counter-espionage targets lay abroad: the headquarters organisations of the enemy organisations, their stations in occupied and neutral countries, their recruitment of agents and dispatch to British or other territory. A great deal of enemy intelligence and subversive activity might never involve

British territory at all: for example, the watch from neutral countries on British ships and convoys; sabotage of British ships in
neutral ports; the dispatch of enemy agents to countries that were
allied or friendly to us; counter-espionage activities by *Abwehr* III
against SIS or SOE or our allies; German intelligence relations
with neutral governments. To this must be added what became
much more important later, the kind of shorter-range secret
intelligence operations that take place when two armies are
opposed in the field: agents left behind as the enemy advances,
line-crossing operations and so on.

The territorial division of the counter-espionage function
between MI5 and Section V was therefore somewhat unreal,
and a demarcation dispute was inevitable. There were three
sensible solutions: first, that MI5 should take over the whole of
counter-espionage abroad as well as at home and where necessary set up its own stations and communications, with all that
that involved in expert knowledge of other countries and their
languages; second, that Section V should expand within the
existing demarcations of function and expertise; third, that there
should be some kind of amalgamation of MI5 and Section V, or
a pooling of resources and tasks. By the time I arrived, I think
the principle had really been decided in favour of the second
solution; at any rate, Section V was expanding fast. This was
due partly to the logic of the thing, though the issues were fairly
evenly balanced, but perhaps more to the determination of one
man: Felix Cowgill, the head of Section V. It was Felix who fought
off the MI5 challenge and, equally important, set about getting
the necessary staff. Plenty of battles still lay ahead. But in my
own view MI5 were not great empire builders at heart, as empire

builders go; they wanted to do their own job, but realised that increasingly it depended on what was happening abroad. If we were able to give them the necessary service, they seemed willing in the last resort to see the division of functions left unchanged.

In late 1941 the difference in resources between MI5 and Section V was still very great. MI5 had been built up rapidly in 1939–40 when people believed in fifth columns, and when thousands of refugees were being interned. It was a time when stories of German parachutists dressed as nuns, Charlie Kunz the bandleader passing information to the enemy through broadcast foxtrots, and Lord Haw-Haw's infallible knowledge of when the town hall clock had stopped found easy credence. Although the larger lunacies had been discounted by the end of 1941, MI5 still had a swollen staff and were able to write four-page letters to us about mildly suspicious sentences appearing in a letter examined by censorship, whereas we were desperately pressed to deal even briefly with all the hard overseas intelligence that was beginning to be thrown up.

The best of our sources was already the ISOS messages, even though at this time it covered only a small proportion of German intelligence telegrams. At the end of the year there came a radical change. I was staying down in Dorset for Christmas when Kim rang me in the guarded language used on the open telephone: 'You remember the possibility we discussed that you might have a tremendous increase of work? Well, you have.' I returned to St Albans to find the first decoded messages from the machine cypher links on my desk. Within a few weeks I was having to study anything up to 120 a day: nearly all were *Abwehr*, a few SD. (I should mention that the term 'ISOS' strictly referred only to the hand cypher material, while the machine cypher material was given the code-name ISK;[†] but unofficially ISOS continued to be used as a generic term for the lot, and I shall so use it here.)

Although ISOS was distributed also to MI5, to specialised sections in the three forces ministries and to a few other people, it had been agreed by the chief that the prime responsibility for action on it lay with Section V. This responsibility was in turn delegated to the appropriate geographical subsection. In practice most of the opportunities for doing anything with the information, as opposed to merely studying it, lay with Vd. This is because Spain and Portugal were neutral European countries in which both the Germans and SIS maintained stations, and which gave the Germans their best outlet to Allied territory. In addition the harbour and Strait of Gibraltar were themselves important intelligence and sabotage targets. Since Spain and to a lesser extent Portugal were friendly to Germany, conditions were highly favourable for the *Abwehr*. But the situation also gave us opportunities for counter-action. The other neutral European countries were on a different footing: Sweden and Switzerland were largely cut off from the west, and Turkey was somewhat remote.

While ISOS was potentially of enormous value to us, the handling of it was hemmed about with difficulties. There was nothing like a 100 per cent 'take' of cyphered messages. *Abwehr* radio transmissions might be missed by the British interceptors, or received in a garbled state owing to bad atmospheric conditions.

---

†   *Editor's note:* In the names ISOS and ISK, the IS stood for 'Illicit Signals'. OS stood for Oliver Strachey, brother of Lytton Strachey, and K for Alfred Dillwyn ('Dilly') Knox, brother of Ronald and E. V. Knox. Strachey and Knox were two of the Bletchley immortals.

Of those intercepted, the cyphers might be uncrackable for short or long periods. In addition, a great deal of vital information would be sent through the diplomatic bags between the German consulates and the embassies at Madrid and Lisbon, or between the embassies and Berlin; the bags were of course inaccessible to us. Frequent visits by Berlin officers to the peninsula, or by local *Abwehr* officers to Berlin, and the use of the telephone, all helped to reduce the *Abwehr*'s dependence on cypher telegrams. The messages themselves were often couched in deliberately obscure language, and both officers and agents were normally referred to by cover-names (not to be confused with aliases, i.e. the false names they might be using in public).

More important, our first consideration had to be the security of the source. It was, of course, absolutely vital not to let the Germans even suspect we were reading their cyphers. More than ever this became necessary when the machine cyphers were broken, since these, we were given to understand, operated on the same principle as those used by the German armed forces for their high-grade cypher messages; much has now been published about the Ultra source and its incomparable value to the British and American governments and armed forces. It was impressed upon us that, whatever else we might do or fail to do, the one crime we must never commit was to endanger the ISOS source. I should make it clear that although the risk was much more serious in the case of machine material than with the lower grades of cypher, we treated all kinds with equal care. We did not want to give the Germans the slightest reason to begin examining their cypher security.

As the ISOS officer in Vd it was for me to study all the intercepts affecting our area; piece together and try to make sense of

the dozens of different German operations and activities that
were going on simultaneously; identify the large cast of characters, mostly referred to only by cover-names; pursue enquiries
abroad with a stream of telegrams and letters to our stations
in the peninsula, in Tangier and sometimes elsewhere; keep in
close touch with other departments concerned, particularly MI5
over anything that involved or might involve British territory;
and gradually build up an order of battle of the many German
intelligence stations and sections in the area. The work involved
study not only of the ISOS but also of voluminous reports from
the stations, interrogation reports from MI5, back files in the
SIS registry and much besides. For the first fifteen months or so
I had no assistant. Kim followed the material as well as he could,
but one could not learn much from merely skimming through
it. The most important message of the day might be something
like 'Your 129. Yes.' Who sent a message and to whom was often
more important than the message itself, and could be a valuable
indication of the nature of a German intelligence operation, or
even of vital changes in *Abwehr* or SD structure and hierarchy.

Most of the messages did not make much sense by themselves.
This had its advantages. The chief had a tiresome assistant who
was supposed to run through the material for anything that
ought to be brought to the attention of his master. Before long
he was reduced to ringing me only when something like a titled
name caught his eye. Otherwise he left me in peace.

The very heart of the whole problem was to marry up ISOS
with what was called ground information, i.e. reports from our
stations abroad and other non-cryptographic information. ISOS,
purely by itself, was of little practical use. It could tell you a good
deal about headquarters organisation, chains of command and

communication, levels of activity, and, within limits, intelligence operations; and it was very useful towards the end of the war for the picture it gave of the collapse of the politically unreliable *Abwehr* command and its takeover by the SD. But by itself it did not usually tell you the real names of *Abwehr* officers and agents, and was liable to give a very incomplete or misleading impression of what was going on. It was also easy, particularly in the early stages, to misinterpret the material. Kim relates in his book the story of the 'ORKI companions', a fabulous nonsense which was in progress when I arrived. The story has, I think, more significance than has previously been realised, but it would interrupt the narrative unduly to go into all the details, which are given in a footnote to this chapter.

An important part of the business was identification of those appearing in ISOS under cover-names. Often it was simple. A message would say, perhaps, that HERMANO was flying from Madrid to Barcelona or Berlin on such-and-such a date. Our stations could normally supply passenger manifests for Lufthansa or Iberia airlines as a matter of course. When the appropriate list came in, usually with surnames only and often misspelt, you scanned it for likely names. Perhaps the list for that day would be missing, or incomplete, or HERMANO might have decided instead to go by train or car. But with luck there would be one or two likely candidates on the list. Unless there was urgent need, you then waited for another announced journey, or it might be a hotel booking, for with the larger hotels we could usually get hold of the nightly guest lists. If one of the likely names appeared again, and if (as usually happened) you had other ground information on him, the identification was probably safe.

Sometimes the situation was much more urgent, and the

station had to be brought in to make investigations within the limits imposed by the overriding need not to compromise the ISOS source. One of the first such cases, in early 1942, concerned an agent with the cover-name PASCAL, of whom we knew little except that he had stayed at a small hotel in the Barcelona area on or around a particular date, and was being sent, at any rate in the first instance, to South America. The hotel was not one we had regular tabs on. Then came an ISOS message saying that the *Abwehr* had bought a ticket for PASCAL on the SS *Marqués de Comillas*, at a cost of (let us say) 14,875 pesetas. He was about to sail. Our Madrid station managed, first, to get guest lists for the obscure hotel, and secondly to pin the ticket cost down to one or other of six people. This was more difficult that it might sound, since there were apparently several options and extras contributing to the total ticket cost of each of the hundreds of passengers. One name appeared both on the hotel list and among the six passengers. Because of the need to exercise extreme discretion the enquiries had taken several days, and the boat was on the point of docking in Trinidad when the identification was made. We and MI5 sent Trinidad a Most Immediate signal, and poor PASCAL, who probably never even knew what his ticket had cost, was taken off the boat for interrogation. He was carrying compromising equipment and soon confessed. For the rest of the war he was interned in Britain. Several of his companions in internment were caught in the same kind of way.

Many identifications were difficult. Some of the characters never travelled, never moved outside the metaphysical ISOS world. It was a long time before we were able to put a name to FELIPE, of the *Abwehr* headquarters in Madrid, who was of particular interest because he specialised in sending agents to

England. Cover-names of staff were often changed, so that you had to identify a cover-name with its successor before you could proceed. In addition, most of the more important *Abwehr* station officers were living under aliases in Spain or Portugal, and could not readily be identified with previous records from other countries. Some of our identifications would remain on the 'tentative' list for months before the final clincher arrived. Occasionally it was child's play: for instance, a message from Seville to Madrid containing a cover-name might be passed on to Berlin with the real name substituted. In the course of two years or so several hundred German intelligence staff, agents and contacts in Spain, Portugal and north-west Africa, appearing under cover-names in ISOS, were finally identified with 'real' people.

But the agent-running activities of the *Abwehr* in the peninsula were less important and less damaging to Britain than their ship-watching activities in the Strait of Gibraltar, to which the Spanish authorities were not so much turning a blind eye as giving active if undeclared assistance. The *Abwehr* station at Algeciras reported all comings and goings in the port of Gibraltar, and together with the station at Tangier covered the passage of Allied naval units, convoys and other shipping through the strait. But *Abwehr* observation did not, at that time, extend to the hours of darkness. It was I think in February 1942, soon after the machine cypher had been cracked, that we saw the first cryptic ISOS message about 'Bodden'. This enterprise appeared primarily to involve infrared searchlights, cameras and heat-sensing apparatus beamed across the Strait of Gibraltar between two German-manned posts on either side of the water; but radar equipment was also mentioned, and a '*Lichtsprechgerät*' or 'light speech apparatus'. (This last, if I understand it correctly, made use of a visible light ray, or more probably an infrared one, modulated to carry a voice transmission in the same way, very broadly, that a radio wave of more conventional frequency is modulated. It would be almost impossible to intercept, unless one could position oneself exactly in the line of the very narrow beam, and had some rather exotic equipment.) After ten or twenty ISOS messages had accumulated, bristling with German electronic terms, it was clear that first-class technical advice was needed. Felix suggested I should take the whole problem to R. V. Jones in Broadway.[1] Jones's official title there was IId, that is to say he was nominally one of several desk officers in the Air Section, but in fact he held a more or less autonomous post in charge of technical intelligence; he also held a comparable position in the Air Ministry intelligence branch. Though still only twenty-nine, he was already famous for his exploits in 'bending the beam' used by the Luftwaffe in bombing Britain. (This is probably an inaccurate description of what he actually did, but it is what we believed.) The first thing I saw in his room, apart from his own young and cheerful face, was something that looked like a rather complicated piece of radio equipment. This turned out to be the German radar set (or part of one) that British commando troops had just captured in the Bruneval raid.[2] The official reports in the press had said the radar was destroyed, but here it was. Jones and his number two were cock-a-hoop. We turned to the ISOS I had brought, and it was obvious I had come to the right place. From then on I consulted Jones regularly about Bodden.

Kim describes in his book the political steps we were subsequently able to get the Foreign Office to take through our embassy in Madrid, which finally compelled the Germans to close down the whole Bodden operation. I hesitate to pit my memory against his, because I am relying entirely on what I can remember of these events of more than thirty-five years ago, whereas Kim, writing in Moscow, had presumably been able to consult directly or indirectly the reports which I imagine he made to the Russians at the time. My own recollection is that the first démarche to the Spaniards, made in 1942, concerned not so much Bodden as the presence and activities of so many German *Abwehr* officers in Spain under diplomatic cover, a large number of whom we named with details of the posts they held. We would certainly have laid emphasis on the unusual concentration of Germans, offices and observation posts in the Strait of Gibraltar, but I doubt whether we could have said very much about the Bodden plans or any special technical apparatus; we had no knowledge of these except from ISOS, much of which was still difficult to interpret. The Germans were eventually forced to abandon Bodden, but not as far as I recall for several months – perhaps after the Allied landings in north Africa of November 1942.

There were, I think, three or four British démarches to General Franco in 1942 and 1943, all based primarily on ISOS, with the support of ground information for identifications and for a number of other details. It is remarkable in retrospect that we were allowed to do so much with this secret material, in the light of the absolute need to protect the source and the knowledge that the Spaniards would pass our protests verbatim to the Germans. Perhaps it was because no one above the level of Kim fully understood what we were doing. The prevalent wisdom had been that no action must be taken on ISOS unless there was some kind of confirmation from ground sources. This, it was thought, would give 'cover' for the use of ISOS. We reasoned that the only thing that mattered was what the Germans would think. Would they jump to the conclusion that we were reading their signals? Or would they think rather that the ubiquitous and omniscient British Secret Service had pieced it all together from its countless agents throughout the peninsula, if not in Berlin itself? We reckoned that, provided we were certain that any German we mentioned really existed in the name and position we gave for him, it did not matter whether we had information on him from the field or not: after all, how were the Germans to know what reports we had? We felt confident that our use of ISOS, unprecedented though it was, would not endanger the source.

The text of the first démarche was drafted by Kim, though later I had a hand. Patrick Reilly of the Foreign Office, by now seconded to the chief as personal assistant, gave valuable help. Kim evolved a fine Augustan style in which indignation at the outrageous behaviour of the Germans, and pain that the Spaniards were allowing their neutrality to be thus compromised, were nicely blended. Once the first protest had been made, with no adverse effect on ISOS, we became increasingly bold until finally we were able to present Franco with an almost complete order of battle of the *Abwehr* stations in Spain and Spanish Morocco. Later we saw the whole list go over the air from Madrid to Berlin, but no one at either end ever suggested that cypher security might be to blame. One of the possible reactions to be expected was that the Germans would retaliate by similarly denouncing SIS staff in Spain; some Broadway officers made much of this at first but they were overridden. We were confident (partly on the basis of ISOS) that German knowledge of SIS in the peninsula was sketchy. Sure enough they eventually produced a list, a strange concoction naming one or two actual SIS staff and agents, lost among a much larger number of irrelevant names, including people who had died or left Spain. Nobody on the British side took much notice, and the Spaniards did not press it. They did, however, press the Germans as a result of our protests and sometime in 1943 a large number were withdrawn from Spain, including most of those in the south.

Why did Spain, which was openly committed to supporting the Axis, pay so much attention to our démarches, first presented in mid-1942, when the Germans were riding at their highest, pressing towards the Caucasus and along the north African coast and sinking a frighteningly large proportion of our shipping? The truth was that Franco (whom Kim always regarded as exceptionally astute) was prepared to help the *Abwehr* only so long as it maintained reasonable secrecy about its staff – most of whom were commissioned or non-commissioned officers in the armed forces – and its operations. We knew, the Spaniards knew and the Germans knew that our information was true, and that what the Germans were being allowed to do was totally incompatible with neutrality, however nominal. A protest in 1943 to Portugal had much less success: the Portuguese considered they had behaved with reasonable neutrality, and their consciences were fairly clear.

It is easy to see your own job, and your performance of it, in a very rosy light. Throughout 1942 and most of 1943 I reckoned I had the key job not only in the Iberian subsection but in all of Section V. Indeed I would not have changed it for any other post in the whole counter-espionage world. Never before or since did I have a job that seemed to suit me so exactly. R. V. Jones once said to me (anticipating computers) that the ideal intelligence assessment officer would have a brain as big as a room, capable

of absorbing and synthesising the entire field of relevant information, and I would say that the description applied more nearly
to Jones himself than to anyone else I met in the war. I was not in
that class, but such capacity as I had at the time for ingesting and
retrieving names, dates, places, figures and facts now paid off.
On top of that, I was working with congenial colleagues under
Kim whom we all respected and liked. I have said little so far
about these colleagues, who had to cope with the bulk of the
material coming from the stations and elsewhere, the requests
from MI5 and a hundred other things, and who had a knowledge
of the area and its languages which I totally lacked. Over all this
Kim – himself familiar with Spain, its leaders and its language –
presided with a benign and unruffled wisdom.

Life was far from overserious. Counter-espionage has an
advantage over most other intelligence work: its subject is people,
and a very mixed bag too. Anything funny, lewd or otherwise
interesting was shared among all of us, working as we were in the
same room. Kim was very much a part of this. Yet again I was
fascinated by the change that had come over him. Section V had
more than a normal share of enemies but Kim seemed to get on
with everybody. In his dealing with others he appeared the very
opposite of his uncompromising and often cantankerous father,
and quite different from his own earlier self. Yet Kim himself
could also be uncompromising on anything he considered
important. Somehow he usually got his way without antagonis-
ing the other party, often without even letting him realise there
had been a conflict. One of his weapons was that he was always
well informed on the subject he was talking about; all too many
officers in SIS and indeed elsewhere had a marked aversion to
reading papers really thoroughly.

The files in the SIS Central Registry (which was located in St Albans at a house two fields away from Glenalmond) went back to the early 1920s. We saw much of them because every new name that came up was automatically 'traced' in the registry: one was constantly receiving huge bundles of files with any likely – or unlikely – traces flagged. I cannot say that these pre-war records really justified to us the reputation SIS had achieved in the world. In the Section V field, concentration on the communist target meant that very little had been done about German intelligence by the time the war began: even obvious basic work, for example the assembling of overt material such as German telephone books or other reference publications while they were still easy to obtain, had been neglected. To judge by the stories of our colleagues who had joined in peacetime, pre-war SIS had considered secrecy an end in itself. There had been a mindless concentration on the inessentials of security: just about the two worst offences you could commit were to let your wife know what your real job was, and to tell any of your colleagues your salary. The war had swept away a lot of this nonsense, but we were still paid our monthly salaries in crackly white fivers. The security effect was the opposite of what was intended; you were pinpointed either as a black marketeer or as someone in the Secret Service. Once when I wanted to raise a small overdraft at my bank I went to see the manager and explained that my only source of income was the small batch of fivers I deposited monthly. 'Ah yes,' he said with a knowing grin, 'we have several customers like you.' I don't *think* he meant I was a black marketeer.

We in Vd were all extremely busy. In my own job alone there was enough work for almost any number of people. Twenty of us could easily have been employed in following up all the possible leads and subjects that ISOS produced in our area; but even if war priorities had justified a large increase (which clearly they did not) and good staff had been obtainable, there would have been no point in generating more enquiries than could be handled by our stations abroad. Every day brought its excitements and its new problems. I insisted on taking one day off a week, and seldom came back without being told by Kim that as usual a crisis had arisen in my absence. There was a crisis every day, I replied; he was just seeing one in seven.

Almost every evening the two of us took work home. We would continue at Glenalmond till about seven, then fill our briefcases and go. The bus went almost from door to door, with a pub at each end. What drinking we did at St Albans, which was nothing remarkable, was mostly at one or other of these two pubs: there was little drink at The Spinney itself, and no bar or mess at Glenalmond. During the winter of 1941–42 Kim and one or two others from the subsection used to lunch at the White Hart in St Albans and have a few drinks, but they abandoned this eventually, probably for financial reasons. Patrick Seale says that throughout the war Kim seemed to get hold of black market whisky at £4 a bottle when nobody else could.[3] This seems to show a misunderstanding both of the wartime alcohol situation and of Kim's own way of life at this time. To the best of my memory whisky from distillers outside the Scotch Whisky Association was often available in the shops towards the end of the war at £4 15s. a bottle if you could conceivably afford it, but the ordinary person established himself with one or more retailers and bought the occasional bottle at the unofficially controlled price of something over a pound. Kim could never have afforded to make a habit of buying whisky from his own pocket at £4 or £4 15*s*. a bottle – say £20 to £30 at present prices† – and it would surely have been far too risky to take subsidies from the Russians for the purpose. Our drink at St Albans was usually draught bitter, sometimes laced or chased with a small gin: the object was to make the alcohol go as far as possible. It was not until the arrival of the Americans in force from about 1943 onwards that drinking became a little easier.

I still have nightmares thinking of the risks we took in carting all those top secret papers through buses and pubs. I don't think there were specific rules against it, but the penalties for losing the stuff would hardly bear contemplating. Sometimes I would have ten or more ISOS files, among other papers, while Kim's batch might well include a thick wad of BJs,[4] the equally sensitive diplomatic intercepts; it was a time to catch up on reading. I sometimes wondered why he bothered so much about BJs, which with well-defined exceptions were only occasionally of interest in our peculiar world, but if I thought of it further I must have concluded that someone needed to comb through them and he was the best person. I suppose now that he may have been concerned also to note BJs of interest to the Russians, perhaps even to abstract or 'borrow' the useful ones – there was precious little security control over papers of this kind, of which several copies were circulating.

Soon after we arrived back we would be sitting down in the kitchen to a meal prepared by Aileen. In the early days we had the occasional services of someone we called 'the poacher', though I dare say his offerings were legitimately come by; but

---

† *Editor's note:* The 'present prices' are from the late 1970s. In 2014 Milne's wartime prices equate to around £150 and £180 respectively.

his pheasants soon became chickens, then rabbits, then nothing. We still ate fairly well, on our purely civilian rations. Aileen was a reasonably good cook and even her Woolton pie was edible.[†] Neither we nor anyone else in Section V did much entertaining. Nor did we seek outside distractions. In twenty-one months Kim, Aileen and I went to one old Marx Brothers film. At The Spinney we had a radio and a rather primitive gramophone with twenty or thirty records. But here was a potential source of discord. Aileen, who was tone deaf, hated most music, and Kim was thereby deprived of something he had always needed. Later he must have asserted himself, especially in Washington where he bought many LPs. But in St Albans we had almost no good music.

It was a casual domestic life, but at the same time a very regular one: off to work each morning at the same time, back between seven and eight. Kim went up to London once or twice a week but would be home by evening. But after I had been four or five months at The Spinney life changed abruptly. I came back from a day off to be told by Kim that Aileen was ill, a nurse was being brought in and my room was needed. Within a day or so I was billeted on a household of elderly people whose lives had been little affected by the war. Although their financial reward from my presence was small, they benefited from my ration book. All I ate there was a light breakfast: in the evenings I would get a bite at a pub, then go back to the office. It would have been a miserable interlude indeed if the work had not been so exciting. After three months Aileen was deemed to have recovered. The

---

† *Editor's note:* Woolton pie was a wartime vegetable pie recommended by the Ministry of Food and named after the Food Minister, Lord Woolton.

nurse left, and I returned, thankfully, to the prams and sewing machines and deckchairs of my room at The Spinney.

Kim describes in his book the farcical affair of the 'ORKI companions', which was near completion when I arrived in Section V in October 1941. I had no part in it. I summarise it here because with hindsight one can see a significance which nobody (other than Kim) could have appreciated at the time, and of which Kim says nothing in his book. He tells us that ISOS revealed, in September 1941, that the *Abwehr* in Spain was sending two agents named Hirsch and Gilinski, the first accompanied by his wife and mother-in-law, to South America. Shortly before their departure from Bilbao by ship, the *Abwehr* station there sent a cypher message to the *Abwehr* in Madrid to say that (in the English translation issued by Bletchley) Hirsch and his 'ORKI companions' were ready to leave. Kim appears to have leapt to the conclusion that 'ORKI' might be an abbreviation for a group of revolutionary (anti-Stalinist) communists, probably Trotskyists, who were presumably being sponsored and exploited by the *Abwehr*. (He does not mention this, but according to what he told me later, he – or some assistant – unearthed a reference to an organisation of this kind called RKI, and I understood from him that it might also have been called ORKI in the same way that the GPU was also called OGPU.) Kim, breaking several rules, managed to arrange that, in addition to Hirsch and Gilinski, at least a dozen people on the passenger list whose names suggested a possible link with dissident communism, or perhaps were merely Slavonic, should be arrested and interrogated in Trinidad. They were detained – most I think for quite a long time.

When some months later I found myself looking back at this incident I was completely flummoxed. It was totally unlike anything else the *Abwehr* was doing, and the evidence ludicrously insufficient for the kind of action that was taken. I had also noticed that when GC&CS came across a short indecipherable passage in ISOS they were liable (in the text as issued) to show the relevant 'corrupt' letters in capitals, in the middle of an otherwise intelligible message. I had noticed further that, in the type of cypher used by the *Abwehr* substations in Spain, a 'corrupt' passage often consisted of correct letters alternating with 'corrupt' ones. I asked GC&CS whether 'ORKI' could be 'DREI', i.e. 'three'. They checked, and agreed at once. In other words, the message simply referred to Hirsch and his three companions (wife, mother-in-law and Gilinski).

It seems very likely that, because of the imagined Trotskyist connection, Kim saw a great opportunity to score a success with the Russians. He would certainly have wished to discuss it with them. They would have been extremely interested if the Germans really were helping dissident communist groups in this way, and they may have pressed Kim to take the action he did. In the state of ignorance prevailing in Section V at the time, this would have scarcely have aroused suspicion. I wonder if it was the Russians who put him onto the possible interpretation of RKI/ORKI, or whether it emerged from a study by Kim and others of ancient Central Registry files – or perhaps both. Even if Kim did not have the opportunity to consult the Russians, he must have seen a chance of presenting them with a coup. Subsequently – as in his book – he made a joke of it, and even claimed it as a triumph of sorts, although in fact it was an utter fiasco. He seems to have acted miles out of character and indeed common sense. My conclusion is that he could not conceivably have behaved in this way if he had not been pursuing something of value, as he saw it, to the NKVD. I am happy to say that we never treated ISOS so recklessly and crassly again.

ON THE MAP

By the summer of 1942 Section V was beginning to take on a different look. The number of officers and secretaries was steadily increasing. The flow of ISOS was now five or ten times what it had been a year earlier. Abroad too we were expanding. In the early part of the war SIS overseas stations had been all-purpose, trying to produce intelligence of all kinds, military, political, technical and counter-espionage. But counter-espionage had had very low priority. In 1940–41 Felix Cowgill succeeded in arranging for specialist counter-espionage officers to be posted to the Madrid and Lisbon stations. Although nominally subordinate at this time to the existing head of station, they became in practice (and later officially) independent, with their own offices, staff and cyphers. Now other officers from Section V were being sent abroad to open their own stations. We were beginning to become almost a separate service from the rest of SIS, though under the same general management in London and having very close links both at home and in the field.

There is no doubt that Cowgill was the man chiefly responsible for putting Section V on the map. History so far has given him a raw deal. He was caricatured in the original *Sunday Times* articles, and not very fairly treated in Kim's book. Not that I am in a position to throw stones at the authors of either: my views of Felix became very critical as the war progressed, and in the end I was, I suppose, a beneficiary of his downfall. Certainly he had large faults, two in particular. One, much commented on in the Philby literature, was that he made an altogether inordinate number of enemies. Anyone who tried to build up a large department from almost nothing in the cut-throat world of wartime intelligence was bound to make enemies, but Felix seemed to go far out of his way to antagonise people. A more serious fault in my view was that his judgement on intelligence matters was not always sound, and he did not fully appreciate the changing pattern of the work. It would indeed have needed one of R. V. Jones's ideal intelligence officers with an outsize brain to keep up with all that was coming in, but Felix's operational judgements and ideas became increasingly remote from reality. His considerable gifts lay in a different direction. A section chief without his drive, stubbornness, courage, capacity for hard work and interest in administration would not have succeeded in preserving and increasing Section V's role and getting the necessary staff in the crucial years of 1941 and 1942. Kim, with all his great abilities, could not have done the same job.

It is interesting to speculate on the kind of animal Section V might have become if Kim had been in charge in those years. Probably it would have been much smaller and more closely knit with MI5, perhaps in a joint working organisation; it would have had good staff and would have done an efficient job; but in the end it would not have made such a mark. Kim congratulates himself in his book on having helped to abolish Section V after the war. But there would not have been so much to abolish if it had not been for Felix Cowgill.

In two of his projects Felix showed himself more far sighted than Kim or me or most other people in Section V. These were, first, liaison with OSS (Office of Strategic Services, the American counterpart of SIS) and, second, the establishment of Special Counter-Intelligence (SCI) units in a number of military headquarters in the field. Though both belong more fully to a later period of the war, their beginnings were in 1942. Contact between SIS and OSS had begun even before OSS was properly established and collaboration was of course inevitable after Pearl Harbor. But Felix conceived something far more radical – no less than a joint counter-espionage headquarters consisting of Section V and the corresponding section of OSS, later called X2 – the very name was derived from XB, the code-name used for Section V in our communications with the field. During 1942 the first X2 officers appeared in St Albans, and huts to accommodate them and the later arrivals were built in the grounds of Glenalmond. Most papers could be freely passed between Section V and X2, which also received ISOS although action remained with Section V.

The objections from me, Kim and others were twofold. First, the risk to ISOS, and to SIS organisation and operations generally, would be enlarged. Second, we foresaw that for a long time we would get little or nothing from the arrangement, and would have to spend a lot of our precious time talking to and training the X2 officers. So we did, but in the end it paid off because from November 1942 onwards much of the German-occupied territory liberated by the Allies fell in the first instance to the Americans. Information from captured *Abwehr* and SD officers and agents, and the opportunity to 'turn' suitable agents against the Germans, were immediately available to us. The process was

greatly helped by the establishment of British and American
military SCI units, staffed by officers trained in Section V and
attached to Army Group headquarters or sometimes a lower
formation. The SCI units were equipped with rapid and secure
wireless and cypher communications with Section V, and in effect
were Section V (or X2) outstations in the battle areas. X2 officers
could be attached to Section V's SCI units and vice versa.

It is rather surprising that Kim was not more enthusiastic about
the Section V link with OSS. It was bound to give greater insight
into OSS activities, capabilities and staff identities, and therefore
those of whatever organisation would succeed it in peacetime
– surely a prime Russian target. There is little doubt that the
very close relations established between Section V and OSS/
X2 helped to lay the foundations for later collaboration between
SIS and the CIA, the post-war successor to OSS. Whether Kim
thought this a good thing or not, his acceptance of Section V–X2
cooperation was grudging, though he certainly did not actively
campaign or intrigue against it. He always disliked America and
the Americans, whereas I had a weakness for them, and probably found it easier than he did to work closely with X2 as time
went on. He had better relations with the much more professional FBI, with whom we had a less closely interlocked liaison.

One of the accusations made against Cowgill is that he clung
jealously to Section V information, particularly ISOS. He has
been described as notorious for sitting on information rather
than circulating it. Certainly one of the many besetting sins of
intelligence officers is the overuse of secrecy, ostensibly in the
name of security, but actually to preserve some private empire.
Claude Dansey, vice-chief of SIS in the war, and his special
fief, Switzerland, immediately come to mind. But Cowgill's

opportunities for restricting information were somewhat limited. ISOS, as I have said, was circulated in full to a number of departments, including MI5. Telegrams and reports from stations abroad, including Section V stations, automatically went to Broadway as well as to us, and into Central Registry files. Most other information was not Section V's preserve, and restriction on it, if any, was imposed by others; the great mass of Bletchley information (other than ISOS) came into this category, and indeed we in Section V saw little of it apart from the diplomatic BJs.

There was for a short time a minor exception to what I have said above about ISOS. Felix arranged that some restriction should be placed upon the circulation of ISOS messages which appeared to name or refer to British agents and intelligence operations; at least, I think it was Felix who arranged it, but if so the idea found ready acceptance in Broadway, which disliked the thought that what appeared to be its failures were being gratuitously advertised to the intelligence branches of the Army, Royal Navy and RAF, particularly as the *Abwehr* reports were often untrue. As far as I recall, the restricted series, code-named ISBA, was fairly soon terminated and the total number of such messages was few. We in Vd thought the series was silly and unnecessary.

What Felix did do was to cling with his teeth to the principle that external action on ISOS information should be vested in Section V alone, and that any other department or section, including MI5, that wished to take action would have to do so with the permission and under the close supervision of Section V. Here he was on extremely strong ground. In using ISOS we were juggling with eggs. Anyone who was not devoting as much time and care as we were to the study both of ISOS and of all the information from stations, interrogations and other sources might well do serious damage. I have no doubt that the rules about ISOS were bent from time to time by other departments, but the general principle was maintained.

I am mystified by a statement in Patrick Seale's book: '[Cowgill's] miserly attitude to the treasures at his disposal enraged the customers of Section V, and in particular MI5 who would dearly have liked sight of all the *Abwehr* material rather than having Cowgill release to them only what he felt concerned British security.'[1] With the possible and frankly trivial exception of ISBA, MI5 received ISOS (if that is what is meant by *'Abwehr* material') as soon as we did. Nor was there any serious holding back with MI5 on other material. At some point in, I think, 1942, Felix invited Dick White, deputy head of the intelligence division of MI5, to spend a fortnight with us at Glenalmond. We were instructed to show or discuss with him anything that he – or we – might wish, and we took full advantage of this. (I am also surprised by a statement of Patrick Seale's that two extremely able GC&CS officers, Leonard Palmer and Denys Page, were critical of Cowgill's 'hoarding of their hard-won material'. Hoarded from whom?)[†]

There is no doubt that Felix could be highly obstructive to departments outside Section V, in strong contrast to his attitude towards his beloved OSS/X2. But the larger Section V became, the less this really mattered. The people who actually dealt with

---

[†]   *Editor's note:* Milne is right to say that most ISOS and ISK material went to MI5 but the main problem was not Cowgill's refusal to pass material to MI5; it was his refusal, on misguided security grounds, to allow service intelligence officers involved in the Double Cross operations access to the ISOS and ISK material.

the cases that came up every day were his desk officers, such as Kim, me and many others. I cannot recall having to hold back anything important from MI5. Few if any of us had much stomach for interdepartmental squabbles. There was far too much to do anyway. In Vd, MI5 were regarded as colleagues with whom we were more closely concerned than we were with, say, Ve, the Middle East subsection. Between us and MI5 there was, however, a difference of approach to the work. In Section V we were a bunch of amateurs who had been brought in to man a section which for practical purposes had scarcely existed before the war. However hard we worked, we always – Kim as much as anyone – maintained a rather light-hearted attitude, looking for the funny side even in our most formal correspondence. Although MI5 had also absorbed many people from outside, they remained a solemn-minded professional service whose officers prided themselves on the extreme care and thoroughness with which they handled every matter, however small: counter-espionage was much too serious to joke about. But in two of them – both close friends of Kim's – irreverence was always breaking through.

Dick Brooman-White (not to be confused with Dick White) was head of MI5's Iberian section. By the middle of the war, thanks largely to his own efforts, there was little left for him to do, so he joined us in Section V. Because of internal injuries caused in a riding accident he could not drink, but he was highly intelligent and amusing company. It was ever a mystery how this rapid and almost inaudible speaker managed after the war to make himself understood at the hustings and on the floor of the House of Commons.[2] Tommy Harris, also in the MI5 Iberian section, was a law unto himself.[3] Part Spanish, part Jewish, art dealer, rich, he came from a very different background from most of us. 'Tommy can't read or write,' Kim would say, 'but he's extraordinarily subtle and astute about anything to do with people.' It is true that Tommy never read or wrote anything if he could possibly help it, but he ran the most remarkable double-agent operation of the whole war.[4] He was in some ways Kim's closest friend and Kim named his second son Tomas after him.

It is time to mention the brilliant maverick section headed by Hugh Trevor-Roper, who had come up to Christ Church during my time at Oxford. The search for an interception of enemy intelligence radio messages was carried out by an organisation in Barnet called RSS – Radio Security Service – which then passed the messages on to Bletchley for decipherment. It was logical that a small office should be set up to extract, interpret and process intelligence – chiefly from the deciphered messages but also if appropriate from other sources – which might help the RSS interceptors in their search of the ether for clandestine transmissions (times, frequencies and call signs were constantly being changed). It was also logical that this office, while physically located at Barnet, should form part of Section V, where the intelligence was to be found; hence its title Vw. In the ordinary way the job might have remained on this basis for the rest of the war, filled by a single medium-grade officer. But equally it could provide unlimited scope for study of the *Abwehr* and SD, as a basis in the first instance for giving informed guidance to RSS. It so happened that Felix Cowgill, in organising Section V, had unaccountably neglected to set up a subsection to study the central organisation, personnel, policies, methods and political position of the *Abwehr* and SD. True, one officer was theoretically deputed for this task, part time, but since it should have involved among many other things a study of all the ISOS from all areas there was no possibility of his achieving anything. No one as intelligent and enterprising as Trevor-Roper, in his position as Vw, could have failed to see the opportunity this presented. He gathered around him three other first-class Oxford academics – Gilbert Ryle (who had been one of my philosophy tutors), Stuart Hampshire and Charles Stuart. Although nominally a subsection of Section V, they were for most practical purposes independent (a position that was ratified later in the war when they were formally separated from Section V and given the title RIS, or Radio Intelligence Section).

In so uncharted a field as wartime intelligence, there are bound to be many demarcation disputes and many contenders for any piece of ground. But there is one argument that nearly always silences the rest: if someone is really producing the goods, it matters little what this or that directive or charter may say. Trevor-Roper's high-powered team began to issue broad studies of the German intelligence services of a kind that no one else at the time was producing. It was useless for Felix to object, since he had failed to offer an acceptable alternative; and his own officers were glad to see the job being done. Battles continued for a long time, but in Trevor-Roper, Felix was up against someone who was as prepared to fight as he was and much cleverer about it. On the whole, at any rate at this time, there was little duplication between Vw and the regional subsections of Section V, and I found much profit in my dealings with Charles Stuart, whose area included the Iberian peninsula.

Felix, who was well liked by his staff, ran Section V as a cosy family affair – indeed his nice wife, Mary, and his sister-in-law were working in it. All of us, from Felix himself to the newest secretary, were on Christian-name terms. There is a tendency

anyway for this to happen in intelligence circles, partly for security reasons and partly because of the feeling you have of shared
secrets and of isolation from the outside world. Section V, big as
it became, never entirely lost this family atmosphere. There was
a minimum of administrative tail. A factotum called David, with
one assistant, looked after the building, slept there at night and
presumably organised things like office cleaning. A middle-aged
lady, widow of a former SIS officer and probably unpaid, helped
over billeting and ration books. One or two cars and uniformed
women drivers were allocated to the section.

Although most of us, apart from the secretaries, were in
the Army, or occasionally Royal Navy or RAF, we were an
unmilitary lot. One admirably unorthodox colleague was A. G.
Trevor-Wilson, who had been with Kim at the SOE training
school at Beaulieu and who was working in Vd and looking
after Tangier and Spanish Morocco when I arrived.[5] Nominally
a captain in the Intelligence Corps, he wore a strange assortment of uniforms and insignia. The badge on his cap was not
the same as those on his lapels. His respirator came from the
RAF. Sometimes he wore a white shirt with his uniform. Once
he was stopped by a military policeman who told him that the
flash he was wearing on his sleeve was that of a division in north
Africa, and what was he doing in St Albans? Trevor (who worked
flexible hours) used to cycle to the office. If it had been raining,
he would then change his trousers for others equally contrary
to military regulations, a process inevitably interrupted by the
arrival of a secretary. Trevor claimed to have a variety of mysterious lady friends, to each of whom he was known by a different
name. Once when we were walking together in Jermyn Street
he suddenly dragged me into a shop. A woman went by. 'I know

her,' whispered Trevor, 'but I can't remember the *name* I use
with her.' It was said that when Trevor first joined SIS he was
surprised to find that the smallest comment he inscribed on a
paper evoked immediate and deferential attention. It turned out
that he was using green ink, a prerogative reserved for the chief
since the First World War.

Another member of the section was Sammy. He was an affec-
tionate extrovert black-and-white spaniel whom Marie had been
given as a puppy in the autumn of 1940. For a year we had toted
him round from one unsuitable billet or rented house to another,
with intervals of parking him on long-suffering relatives. Soon
after arriving at St Albans I brought him to The Spinney, where
Kim and Aileen took him in unenthusiastically. When Aileen fell
ill Sammy had to leave with his master. There was nowhere to
put him but Glenalmond, and here at last he came into his own,
the Section V dog. When he was not out in the garden or fields
getting filthy, or making the rounds of the other subsections, he
was generally curled up asleep in my pending tray. The weekly
meeting of Section V in the conservatory, or 'snake pit', was not
deemed to have properly begun until Sammy, tail cocked high,
had trotted in and taken his place. One summer's day there was
an official visit from the Director of Naval Intelligence, looking
as smart as only a naval officer can – I retain an impression,
which cannot possibly be accurate, of white ducks. While we (in
Vd) were gathered round him, trying to explain what we were
doing, an eager mud-caked figure hurtled through the open
ground-floor window and leapt straight at the DNI's resplend-
ent chest. Admirals don't usually take kindly to being landed
on by muddy dogs belonging to Army lieutenants, but Admiral
Godfrey was magnanimous. Sammy was the nearest thing we

had to a watchdog at Glenalmond – Sammy, who thought the entire human race was perfect, even if a few of its members were more perfect than the rest. If parachutists dressed as nuns (or nuns dressed as parachutists) had descended on Glenalmond, Sammy would have been the first to welcome them.

Some writers have suggested that SIS and other intelligence organisations were a kind of upper-crust preserve, effete, riddled with class prejudice, only too ready to cover up when one of their members came under suspicion. A novel written about Kim, called *Gentleman Traitor*,[6] symbolises him on the cover by showing, of all inappropriate things, a bowler hat. Well, it makes more interesting reading than the truth, which is that in Section V at any rate we were a mixed but mostly middle-class lot. We did indeed have a baronet, laird of many a broad Scottish acre, and later a peer of the realm and even a cousin of the present Queen joined us. But mostly we came from a rather ordinary variety of jobs and backgrounds, such as the Indian police, schoolmastering and commerce. I do not even know where most of my colleagues in Section V went to school or whether they went to university. I do know that several of them had spent a great part of their lives abroad; their knowledge of foreign countries and languages was an important reason for their recruitment into Section V. Perhaps some of the secretaries tended to be well bred: however, as they also tended to be rather good-looking, and hard-working into the bargain, their origins could be overlooked.

In these years of 1942 and 1943 Kim was riding high. He was rapidly making a name for himself, even among hard-core enemies of Section V in Broadway, as an intelligent, reasonable and effective person with whom business could be done. The Foreign Office, in the person of Peter Loxley,[7] who was our main link, were beginning to like him very much. He was MI5's favourite son. In Section V he was popular with his colleagues, and usually adored by the secretaries. Felix trusted and later promoted him; there was no hint yet of the future rift. But Kim had his own views about some of the people he was dealing with, especially in Broadway, which had more than its fair share of placemen, hangers-on, second-raters, former naval captains who were popularly reputed to have hazarded their ships, and plain duds. His book contains some of the acid opinions he – and many of us – expressed at that time.

At home his life with Aileen seemed to be happy. I didn't know they weren't married. Vaguely it registered at the back of my mind that Aileen, with all her reminiscing, never spoke of any wedding day, and no anniversary was celebrated. With that, I put it out of my thoughts; it mattered little anyway. They probably assumed Marie and I knew, but in fact I first heard of it in 1945 from Dick Brooman-White. According to Aileen, she and Kim first met through Flora Solomon,[8] under whom Aileen had worked in the staff welfare department of Marks and Spencer before the war. Already by May 1940 the Kim–Aileen affair must have been well established, because Aileen used to describe how she travelled to Paris to see him and arrived on the very day the Germans launched their drive into Belgium and Holland.

Life at The Spinney continued to revolve around our Section V work. At one point I had to stop bringing papers home with me for about a fortnight because I found I was dreaming about the work all night and every night. We made little use of the garden, except for one attempt to grow garlic. Kim's philosophy of gardening was simple: if a certain amount of fertiliser was good for a plant, then ten times the amount was ten times as good.

In the summer of 1942 there was an addition to the household, a French bulldog whom we named Axel after a favourite ISOS character, the *Abwehr* guard dog at Algeciras. We used to have boxing matches with this seemingly ferocious dog, sparring with him and mock-punching him on the face. One evening Guy Burgess came to dinner. Guy seldom managed to get through an evening without doing something mildly shocking. Boxing Axel was not enough; he had to kiss him repeatedly on his snarling, slavering mouth. Another visitor was an American journalist, an old friend of Kim's from the Spanish Civil War. I can no longer swear to his identity, but I think it was Sam Brewer, whose wife Eleanor Kim was eventually to marry. On another occasion Victor Rothschild, MI5's anti-sabotage expert and an old friend of Kim's, came down to St Albans and Kim and I arranged to have dinner with him at a hotel. 'One doesn't often dine with a Rothschild,' said Kim, and we had visions of black market steaks, done rare, washed down with Château Lafite. Rothschild, very reasonably, entertained no such fantasies. We went Dutch, ate *table d'hôte* at the controlled price, and drank draught bitter.

Somewhere about the beginning of 1943, Kim's young sister Helena, aged nineteen, joined both Section V at Glenalmond and the family at The Spinney. With her mother's red hair, a fair measure of her father's and brother's brains and a lively sense of humour, she was an acquisition to both places. She was assigned to subsection Vl, a roomful of girls responsible for keeping cards on all the thousands of names that appeared in ISOS. A formidable lady ran the team with efficiency, humour and an iron hand. Helena and the others wrote a poem about their lives (in V1) of which I remember but two lines:

You can't have 'flu –

You're much too new.

Helena had high expectations of both her brother and me. 'When you're Sir Kim and Sir Tim…' she would say. I fear that each of us missed her target by a wide margin.

The ISOS source continued to provide much more information than could possibly be followed up in full detail. At the same time our stations were providing an ever-increasing flow of intelligence, some from double agents, that is, *Abwehr* people whom our stations had managed to recruit for our own purposes. By now it was unlikely that any German agent dispatched from the peninsula would reach British territory – or, very often, other territories – without our knowing about it in advance. The first possibility to consider in the case of an agent coming to Britain was whether he would make a suitable British double agent after his arrival, feeding doctored information back to the Germans. This would primarily be a matter for MI5 to handle, in conjunction with the interdepartmental committee which dealt with double-agent and deception material policy. But a number of agents launched from the peninsula were, like PASCAL, destined in the first instance for other countries. If in their travels they passed through British colonial territory, they would normally be arrested, sent to Britain and interned for the rest of the war. One unfortunate fellow was caught because his name – with no details at all of what he was doing or why the *Abwehr* were interested in him – turned up in ISOS within a few days of his appearing in a long travel permit list which I happened to have been looking through. He was taken off a boat at Trinidad and interrogated, admitted nothing, was sent to England by sea, and halfway across jumped overboard and was lost.

Double-agent operations were among the greatest successes of British counter-espionage during the war. ISOS was often immensely valuable as a check on how the Germans were reacting to such operations, whether their suspicions had been aroused and what their estimate of the agent's value might be. In certain circumstances ISOS could also be used as a check on the loyalty (to the British) of the agent himself. If he were trusted he might be sent on a visit to Spain or Portugal from England with sufficiently interesting information to ensure that a telegram would be sent to Berlin; the resulting ISOS would show at once if he were acting disloyally or had been rumbled by the Germans. Although Section V's role in UK-based double-agent operations was mainly in support of MI5, it was an important role and one in which Kim himself played a large part.

One of the characteristics of the *Abwehr* was that it was highly decentralised. In addition to operations mounted from or in Spain and Portugal by the local *Abwehr* stations, the two countries were used as stepping stones to the outside world by a large number of other *Abwehr* stations in Germany and German-occupied territory – the ASTs or *Abwehrstellen*, which were main stations, and the NESTs or *Nebenstellen*, which were subordinate to ASTs. Each of these – AST Brussels, AST Hamburg, AST Paris, NEST Cologne and many others – had its own agents, and Spain and Portugal were favourite territories for their deployment or transit. In addition each station, like the headquarters, was divided into *Abwehr* I, II and III, and *Abwehr* I further divided into I/H (army), I/Luft (air force), I/M (navy), I/Wi (economics), I/TLW (technology) and so on. Thus there were literally dozens of different sections whose independent operations had to be sorted out. Some of these stations and sections specialised in particular lines. For instance, AST Berlin (not to be confused with the overall *Abwehr* headquarters in Berlin) specialised in agents of Swiss nationality. AST Berlin also had a nasty little habit of using two cover-names indiscriminately for each of its people, sometimes even in the same message, which caused confusion at first. The local *Abwehr* organisations in Spain and Portugal were supposed to give assistance to all these outside activities, but clearly resented them, particularly when our protests and harassment began to take effect and the *Abwehr* had to walk delicately.

We made a close study of the German sabotage organisation in Spain, that is, the local staff and agents of *Abwehr* II. Their main targets were British shipping in Spanish ports and Gibraltar. In late 1941 a time bomb placed by this organisation among the cargo of a British merchant ship in a port in south-east Spain had resulted in the death of many seamen. The Germans had not managed to repeat this kind of success but had been able to maintain an organisation in the area. One day ISOS messages began to come through which showed that *Abwehr* II were planning to place a bomb on a named British ship about to visit Gibraltar. *Abwehr* II were in the habit of couching their operational messages in mildly cryptic language; it was not, one assumed, that they alone in the *Abwehr* doubted the security of their organisation's cyphers, but rather that they did not want to have any too obviously incriminating and politically embarrassing messages sitting around in their office files. In this case they were using medical terms: 'doctor' for the agent who was to place the bomb, 'patient' for the ship, 'medicine' for the bomb and so on. The doctor, we learnt, would be visiting the patient and prescribing medicine in a Spanish port near Gibraltar. The ship was then due to spend a few hours in Gibraltar and sail on. Gibraltar had made it clear to us that if they were to find the bomb they would have to order the ship to unload her cargo on the quayside, where it would be examined crate by crate under the eyes of the dock workers and, in effect, those of the *Abwehr* station at Algeciras. In spite of the risk to ISOS, this action had been authorised if necessary. It so happened that on the night of the ship's arrival in Gibraltar I was duty officer at Glenalmond. It had been arranged that the ship would be held overnight on some easily arranged pretext and searched at first light. Sometime after midnight Bletchley teleprinted a message they had just deciphered: the doctor, it seemed, had had to call off the visit to his patient. Here was a dilemma: the interpretation of the message, while very probable, was less than certain, and there was also the slight possibility that the Germans might after all have subsequently found a way of placing the bomb. On the other hand, risk to ISOS had to be avoided. While we thought it likely that if the Germans saw crates being unloaded they would assume a leak from their organisation or some other cause rather than cypher insecurity, we could not be sure. If they had indeed cancelled the operation, and then saw the cargo being unloaded, they might be less inclined to assume a leak.

Normally something of this kind, involving risk either to ISOS or alternatively to human life, would have been put to Kim and Felix and discussed with the Admiralty and others concerned. But a decision had to be taken before morning. I think Kim was away from St Albans that night. Felix, on the other hand, was reputed to stay up every night till three or four, reading papers at home, and it was now only half past one. The matter was not one that could be dealt with on the telephone, so I jumped into the duty car and drove over to Prae Wood, a large house about a mile away formerly used as Section V offices, where Felix was now living. I rang the bell: no answer. I rang again, and again. I took a handful of stones and threw them at what I fancied to be Felix and Mary's window. I threw more stones. The silence was absolute. I felt completely alone in the world. For a moment I clutched at the idea of going back to Glenalmond and telephoning, in the hope that this might wake Felix. Then I faced what I had known all along: that I was only trying to push on to someone else a judgement which in the last resort I was in the best position to make. All that Felix – or Kim – could have said was, 'Well, you're supposed to be the expert; what do *you* think?' I drove back to Glenalmond and signalled Gibraltar to let the ship go. All through the next day I held my breath, but there was no explosion.

It is the custom now to deride the *Abwehr* as a net liability rather than asset to wartime Nazi Germany. There is a measure of truth in this. Many *Abwehr* officers were at most only lukewarm about national socialism, and some were strongly opposed. Even those officers who weren't politically minded preferred the good life in Madrid, Lisbon and elsewhere to the Eastern Front, and therefore had a special vested interest in exaggerating the value of their work and closing their minds to any suspicion that an agent might be inventing or embroidering his reports or actually working as a double agent for the British or Americans. But at this time, halfway through the war, the *Abwehr* was by no means a spent force. The crews of Allied convoys struggling through the western Mediterranean, murderously bombed as a result of reports from the *Abwehr* observation posts in the Strait of Gibraltar, would no doubt have agreed. So too would those many Allied agent networks in occupied Europe whom *Abwehr* III succeeded in uncovering. One can only speculate how the *Abwehr* would have performed if ISOS had not been available to us; it seems likely, for example, that some of their agent operations in Britain might have escaped detection for a considerable time.

Only once, as far as I know, did the German intelligence services seriously suspect that their cyphers were being read. An urgent message from Madrid to Berlin said that a Royal Navy ship had stopped exactly athwart the secret German infrared beam across the Gibraltar Strait. The *Abwehr* in Madrid, fearing that the British might have been reading their cypher to Tangier, changed it immediately. For a short time we thought some flaming idiot had been taking an unauthorised initiative with ISOS, but after enquiry we were assured that the ship had stopped for an entirely innocent and coincidental reason. I am still not entirely convinced. Bletchley broke the new cypher within a month. Nevertheless, the incident reminded us that the Germans were by no means blind to cypher security. On another occasion we had a bad moment when an ISOS message from the *Abwehr* at Algeciras to Madrid began, 'To our friends in the British Secret Service...' Then we realised it was 1 April.

A more serious danger was that, with so much evidence that the British were uncannily well informed, the Germans might try to test the security of their cyphers by setting a few traps. It would have been easy to name some innocent traveller and then sit back to see whether we detained him for questioning, or to mention an arbitrary address and keep watch from nearby for signs of interest. But nothing of the kind ever happened.

I don't think Kim ever visited Bletchley, but I went there once. Denys Page, who had been one of my classics tutors at Christ Church, was in general charge of the ISOS hut; Tom Webster, who had also been my tutor, was personal assistant to Commander Travis, the head of GC&CS. But my chief contact at Bletchley was Leonard Palmer, whose function in relation to the cryptographers was somewhat akin to that of Hugh Trevor-Roper in relation to the interceptors: it was his job to know what was going on in the German intelligence world, so that proper guidance could be given to the cryptographers and translators. I had also come to see my sister Angela, the same who had worked briefly with Kim in 1936 on the magazine venture, and who was now employed in the naval hut. Both before and after the war Angela earned part of her living by writing for *Punch*. Bletchley offered her and one or two like-minded friends a rich field for light verse:

Commander Travis is my guide.
I shall not want with him beside.
He for my wandering footsteps hath
Laid everywhere a concrete path…

And so on. But eventually she went too far. The output of Bletchley expressed itself in massive daily sheaves of teleprint. It was the custom of one of Commander Travis's assistants to go through the material every day and pick out nuggets to show him. Angela, who for some reason had conceived an antipathy to this assistant, not only wrote derogatory verses about him, but with the help of friends had them teleprinted in the same format as the Bletchley output and inserted into the daily batch.

Soon afterwards she left Bletchley and joined the Foreign Office Political Intelligence Department, which presented less temptation to scurrility.

At Glenalmond the Iberian subsection, like the rest of Section V, grew larger. Eventually we had ten officers all working in the single room. One of these was the long-awaited assistant on ISOS, who arrived at the beginning of 1943, just in time to help with all the extra work arising from the north African landing of November 1942. Kim's area, and therefore mine, had been enlarged to include the new theatre of operations. Three of our original colleagues in Vd were now attached to various headquarters under General Eisenhower's command, each with his own rapid cypher communications to Section V. Much of what they reported tied up with ISOS, and much of the ISOS needed investigation through them. Desmond Pakenham,[9] the new ISOS assistant, not only was an amusing companion with a nice turn of phrase but took over much of the work.

Another area which took our attention in Vd for a short time was the Azores. Secret plans were being made in the summer of 1943 to establish a British and American base there, with Portuguese agreement, and it was arranged that a Section V officer would be attached to the force. He had previously been in MI5, but joined us in St Albans at about the beginning of June and was invited by Kim to become yet a further inmate of the rather crowded Spinney. Our chief reason for sending a man to the Azores was that the *Abwehr* in Lisbon had recently established an agent there (of Portuguese nationality) with wireless and cypher communication. Although we had not yet been able to identify him we wanted to nobble him as soon as possible. When therefore the expedition was launched in October 1943 it was accompanied not only by our officer but also by a radio direction-finding van capable of geographically pinpointing the source of transmissions. As soon as the troops landed the van was sent into action, but before the technicians had got the definitive fix the agent sent a final message, duly decyphered by Bletchley, which ran something like this: 'Can see D/F-ing van at end of my street. Closing down.' With no further transmissions to work on, it was some weeks before he could be identified and arrested.

I am very conscious that so far I have struck no sort of balance between my own work and that of other officers in the subsection. Many of the cases we were investigating came up first from the stations or other non-ISOS sources and would be dealt with by my colleagues; I would keep an eye open for ISOS reflections, an obvious criterion of the importance of a case. But a number of potentially dangerous operations might show up relatively little in ISOS, if at all. This was true, for example, of the many Spanish and Portuguese seamen recruited by the *Abwehr* to report on what they might see of Allied warships or merchantmen. The neutralisation of these operations was brought to a fine art by the Vd officer dealing with Spain, in conjunction with the Ministry of Economic Warfare.

I am also very aware that I have said nothing at all about the work of other subsections, of which I knew or at any rate can remember little. This was nothing to do with restrictive security or application of the 'need-to-know' principle. On the contrary we were encouraged within reason to share experiences and expertise, quite rightly in my opinion: in wartime there is often more to be gained from spreading knowledge within an intelligence organisation than is likely to be lost from increasing the security risk. But with the occasional exception of Turkey, there was not much parallel between our area and elsewhere, and I am afraid I was too immersed in my own work to bother much about what others were doing.

The job was so absorbing and completely time consuming that I would have found it almost impossible to imagine it could take second place to even more important work. Yet, one supposes, that is how it was with Kim. Sitting opposite me in the office, puffing at his pipe, with a faraway look in his eyes, he seemed to be planning some new initiative with the Foreign Office, some far-reaching scheme to discuss with MI5, some comprehensive instruction to the field. More probably he was putting together in his mind a report to the Russians, or wondering what, in furtherance of their interests, his next move or manoeuvre should be. I have no idea whether his contacts with the Russians were always direct or sometimes carried out through an intermediary, how frequently they took place and where, whether his reports to them were oral or written, whether he ever photographed papers for them or lent them copies to photograph and return, or what. He surely could not have had any contact with them in St Albans itself; there he was always to be found either at Glenalmond or at The Spinney, or travelling between, or in a pub with others of us. I assume that his contacts took place during his regular visits to London. But where? In a pub or restaurant? At a Russian safe house? In Guy Burgess's flat? Whatever the nature of the contacts, they must have been quickly and efficiently managed, for his visits to London seldom lasted more than a day, travel included, and he always had a number of people to see and meetings to attend in Broadway, MI5 and elsewhere. If one tried to get a message to him on the telephone there were no unexplained gaps in his timetable. As to photography of documents, it certainly could not have been done either at Glenalmond, where privacy was nil, or at The Spinney, which was equally public and where nothing was ever locked. In any case Aileen would have had to be in the know, which I'm sure she wasn't.[10]

I have searched my memory for incidents which might with hindsight be seen to have some significance, but apart from the case described in the footnote to the previous chapter, little emerges. Only once did he and I have anything like a disagreement in Section V. I have forgotten the subject, but I remember being surprised that Kim, who was normally so reasonable, was suddenly being utterly perverse. Perhaps he thought the same about me. But I have a faint memory that it may have been to do with Poland. Had I stumbled on something that meant more to him than to me?

Sometimes it struck me as strange that Kim was prepared to leave so much of the most interesting work to me. If I had been in his place I would have grabbed ISOS for myself with both hands. (When I did eventually succeed him as head of the subsection I continued to deal with ISOS as a main part of my function.) One might now surmise that he was content with the arrangement because it left him with more time for extramural activity. But I think this unlikely; the division of work made good practical sense, and enabled him to give proper time and attention to directing the work and policy of the whole subsection. I think too that he regarded himself as not having an 'ISOS mind', which he saw as slightly peculiar.

I seldom saw Kim even slightly disconcerted. Once, the officer who dealt inter alia with vetting questions and acted as a kind of security officer came up to him. 'Sorry to bother you, Kim

– mere formality. It's about your wife's application for a job –
she's quoted you as a reference. I just need the usual good word.'
Kim looked utterly blank. Then his face lit up. 'Oh, you mean my
first wife… Yes, she's OK.' Presumably Lizy, who had returned
to England soon after the war began, had not let him know that
she was giving him as a reference for some job she was seeking,
and I imagine they were not in touch.

Kim had moved a long way by now from the asceticism of
school and university days. Yet he still seemed to have little interest in physical comforts or luxurious surroundings. I think he
bothered less about personal possessions than anyone I have
known. If I had been in the habit of borrowing his clothes, or
even his toothbrush, I don't suppose he would have minded in
the least, assuming he noticed. He was very easily bored, especially by pretentious or snobbish conversation or by social small
talk. One always knew when Kim was bored: he would go very
solemn, his voice would drop an octave and he would say, 'That's
extremely interesting.' He was not a good actor when it came to
the minor exchanges of life, however adroit he may have been
over anything to do with his great central secret.

Kim had a few foibles. One, trivial in itself yet unexpected in
someone so sane and well balanced, was that he had an extraordinary aversion to apples – the sight, the smell, even the thought
of them. I was once rash enough to allocate the code-name Apple
to some intelligence operation, but had to change it at Kim's
insistence. Some years later in Istanbul I saw him angrily seize
a bag of apples which the nannie or cook had surreptitiously
bought for the children and hurl it out of the kitchen window
into the Bosphorus. His third wife, Eleanor, in her memoirs, says
that after she returned to America finally from Moscow, she sent

Kim a Beatles record, 'Help!'[11] If it was on the Apple label, it would not have lasted long.

He, I and the others followed the course of the war very closely, especially on the Eastern Front, where the main fighting was taking place. While none of us seemed to discuss basic political beliefs, we often talked about the practical politics of the war. Kim had been critical of Churchill in the winter of 1941–42, and appeared to welcome any strong independent vote in a by-election, which of course was the only way in which anti-government feelings could be expressed at the polls. But he acknowledged that Churchill's unequivocal broadcast on the evening of 22 June 1941, pledging immediate support to the Russians in their fight against Germany, showed a sense of greatness; we used to wonder what Chamberlain would have said. Sometime in mid-1942 Kim delivered himself of a rather uncharacteristic statement: 'You know, I'm beginning to think we're going to win this war.' No doubt 'we' meant the Allies rather than Britain, but this was not the way he usually spoke. He never seemed to identify himself with his country, even over sport. Although Kim was a very English person, and much more at home in congenial English company than any other, he showed little affection for England or its countryside, cities, institutions and traditions. He had some regard for the qualities of English people as a whole, but much contempt for middle-class virtues and middle-class likes and dislikes. Though he never lacked physical or moral courage, one could not imagine him making patriotic gestures. Perhaps there should have been a clue in all this to his real feelings. But England is full of people who appear to have little patriotism yet would not dream of spying against their country.

Though not an intellectual, if I understand that term correctly, and still less an academic, he was very much one of the middle-class or upper-middle-class intelligentsia. Once at St Albans I said to him that I usually found it difficult to feel entirely at home with working-class people. 'Really?' said Kim in surprise. 'I find it very easy.' In fact I doubt if he ever had much to do with working-class people in his life, except in a small way at Cambridge. Although over the period 1935 to 1955 I met many of Kim's friends, I do not recall any who did not have an 'educated' accent. His acquaintances came from a rather narrow social class, though they embraced a wide range of types within that class. While this may have helped his position as a Russian spy, I doubt whether it was in any sense dictated by that position; even if he had never been a spy I think he would have had the same sort of friends.

The St Albans time was drawing to a close. By the spring of 1943 Section V was beginning to be heavily involved in the war fronts that were opening up. The Allies were about to move into Sicily, and then Italy. Next year it would be western Europe. All this necessitated much planning with the War Office, the various commands that were being set up, MI5 (who were represented in the SCI units), the Americans, Broadway and others. We were beginning to feel more and more that we were out on a limb in Hertfordshire: power and action lay in London. An opportunity arose to move to Ryder Street in the St James's area, a minute's walk from MI5, but Felix Cowgill was strongly opposed to such a move. He foresaw that the character of the Section V he had built up in its country isolation would be threatened by a transfer to the London mêlée, and that he himself would find it more difficult to cope with his enemies. There were several Section

V staff who wanted to stay in St Albans, perhaps for the same sort of reasons as Felix, perhaps because they now had strong domestic roots in or around the town, perhaps simply because they did not know London. But, when it was put to a vote, most of us opted for the move. I was much in favour, both for the reasons I have given above and on personal grounds. Kim also had personal grounds of a different kind: he would be nearer to the centres of power and better able to carry out Soviet aims. He was one of the strongest advocates of the move. As so often in this story, he was pressing for something which made admirable sense in itself but which one now sees he wanted primarily for different reasons.

July 21st was set as the date of the move. Kim, who had a monthly tenancy on The Spinney, decided to give it up at the end of June. He and Aileen and the two children – a third was on the way – went to Dora Philby's flat in Grove Court, Drayton Gardens in South Kensington. (Either then or later Dora moved upstairs to another flat.) I moved to the flat near Chelsea Town Hall which Marie had taken a year or so earlier. For three weeks Kim, Helena, I and others commuted in the wrong direction, leaving St Pancras for St Albans in the morning and returning to London at night.

One sad casualty of the move, for me at any rate, was Sammy. Marie and I tried to keep him in London for a time, but with both of us working it was not a practical proposition. Eventually I handed him over to the assistant of David, the Glenalmond factotum. Sammy had conceived an inordinate attachment for him and he could offer him a decent home in the suburbs. Kim spoke his valediction. 'David's dogsbody's dog,' he said unfeelingly.

RYDER STREET AND BROADWAY

Before the war 14 Ryder Street had been the home of the Charity Commission, as it is once more.[†] Even for London offices of the time it was old fashioned. The lift was more primitive than Broadway's museum piece. Many of the rooms were small, high ceilinged and heated by little coal fires. For lack of a suitable large office the communal life of the Iberian subsection had to be broken up and we were housed two in a room. But there was compensation in all this: my room-mate for a time was Graham Greene, who had recently taken over the Portuguese desk when its former occupant was posted to Lisbon. Graham had returned from his post as SIS representative in Freetown at about the end of 1942 and was assigned to Section V. At Glenalmond he had been engaged in a solitary pursuit, the production of the Portuguese 'Purple Primer'. A Purple Primer was a 'Who's Who' of all known enemy intelligence officers, agents and contacts in a particular country, and was intended partly for current reference and partly for mopping-up operations after the war. It cannot have been one of the most rewarding experiences of Graham's life, but he stuck to it tenaciously and completed it, on

---

† *Editor's note:* The Charity Commission has since moved to 1 Drummond Gate, Pimlico.

the basis of evidence then available, before we left Glenalmond. Kim wrote an introduction. Later I had the task of amplifying and updating the work. Perhaps this entitles me to go down in history as the co-author, with Graham Greene and H. A. R. Philby, of a volume privately published, in limited edition, with numbered copies.

In Ryder Street Graham brought his own particular style to the handling of Portuguese matters. He was not greatly interested in the intelligence war, perhaps because it was now beginning to go so much in our favour, but anything in the nature of human injustices caught his imagination and his pen. He bombarded everyone for weeks with pleas and arguments on behalf of a former SIS agent who had ended up in a Lisbon jail, allegedly for activities on our behalf, and in whom we had now lost interest. Graham's marginal notes on incoming correspond-ence, inscribed in a fine compressed hand in which he appeared to have omitted to move the pen sideways as he wrote, were a pleasure in themselves. 'Poor old ——,' he noted on one letter from the Broadway man in Lisbon, 'bashing about like a bull in a china shop, letting in great glimpses of the obvious.' I had less to do professionally with another luminary of Ryder Street, Malcolm Muggeridge, who had likewise returned from a post in Africa, in this case Lourenço Marques, and was to lighten the later months of our war with malice and wit.

At the time of the move to London I had already been Vd1 for nearly two years; Kim had been head of the subsection a few weeks longer. Neither of us had had any promotion within the service. However, Felix Cowgill had had some success in improving the status of his officers, and I think we were getting a little more pay than at first. There had also been some improvement – though this, of course, did not affect Kim as a civilian – in the military ranking of Army officers in Section V. Felix had had a hard struggle to achieve this. A Brigadier Beddington in Broadway, who supervised Army staffing and promotion matters in SIS, had made it part of his life's work to block all attempts to rationalise the Section V military establishment and place us on a more even footing with the people we were in touch with in the forces ministries, MI5, the Army commands and many other places. In November 1942 there had been a breakthrough, and I had gone up to captain, but I continued to wear civilian clothes and never used the rank. A captain was still nobody, and I was better able to deal with outside people if I appeared to be a civilian.

In September 1943, having secured an enlargement of the Section V establishment, Felix announced some promotions. A new post was created for Kim, with the designation Vk (the K stood for Kim), overseeing Vd and several other subsections. I became head of Vd in his place, though I continued to spend much of my time on ISOS, and Desmond Pakenham moved up to Vd1. The post of Vd now carried with it the rank of major. The higher status, and the condition of my civilian clothes, induced me to get out my battledress, and Marie was able to unpick the second lieutenant's single pip and substitute the major's crown without having to bother about the intervening stages.

Sicily had fallen to the Allies in July–August 1943, and Mussolini had been deposed by his compatriots and incarcerated in a mountain fastness. At the beginning of September our troops had begun landing in southern Italy. In Ryder Street a new subsection, Vt, was set up to handle Italy, and a brilliant recruit, Colin Roberts of St John's College, Oxford,[1] was brought in to deal with ISOS in the Vt area; he and I looked after it jointly until he was ready to take over.

It was during this time that one of the might-have-beens of the war occurred. The cypher used between SD headquarters in Berlin and their station in Rome had just been broken by GC&CS, but for the first week or two, as so often with newly broken cyphers, the decoded messages reached us in random order and with many gaps. Evidently something big was being planned, involving a specialist commando under Otto Skorzeny.[2] But one or two vital earlier messages were missing, and it was not until after Skorzeny and his men had landed on the Gran Sasso and 'rescued' Mussolini that Bletchley manage to unbutton them. Had they broken the SD cypher a few days earlier, or had Skorzeny attempted his snatch a few days later, means might conceivably have been found to forestall the operation. Mussolini would not have ended the war hanging upside down with Clara Petacci in a Milan square, and might have stood trial as a war criminal instead.

Now, of course, I was seeing much less of Kim. He was working in a different room, and concerned with several areas besides my own. After office hours there was not much time or energy for social life. But the lunch hour usually found Kim, me and a few companions in one or other of the many pubs within three minutes' walk of 14 Ryder Street. Our favourite was the Unicorn, at the corner of Jermyn Street and Bury Street. Here on one occasion Kim and I were sitting at the bar when a man walked in whom I recognised as a former contemporary of ours at Westminster, from another house. He caught sight of Kim, and without noticing me went up to him and said, 'Good Lord, aren't you Milne?' 'No,' said Kim, 'he is.' I can think of no

Tim Milne, 1929.

Tim Milne (front row, second from right) and Kim Philby (front row, first from right) on stage at Westminster School, 1928.

Tim's wife Marie with Tim's grandfather, the renowned author A. A. Milne.

A rather pensive Kim Philby, 1933, shortly before he was recruited as a KGB agent.

Commissioned into the Royal Engineers in 1940, Tim was recruited into MI6 only a year later by his childhood friend Philby.

Kim and Aileen Philby's son Harry with Tim's wife Marie and their daughter Catherine.

The Cambridge Four: (clockwise from top left) John Cairncross, Anthony Blunt, Guy Burgess playing the piano at a friend's house in Moscow and Donald Maclean.

А report written by the KGB's London *Rezident* created from information provided by Source SOHNCHEN (Philby's KGB code-name). It details the locations of various secret British intelligence and Special Operations Executive bases.

HALL, near BLETCHLEY, the W/T Headquarters of the S.I.S; then was transferred to Section V. He is in charge of section VB4 and attends personally to France.

b) Mr NICHOLAS ELLIOTT. 24 5 ft 9 in, brown hair, prominent lips black glasses. Ugly and rather pig-like to look at. Good brain, good sense of humour. Likes a film but was recently very ill and now, as a consequence, drinks little. He is in charge of HOLLAND.

c) ERIC DUVIVIER. 24, face curled hair, blue eyes, very prominent nose fresh complexion, 5 ft 9 inches tall fairly broad-shouldered. He is half-, or wholly, BELGIAN He is clever, hard-working. He is in charge of BELGIUM.

Kim Philby's uncomplimentary hand-printed report to Moscow Centre on Nicholas Elliott, who believed himself to be a friend of the KGB 'master spy'.

The author Graham Greene, who worked alongside Milne and Philby in MI6.

Philby gives a press conference at his mother's London home after then Foreign Secretary Harold Macmillan told Parliament: 'I have no reason to conclude that Mr Philby has at any time betrayed the interests of his country, or to identify him with the so-called "Third Man", if indeed there was one.'

Macmillan, who as Foreign Secretary cleared Philby of being the Third Man and was Prime Minister when Philby admitted spying and defected to Moscow.

BELOW LEFT Nicholas Elliott, who ran Philby as a freelance agent in Beirut and went to the Lebanese capital to interview him after it emerged that Philby was indeed a Soviet spy.

BELOW RIGHT Dick White, who sent Elliott to Beirut to interrogate Philby.

Kim Philby in Moscow with his Russian wife Rufina and members of the KGB.

Milne, MI6 head of station in Tokyo, 1961.

Tim with his brother Tony in 1980.

obvious reason why somebody whom each of us had known only slightly at school and whom neither had seen or heard of since should have mentally associated us to the point of confusion. The newcomer seemed as mystified as we were.

Some accounts suggest that Kim travelled a good deal at this period, visiting our stations in Spain and Portugal several times and even the Middle East. I recall only one visit by Kim to the peninsula and none elsewhere, as long as he was in Section V. But there was plenty for him to do in Ryder Street, especially in supervising the new Italian subsection and in planning the Section V contribution to the forthcoming Overlord operation. It was also in these first few months in Ryder Street that a most interesting case arose which Kim made very much his own and which he describes in detail in his book. A German Foreign Office official, code-named WOOD,[3] was supplying Allen Dulles, head of OSS in Switzerland, with *en clair* texts of telegrams between German embassies and Berlin, most of which were not available through Bletchley. Each time he came to Berne he deposited a batch of telegrams on Dulles's office. For complicated reasons it fell to Kim to handle the processing and distribution for British customers of this voluminous and extremely valuable material. It was through WOOD that we first learnt about CICERO, the valet to the British ambassador in Turkey, who for a few months supplied so much information to the Germans in Ankara. CICERO was run by the SD, whose cyphers between Ankara and Berlin were not being read by Bletchley. But the German ambassador in Ankara, Franz von Papen, also sent a few telegrams about him to the German Foreign Office, and it was these that WOOD produced. While they did not name or directly pinpoint the SD agent, there was enough information for the British investigators to get

uncomfortably close to him and frighten him off for the rest of
the war, though it was not until the Americans captured CICERO's
case officer, Moyzisch, after VE Day that we learnt the full truth.
Seldom has a case had such an all-star cast: CICERO, probably the
best German agent of the war; WOOD, one of the most remarkable Allied agents; Dulles, perhaps the most celebrated of OSS
officers; and Kim, described (by Dulles) as 'the best spy the
Russians ever had'.

Though I did not know it, my time in the Iberian subsection
was coming to an end. In February 1944, I went down with severe
sinus trouble and a high temperature, and as recovery was slow
I was packed off to Dorset to convalesce. Arriving back in Ryder
Street on 1 March, I found I had made a sideways move and was
now in charge of a new subsection, Vf, dealing with Germany.
Felix Cowgill was belatedly making good his original omission
to do anything about Germany, and handsomely. Within a few
months Vf numbered twenty or more officers. They included
three or four first-class people, a larger number who were
competent without being outstanding, and one or two elderly
has-beens who were so abysmally useless that all one could do
was to put them onto relatively unimportant matters where they
could do no serious harm. This was not too difficult to arrange
because Vf had no stations to deal with and no current casework
to handle. One of our main tasks was to assemble in easily available form all information about German intelligence services
and their members that might be useful to the Allied forces
when the time came for them to enter and govern a large part of
Germany; it was anticipated that by then *Abwehr* and SD officials
who had not yet been captured either would be found corralled
within Germany or could be repatriated there by arrangement

with neutral countries. Our field included the Gestapo (who had not hitherto come much within our purview) and several other departments concerned with aspects of intelligence and security. Of course, the work was nothing like so exciting as it had been in Vd. We had no telegrams to send, no spies to catch or turn, no démarches to make.

But in truth the counter-espionage war against the Germans was already near to being won. The *Abwehr* was in disarray. On top of the humiliations it had suffered at our hands in Spain – to the personal disadvantage of Admiral Canaris, the head of the *Abwehr*, some of whose earlier prestige had arisen from his close friendship with Franco and other Spanish leaders – three *Abwehr* officials in Turkey defected to the Allies early in 1944. Soon after this, slight changes began to be noticeable in the designation of certain addressees and signatories of *Abwehr* messages. The phrase 'Mil.Amt' appeared – i.e. *Militärisches Amt*, or Military Office. It eventually emerged that the politically unreliable *Abwehr* had been put under the command of the SD and was now designated as the SD's 'Mil.Amt'. First to appreciate what was happening were Trevor-Roper's section, from their central vantage point. If Vf had been properly established by then I hope we would have been equally quick. But to anyone concentrating on Spain, Portugal and north Africa the change was distinctly unexpected. There the SD had been ineffective. Only their man in Tangier remains in memory, not for any achievements but for his big mouth. After the Allies landed in north Africa, he was forever promising Berlin that he had a team ready to assassinate Eisenhower in Algiers or an agent who could penetrate this or that headquarters. At first he had a slight nuisance value, but was soon discounted. Elsewhere the SD were of greater consequence: I have already mentioned the Skorzeny and CICERO operations. The political significance of this take-over of the German General Staff's secret intelligence service by the rival Party organisation, at a time when German forces were in retreat, was unmistakable.

Although I had left the Vd subsection (now headed by Desmond Pakenham), Kim as Vk was still my immediate boss. A subject which was increasingly occupying our attention was that of anti-Hitler plots within Germany and attempts by the plotters to gain the interest and support of the Allies. I put one of my officers, Noel Sharp, on to the subject full time. As early as the summer of 1942 Otto John,[4] on one of his visits to Madrid as Lufthansa's legal adviser, had begun to give information to an SIS agent (on the Broadway side, not Section V) about a group, including Ludwig Beck, Carl Friedrich Goerdeler and others, which was said to be planning to overthrow the Hitler régime. In the two years that followed, other emissaries such as Adam von Trott and Hans Bernd Gisevius amplified the information in other neutral countries – as did John himself on further visits to the peninsula. The broad political aim of the group was to set up a government which would be friendly to Britain and America and ready to make peace.

A myth has grown up that Kim, in the Soviet interest, managed to stifle reports of this kind or at least to get them regarded as unreliable. I have no doubt that if he had seen in this situation an opportunity of helping the Russians without danger to himself he would have taken it. But he was not really in a strong posi-tion to influence events. For one thing, the plotters were in touch with the Americans as well as the British. Within SIS, it was for Section I, not Section V, to decide what political information should be circulated to the Foreign Office and other Whitehall departments. To the best of my memory John's reports were indeed so circulated by Section I, with the reasonable comment that as the source was not a regular SIS agent the reports could not be vouched for. I assume that something similar happened to the reports from the other emissaries. Section V's primary role was to examine whether there was any evidence that the whole thing was a plant by a German intelligence service, or alternatively that the German security service had penetrated the group and were aware of what was going on. It soon became apparent that there was no evidence for the first possibility. Although, as we could see from ISOS, some of the emissaries were technically *Abwehr* agents, this meant nothing. Almost all Germans who visited neutral countries frequently were likely to be given some sort of brief by the *Abwehr* to report any useful information that came their way. We found it harder to judge the second hypothesis. It seemed impossible that the Gestapo and SD, with all their resources and ruthlessness, had never, in the course of two years and more, had an inkling of what was going on when we were picking it up all over the place. Perhaps the plotters were deliberately being allowed a lot of rope by the Gestapo and SD. The general attitude in London was cautious. One reason was that, in November 1939, SIS had fallen head first into a trap laid by the SD at Venlo, on the Dutch–German frontier. Two SIS officers, lured by a bogus resistance group, had been captured by the Germans. (The leader in that operation had been a young man called Walter Schellenberg, who was now incidentally in charge of the Mil.Amt.)

Nevertheless Noel Sharp and I found ourselves getting increasingly interested in and optimistic about this group of plotters, and

I don't recall any contrary view from Kim. The real objections to giving encouragement to these and similar feelers came from the Foreign Office. It was fixed Allied policy to reject anything that could be interpreted as an attempt to drive a wedge between the Western Allies and Russia. There may also have been reluctance in the Foreign Office, and indeed elsewhere, to believe that this was more than a small bunch of amateurs unlikely to achieve anything. Not long after the bomb attack of 20 July 1944 several of us, as was our custom, were listening to the news in the hall of 14 Ryder Street. Noel and I looked at one another open mouthed as so many familiar names were reeled off, of plotters now dead or in custody. Perhaps the Gestapo had already had some of them in its sights, but it had not managed to prevent Claus von Stauffenberg's bomb (provided by accomplices in *Abwehr* II, from captured SOE stock) from going off under Hitler's conference table.

Noel Sharp, who later became keeper of the Department of Printed Books at the British Museum, has confirmed to me lately that he had no evidence, impression or suspicion either that Kim tried to suppress or get classed as unreliable any of the reports we received on this whole subject, or that he was playing any game of his own, least of all in respect of the 20 July people. It is also relevant that Kim was largely responsible for the dispatch of Klop Ustinov (father of Peter) to Lisbon in, I think, early 1944 with a specific brief to revive friendships with anti-Hitler Germans he had known in the past – a mission which Klop performed with some success. One of his old friends proved to have connections with the 20 July group, and produced useful advance information.

Other allegations have been made that while in Section V

Kim may have suppressed or discounted information in order to suit the Soviet interest. Trevor-Roper says that late in 1942 his section wrote a paper on the growing struggle between the Nazi Party and the German General Staff, as exemplified in the field of secret intelligence, and on attempts by Himmler to oust Admiral Canaris and take over the *Abwehr*. Kim is said to have forbidden circulation of this paper on the grounds that it was merely speculative. I do not recall the incident exactly but feel sure that the interpretation of his attitude is unjustified. There was indeed a long-standing argument between Trevor-Roper's section and the rest of Section V – particularly Vd – on the importance or otherwise of the SD, but it was a perfectly genuine disagreement. I have already indicated that in the Iberian area it was difficult to think of the SD and the *Abwehr* as two rival intelligence services of comparable weight. In the end Trevor-Roper's section was vindicated, in that the SD was able to use its political muscle and take over the battered and disaffected *Abwehr*. But at the time Kim's attitude would have been perfectly reasonable. It is also worth pointing out that he was then head of the Iberian subsection only and had no power to give orders to anyone outside it, although he might have been in a position to veto external circulation of a paper in so far (and only in so far) as it was based on Iberian ISOS.

One book has related a story of an agent of German nationality called Schmidt who had been executed by the Gestapo as a British spy and whose mother, as Allied troops advanced into Germany, wrote to the British SCI unit there demanding compensation.[5] The SCI telegraphed London, but allegedly the telegram was conveniently 'lost' in Ryder Street. After the war, the account continues, captured *Abwehr* records showed Schmidt to have been not only a British agent but also an important Russian one. This author surmises that the telegram may have been deliberately suppressed, presumably by Kim, to prevent investigation of a Russian network. The story does not make much sense as it stands. So far as Kim is concerned, he had left Section V and Ryder Street, and had become head of the anti-Russian section in Broadway, several months before the Allies entered Germany. In any case, a telegram of this kind – of which there would probably have been at least two or three copies – would normally have gone first to a desk officer in Section V, who would then have had the agent traced in Registry. If this showed he had been an SIS or SOE agent, the desk officer would have alerted the appropriate Broadway officer or our link with SOE. Only if the trace had showed a Russian connection – which, to judge from the story, it did not – would Kim's section have been brought in. It would have been very difficult for him, or for that matter anyone in Ryder Street, to suppress all copies of the telegram and all action on and knowledge of the case.

I comment on these three matters not in order to play down Kim's activities for the Russians, far from it, but simply to show that it is not easy to tinker with facts and paper; this applies as much to the Secret Service as to the most public of government departments. Too many people and too many copies are involved, particularly over matters of wide interest like anti-Hitler plotters or *Abwehr*–SD rivalry. You cannot usually make something go away simply by destroying or holding back a piece of paper. It would have been foolish for Kim to expose himself to suspicion on inessential matters by suppressing papers or taking a notably different line from other people. He makes no mention of any of these affairs in his book although he describes in detail other services he was able to render the Russians in his SIS work.

In the summer of 1944 the Russians agreed to the establishment in Moscow of an SIS officer to liaise with their intelligence service (an SOE officer had been there for a considerable time). The interest was primarily on Broadway's side rather than Section V's, but the officer chosen for the task was given a Section V brief as well. We in Ryder Street spent some time putting together information for him to pass to the Russians (not of course extending to raw ISOS) and also some questions: we reckoned among other things that a considerable number of *Abwehr* and SD officers must by now have fallen into Russian hands on the Eastern Front. It was many weeks before our man got anything out of the Russians. One reason was that they insisted on dealing with him only at a very high level, through a lieutenant-general, as good a way as any of ensuring frustration. Eventually a small batch of stuff arrived in Ryder Street, and Kim, I and others examined it. It was pathetic: one might have concluded that in counter-espionage the Russians were no further forward than we had been in 1940 or 1941. One assumes now that while we were getting together our collection of material to pass to the Russians they must already have been in possession of much important Section V information, as much anyway as Kim could provide. No wonder they had no great interest in giving us anything useful (possibly the service our representative was dealing with was not the NKVD but the military GRU; however, I assume that counter-espionage information would have been exchanged with the NKVD).

Felix Cowgill's picture of a joint Section V and OSS/X2 office was now coming nearer to reality. X2 had offices next door to

14 Ryder Street, with communicating corridors. They too had a German subsection, called V/48/F, with whom Vf worked very closely: we divided the work between us. Other X2 subsections, parallel to our own, were called V/48/D, V/48/E and so on, though they had no V/48/K. (The reason for the '48' was that, in our code language, the United States was 48-land.)† The American contribution to the joint stock of counter-espionage intelligence was still fairly modest, but after the Normandy landings of June 1944 and Patton's breakthrough of August–September the American SCI units, manned by OSS/X2 with officers who had been through Ryder Street, began increasingly to produce information from captured German intelligence staff and agents.

Those three months, June to September, coincided with the main V1 attacks. One of the arguments against moving to London from St Albans had been that the Blitz on London, or something like it, might be resumed; but I think most of us felt it was an unworthy argument, when so many other departments were working in central London. It is certainly true that a V1 nicely placed on 14 Ryder Street, even outside office hours, would have caused tremendous dislocation. Although most of the material in our records could in theory have been reconstituted from Bletchley, MI5, the SIS registry, overseas stations and elsewhere, the destruction of our working files and cards would have been a devastating blow. Fortunately all we lost were a few windows and, temporarily, Dick Brooman-White, who was seconded for some months to the special office headed by Duncan Sandys to deal with V-weapon problems.

---

† *Editor's note:* SIS allocated two-digit code-numbers to each country in which it operated. Germany, for example, was 12.

And now, in September 1944, an event of the first importance occurred: Kim was posted away from Section V to head a small new section in Broadway that had been set up earlier in the year to deal with intelligence on communism and Soviet espionage and subversion. It was a subject which for reasons of political policy had been deliberately ignored since June 1941, although the Russians had not been inhibited by any comparable policy of self-denial towards the British. The new section, called IX, was independent of Section V, though both came ultimately under Colonel Valentine Vivian, who had the title of deputy chief of the Secret Service but whose sphere did not extend outside counter-espionage and security. The story of Kim's appointment has been told in some detail in the Philby literature, particularly in his own book. He describes how, under great Russian pressure and with the support of Vivian and the chief's principal assistant, Christopher Arnold-Forster, he obtained the Section IX job and, as a consequence, secured the resignation of Felix Cowgill, who had been expected to take over the section when the war ended. Kim's account gives the impression that this was all a single episode, whereas in fact he was made head of Section IX and moved over to Broadway in September, while Felix remained as head of Section V until Christmas. After Kim's departure Felix appointed me Vk in his place. This was hardly surprising, as I had been successively in charge of the two most important subsections in the Vk area. It was not promotion in the material sense: I remained a major and my salary was not increased. But Vk was probably the second most important job in Ryder Street.

My immediate reaction to Kim's transfer to Section IX, in spite of the change it was to bring in my own fortunes, was sharp disappointment. It was the end of three years' working together.

I had no knowledge of and small interest in his new subject, on which there seemed to be little hard information. As far as I was concerned, the war was still on and the chief enemy was still Germany. I was not yet ready for adjustment to a post-war world.

But a further change was soon on its way. Felix Cowgill resigned at the end of December 1944, and I was appointed head of Section V in his place. I had no experience of administration on the scale that this now involved, with perhaps 200 officers and secretaries in Ryder Street and abroad. On the other hand, there was no obvious alternative candidate. Two or three people with comparable experience and seniority were abroad in jobs where it was important not to disturb them. It might have been possible to bring in somebody from MI5 or elsewhere, but he would have been at a disadvantage and as far as I know the question never arose. The post now carried the rank of lieutenant-colonel, but it was four months before I got the promotion, thanks to a determined rearguard action by Brigadier Beddington.

The *Sunday Times* account of Kim's elimination of Cowgill as a rival has it that, early in 1944, Kim made a bid to take over the directorship of Section V, before the Section IX opening occurred. The article goes on to say that this bid depended on my being given command of Vd, with Graham Greene taking my place as number two in the subsection; however, according to this version, Graham rather upset the plan by declining to take the promotion. So far as my own position is concerned, there is no truth in the story: as I have said, I became head of the Vd subsection several months earlier, in September 1943, when Kim was made Vk. Those moves were not the result of any intrigue, but were voluntarily made by Cowgill when he managed to get his establishment expanded, not before time. It is true that later there was some talk of promotion for Graham (unconnected, as far as I know, with any advancement of Kim) and that Graham, for his own reasons, resisted this; at any rate I recall his taking Kim, me and our administrative officer to the Café Royal for a splendid lunch in order to persuade us that he should stay as he was, which he did. Not long afterwards, to everyone's regret, he resigned. In his introduction to Kim's book he says he did this 'rather than accept the promotion which was one tiny cog in the machinery of [Kim's] intrigue'. I recently asked Graham if he could substantiate this with further details. Unfortunately he could not put his finger on any specific piece of evidence, but he said he had had a definite impression of ambitious intrigue on Kim's part. Evidently he saw more at that time with his novelist's eye than I did (though it is true that I was absent for nearly all of February 1944).

Kim's own account of these events makes no reference to any attempt to take over Section V from Cowgill: he indicates that it was the establishment of the rudimentary Section IX which gave him his opening. Even before the section was formed, he speaks of being 'anxious to get a certain job that would soon become available'. He places this in the early days of the WOOD affair, that is, late in 1943 or early in 1944. The job he had in mind can only have been that of IX, once it was formed – he had already been appointed Vk, and there was no other post in Section V which he could have been angling for and which was soon to become available. After Section IX had been set up, Kim describes the next stages as follows: first, several weeks of discussion between himself and the Russians which resulted in their deciding he must get himself made head of IX at all costs; second, his anti-Cowgill manoeuvres with Vivian,

Arnold-Forster and others; and third, discreetly canvassing the Foreign Office. In this third step he claims to have had a lucky break over an unconnected matter. Cowgill put up a draft of a letter from the chief to J. Edgar Hoover of the FBI which Patrick Reilly, the chief's Foreign Office assistant, rejected as wholly unsuitable and likely to make the chief look ridiculous. At Vivian's request, Kim put up a second and successful draft. The incident helped to establish Kim's political good sense in the eyes of Reilly, by contrast with that of Cowgill.

This all appears to make sense until one realises that, as Robert Cecil (Reilly's successor)[6] has pointed out, Reilly was posted away from SIS as early as September 1943. It can hardly be that the Hoover incident actually occurred later with Cecil playing the part of Reilly, or Cecil would have said so in his article;[†] in any case, Kim is completely specific in ascribing it to Reilly. Nor can it be that the original setting up of Section IX took place as early as the summer of 1943. Kim himself gives the date as 'when the defeat of the Axis was in sight' and his whole account implies that the interval between the establishment of IX and his appointment (in September 1944) was not more than a few months. This agrees with my own memory and with Cecil's account. The likeliest conclusion is that Kim has erroneously transplanted an incident from an earlier period to the summer of 1944. But if this is so, it throws some doubt on the accuracy of his memory of these events, crucial to his career though they were. The Hoover incident also suggests that Kim had his eyes on the future Section IX as early as the summer

---

†   *Editor's note:* Milne wrote this book in the 1970s but it is clear that this section was added later since Cecil's article in the academic journal *Intelligence and National Security* did not appear until 1994.

of 1943 or thereabouts, and was seeking friends who could help him.

I believe that Kim may have overestimated the difficulties he faced in getting the Section IX job, to judge from his story. People were already beginning to realise that Felix Cowgill, with all his drive and administrative and executive gifts, might not be the ideal man for it. Apart from his bad relations with MI5, the FBI and others, I would say that he did not have the background and intellectual outlook to cope with the post-war task of studying and understanding communist movements and parties, their position in their own countries and their relation to the Soviet Union. He was better equipped to deal with the other half of the work, Soviet bloc espionage, but that problem was certain to be quite different from what we had been faced with in Section V. Kim, on the other hand, had excellent qualifications: his sound economics degree, his first-hand knowledge of Europe, his languages, his political literacy, his successful record in the Iberian subsection and his ability to get on with people, especially MI5 and the Foreign Office. In retrospect I suppose that he might even have thought to make a virtue of his former interest in and knowledge of Marxism, a skill which in any case was going to be necessary to the job; it would have been easy enough to say – truthfully, I imagine – that he had made some study of it at Cambridge as a part of his economics syllabus. For all I know he may even have said something of this kind. As for Cowgill, I am not sure that he would have been given charge of the post-war anti-communist section even if Kim had never existed. There were other jobs to which he was well suited. In any case, after-events suggest that he would probably have been sent abroad in two or three years, as was Kim himself at the beginning of 1947.

One author expresses surprise that I did not come forward at
the time of Kim's appointment to Section IX and inform my
superiors that he had held communist views before the war.[7] I
have already described what I knew about his political views
up to April 1933, after which I was out of touch with him for
more than a year; thenceforward he was less and less inclined
in discussion to commit himself to any political creed. In 1944
it did not seem at all likely that he stood where he had in 1933.
People *do* change their views, particularly those who form
extremist opinions at university. This is well understood: previous membership of the Communist Party itself did not debar
Denis Healey from becoming Secretary of State for Defence
and Chancellor of the Exchequer. Moreover, the implication
that SIS should have required different standards of loyalty
from anyone engaged on anti-communist work, by comparison
with anti-German work, is debatable. It is anyway misleading
to imagine that Kim was accepted into SIS during a temporary
wartime phase when Germany was the enemy and nothing else
mattered. When he first joined SIS (i.e. its Section D) in July
1940, the Russians were not our allies and were still regarded
with great suspicion and hostility. It should also be remembered
that while at Cambridge Kim had made no secret whatsoever of
his politics. Some of his contemporaries there were working in or
close to SIS during the war, yet they did not come forward. Nor
did the contemporary (or contemporaries) of mine at Oxford to
whom I am supposed in the early 1930s to have described him
as a communist. Ignorance of what he was doing in Section IX
can hardly have been the reason. The nature of his new work
was very soon widely known in intelligence circles, and in any
case once the war was over it was obvious that he and everyone

else remaining would be involved in anti-communist work. The fact that nobody appears to have come forward in 1944 or later suggests that it was quite unrealistic to expect anyone to do so. It was not Kim's politics at Cambridge that were remarkable, but the fact that he became a Soviet agent.

My job as head of Section V meant that I was further removed than ever from the casework I enjoyed and for the first time since I joined SIS I felt at something of a loss. I soon found, however, that, while some of the problems I had taken over from Felix were real enough, others were not, and could be made to go away by the simple process of doing nothing about them. The central part of the job, in this last year of war when we were having to man or plan for many new stations and SCI units, consisted of arguing for establishments and in fitting people to slots and slots to people. The staffs of Sections V and IX in London and the overseas representatives of the two sections formed a single entity, sharing a small central personnel and administrative section. While the two London sections were independent of each other, the overseas officers were in principle available to carry out either V or IX tasks as required. This situation, which could have led to friction if the heads of V and IX had been bitterly hostile to one another, never caused the slightest difficulty. Kim's staff needs were small – a handful in Broadway, and two or three officers in key stations overseas who would specialise in his field, though it was understood that everyone abroad must be prepared to follow up a IX matter if needed. At this time, nine-tenths of our total V and IX staff at home and abroad were still engaged on counter-espionage work against our Second World War enemies.

Now for the first time I was brought into occasional contact with the chief, Major-General Sir Stewart Menzies. I think I had met him only once before, when he paid an official visit to St Albans. Normally he lived a remote godlike existence in his fourth-floor office in Broadway, never mingling informally with his staff. He had a flat on the premises, and took his breakfast in the office canteen in the basement; if you were night duty officer you were warned to be out of the canteen by 9 a.m. so that the chief could breakfast alone. He was a shy man of considerable charm and political acumen; Kim has well described the chief's remarkable ability to scent and ward off danger arising to his own personal position. In pre-war days he had combined the headship of Section IV (dealing with the War Office) and the task of liaising with the French. He had little or no knowledge of counter-espionage, though he liked to dabble in it if a chance came his way. Once he called me in to say that a fellow member at White's had given him a scrap of information about some suspicious character – would I look into the matter? 'Of course,' he added, 'the chap at the club doesn't know what I do.' He seemed genuinely not to realise that probably the whole of White's knew what he did. Nor was he minutely informed about what went on in his organisation. He once asked me to list all staff who were entitled to see a particular category of highly secret material. 'I don't suppose there are more than a dozen,' he said. There were 180.

The chief had no great liking for representational entertaining, but I persuaded him to give a small farewell lunch for our liaison officer with ONI (the intelligence branch of the US Navy) and his boss, the US naval attaché; the only other person present was myself. We lunched in a private house used by the service for this kind of occasion. Although there were no professional problems to discuss, the chief seemed extremely nervous. Perhaps to cover this, he talked continuously at high speed about a number of subjects, most of which we were supposed not to discuss with the Americans. Fortunately he spoke so fast and so allusively that it seemed unlikely our guests had understood more than a fraction of it.

Kim used to argue that ideally the chief of the Secret Service should be an absolutely smashing girl, with no other qualifications for the job. 'After all,' he said, 'one has to see the chief every now and then, and it's usually rather a waste of time. This way at least you'd enjoy the occasion.' I expect senior civil servants sometimes have the same feeling about their ministers.

The chief's handwriting was so illegible that one almost needed to call in Bletchley to decipher it. Once, Kim wished to inform somebody of the content of a characteristic green ink scrawl. 'The Chief', he wrote, 'has minuted "I do not (two groups mutilated) with this idea".' Let me add that Kim came to have considerable respect for Menzies, as is clear from his book.

In the second half of 1944 a joint War Room, staffed by Section V, OSS/X2 and MI5, had been set up to deal with the counter-espionage information coming in from the war theatres of western Europe, and to give the necessary guidance – and ISOS information – to the SCI units with the various British and American military headquarters. It has been alleged that this very sensible and obvious arrangement was a humiliating defeat for SIS and Section V, who, it is said, saw the most glittering intelligence prize of the war being taken away from them and who even had difficulties in providing staff for the joint effort. Not so. I believe that Felix was opposed to the establishment of the War Room, but almost everyone else thought it a good idea.

One important reason why it was a tripartite affair was because the SCI units as a whole were similarly tripartite – the American units were staffed by OSS/X2 officers and the British ones by Section V and a few MI5 officers. It is true that, with our ever-increasing overseas commitments and the departure of Kim and Felix, we in Section V would have found difficulty in providing a suitable head. Happily, a universally acceptable candidate eventually became available in the person of 'Tar' Robertson,[8] a regular soldier who had successfully headed MI5's remarkable double-agent section for most of the war. He presided over the War Room's mixed bag with tact and efficiency, but the brains of the outfit was probably Section V's Colin Roberts. I am even more mystified by the suggestion that the War Room were dealing with the great intelligence prize of the war. German intelligence services were no longer the menace they had been. As the Allies drove eastwards, the Germans hastily recruited and trained a number of 'stay-behind' agents, French, Belgians and others, usually equipped with radio and cyphers, who were intended to stay put as the battle-line rolled over them and then transmit information to the Germans. In practice, virtually all of them either buried their equipment and went home to live a quiet life, or came running to the British or Americans. A number of them were used by us as short-term double agents. It was all a lot of work, but the German war was nearly won and the excitement of earlier days was lacking.

I did not appoint a successor to the Vk chair but was fortunate enough to get Dick Brooman-White, now released by Duncan Sandys, as my deputy. We sat at each end of a large room and shared out the work. The arrangement meant that one of us would be free to travel when needed, while the other held the fort.

Travel was becoming both easier and more necessary. My first visit, in March 1945, was to Paris (where Malcolm Muggeridge and Trevor-Wilson now enlivened an already complicated intelligence scene), Brussels and Germany west of the Rhine battle-line. At that time there were still fears of prolonged underground resistance in western Europe by hard-core Nazis, and even of a German military redoubt in the Bavarian and Austrian Alps. Another matter of great interest was our future intelligence relationship with several western European countries. Section V had already established liaisons with a number of foreign counter-intelligence and security services and expected to build these up in the future.

Our chief liaison relationship was and remained with the Americans. In addition to the very large OSS/X2 contingent, both G2 (the intelligence branch of the US Army) and ONI maintained small offices in Ryder Street. The chief reason for this was that on the American side, ISOS, like other cryptographic material, lay within the jurisdiction of G2 and ONI, and OSS/X2 had been allowed access only under their general supervision. A fourth American service with which we were in close liaison was the FBI, whose representative in the American embassy visited us frequently. I hope I will not do injustice to these departments and their professional value to us if I mention in this context a further benefit. To put it briefly, we British were starved of liquor. The Americans had plenty and as always were generous with it. This was the rye and bourbon period of my life.

I am brought, by a natural transition, to Norman Pearson, head of OSS/X2. He later became a professor of English and American poetry, and co-edited with W. H. Auden a five-volume work, *Poets of the English Language*. Norman was a hunchback,

but agile and cheerful if occasionally devious. In liaison he was
neither unintelligent nor unhelpful, but his main task as he saw
it was finding out what the British were up to. Liaising with him
was more like liaising with the French than with the Americans.
Unwittingly Marie and I fed his suspicions. She came along
to the Unicorn one day in the middle of 1944 to have a drink
with Kim and me, and announced in all innocence that she had
been sent to a job with the Americans at 71 Grosvenor Street.
'Marie,' said Kim, 'you have touched bottom.' We explained
that it was the London headquarters of OSS. It was some time
before Norman fully accepted that this was not a deep (or rather
a ridiculously shallow) plot to penetrate his service. In fact both
OSS in Grosvenor Street and X2 in Ryder Street used a number
of British secretaries, and the usual barriers of secrecy that exist
between two intelligence services had been largely broken down.

One secret we did try to keep from the Americans for a time
was the nature of Kim's new work and the existence of Section
IX. I cannot remember what sort of feeble cover story was put
around, but it was highly unlikely to fool someone as curious
as Norman, who could see that the star of Section V had been
removed for no good reason. Norman's technique for getting
information on SIS was to take its people out for the evening and
try to get them drunk. Unfortunately, he always got drunk first,
long before the martini stage was over. One evening he invited
me to dinner at his home, along with Kim and Jack Ivens, who
had been a colleague in Vd but was now, after a spell in Madrid,
working in Section IX. Kim had a prior engagement; he joined
us for a few drinks at the Unicorn but was able to cry off for the
rest of the evening, which was obviously going to be a bumpy
ride. In the taxi, before he lapsed into unintelligibility, Norman

managed to mumble something about 'What's happening in the IX theatre?', but that was the full extent of the business side of the evening. We arrived at his maisonette near Victoria and started on pink gins. It was one of those evenings where you finish the bottle of Angostura and have to find another, which we managed to do. Jack and I got Norman on to his bed and then set about cooking the meal, for which his daily woman had done the groundwork. Just as we had everything ready, with a bottle of wine open, we heard a fearful crash from above. I am sorry to say that we finished our chops before we went upstairs and restored Norman to his bed. Then we went back and scoured his cupboards till we found a bottle of Armagnac. Norman won in the end: we two had terrible hangovers, while he bounced into my office first thing as though he'd never had a drink in his life. The story was a favourite with Kim: 'Tell me again about that evening with Norman.'

VE Day brought a total stop to organised German clandestine activity of every kind. There was no hint of continued resistance by any of the organisations we had been interested in, or of the rise of new secret resistance groups; nor was there a whisper from ISOS. There were still hundreds if not thousands of our targets to be rounded up, members not only of the *Abwehr* and SD but also of the Gestapo and several other departments. The main work for this would be done by the armies and their inter-rogation staffs and our units in the field. The other problem that still lay ahead for Section V was the Japanese. At that time it was generally thought that the Far East war would continue for many months. But from the Section V point of view the Japanese were a very unsatisfactory and intangible target. I am no authority on their wartime intelligence activities, but it is fair to say that

outside the Far East and south-east Asia they did not have a
professional secret intelligence service in the normal sense. Their
embassies and service attachés picked up what information they
could, by any means that might be available. A great deal of
Japanese embassy and service attaché cypher traffic was being
read by GC&CS, and in Europe at any rate it was clear that the
Japanese had few secret informants of any consequence. Their
armed forces intelligence branches were active in the battle
areas, but here it was difficult for us in London to contribute
very much. We did send a number of Section V representatives
to the Far East and made elaborate if rather unreal plans to form
SCI units for attachment to several British and American headquarters. But we in Section V now lacked the most important
ingredient of our work: an enemy.

Not so, of course, in Section IX: here it was all just beginning.
The balance of work in the joint V–IX complex began to move
away from the heavy V predominance, but only slowly. Kim and
I thought it was time to take a combined look at some of our V
and IX people abroad and at SIS stations generally. My purpose
was to find out how the Section V officers were coping with the
post-war task of rounding up and interrogating German intelligence and security staff, and whether our officers were getting
the service they needed from London; and to discuss their future
career wishes and possibilities. Kim's purpose, more exacting,
was to examine with the stations the scope for and strategy of
future anti-Soviet and anti-communist intelligence work. In
addition the trip would give us an opportunity to get to know
something of SIS stations abroad, outside the V and IX complex.
There was also the possibility of a little relaxation after four very
hard years. Towards the end of July we flew to Lübbecke in

north-west Germany, one of several small towns where the British had established headquarters. All the larger towns, of course, were in ruins. After a day or two in this depressing area we motored by autobahn to Berlin. For two months after VE Day the Russians had had Berlin to themselves; the British, Americans and French were not allowed in until the beginning of July. By now, three or four weeks later, there were a number of SIS officers in place, including a Section V man, James, a highly resourceful Russian speaker.[9] His chief occupation so far had been to match the Russians in friendly drinking bouts, at which the usual liquor was 'V2 spirit' (actually pure alcohol). With the press-ganged assistance of the *Parteigenossen*, or captured Nazi Party officials, James had managed to organise and furnish an extremely elegant and comfortable flat, to which Eva Braun had posthumously contributed her electric cooker.

It was more than twelve years since Kim and I had arrived in Berlin as undergraduates, on the day when Hitler's triumphant entry to power was being celebrated. Now we were seeing the place in destruction. We paid a visit to Hitler's Chancellery, badly damaged but not totally destroyed. His office was still littered with broken glass and debris. A light bulb, somehow intact, was lying on the floor and I threw it at the huge marble-topped desk, where it burst with a satisfying report: a cheap and childish gesture for which I felt no shame. We went on to look for our former digs in the Potsdamer Straße. Not only could we not find the house, it was not possible to say even roughly where it had stood. Yet for all the scarcely believable destruction in the streets, the virtually complete absence of goods to buy and the lack of any of the normal amenities of life, Berlin was full of vitality, almost optimism. The atmosphere was quite different from that of defeated provincial Germany. In Berlin the citizens were living at the hub of a new conflict, symbolised by the presence of troops from East and West. Incidentally this must have been the first time, outside his clandestine contacts, that Kim had ever seen any Soviet citizens to speak of. One might almost say fellow citizens, given that he claimed to be an officer in the Soviet secret service, although he did not formally acquire Soviet nationality until after he defected to Moscow.

On our last day in Berlin, James gave the two of us and another visitor a slap-up lunch at his well-appointed flat. I am sure that even the Führer never ate better from Eva Braun's cooker. When we got to the trifle, the cook-housemaid produced a fine bottle of hock from the refrigerator. It was not like Kim to gulp wine, but he and James chose to down their glasses together. A second later I and the other visitor would have done the same but for the violent reaction of the first two. They had drunk pure Flit.[†] The poor maid, who for two months previously had been serving the Russians, was horrified. She had no doubt she would be either shot or at best sent to a prison camp. For the next thirty-six hours or more Kim was really quite ill. As we drove back that afternoon along the autobahn he was in a semi-stupor, as though he were not only extremely drunk but unable to pull out of it. He seemed to have little idea where he was. We had two nights at Lübbecke before he was himself again.

After Germany we visited Klagenfurt, headquarters of the British zone of Austria. The head of the SIS station in Germany had arranged for the RAF to fly us down in an American Mitchell bomber. For some reason this involved our becoming

---

†   *Editor's note:* An insecticide.

part of the crew. Kim masqueraded as the bomb aimer, I as the navigator. It was in Klagenfurt that we awoke one morning to the news of Hiroshima. Three days later came Nagasaki and the opening of hostilities against Japan by the Soviets. The war was ending fast. It was also in Klagenfurt that several of us got into a discussion which possibly throws a light on part of Kim's political philosophy. We were talking about Arthur Koestler's recently published *The Yogi and the Commissar*. Yogis were those who went by intuition, 'feel'; commissars by brutal logic, or 'ruthless common sense' as Kim put it. Kim suggested as the archetypal yogi the head of office administration in SIS. He was a breed all too common in Broadway at that time, a man whose mind worked in strange ways and with whom it was difficult to reason. There was general agreement that in a close Broadway field he probably came first. For commissar Kim suggested Stalin. It was clear that he approved of the commissar cast of mind, whether exemplified by capitalists or by communists. He had little regard for those who used intuitions and hunches as substitute for the powers they lacked of intellectual analysis, and admired those who were prepared to put analysis to the test of action.

We motored down through glorious scenery to Trieste. Now we were in another area of conflict with the new communist world, and one of much more professional interest to Kim as head of Section IX than to me. There was time to sun and bathe and think of peace. Driving through Trieste we saw a crowd round a newspaper seller: a man came away with a paper folded down the middle and I glimpsed half a headline, '*Il Giappone* [Japan]…' A few yards later another folded paper conveniently showed the rest: '…*si arrende* [surrenders]'. It was not entirely true, but evidently the end was very near. I celebrated the occasion by cracking a toe-joint against a rock while bathing near the Yugoslav border and had to spend half the night cooling it in that most versatile piece of equipment, the bidet.

We returned to Klagenfurt, motoring along the Gorizia route just west of the Yugoslav frontier. Our plan was to drive back from Klagenfurt through the American zones of Austria and Germany to Lübbecke. A 'Cap/M' or captured German military car was provided, with British driver. As we appeared to lack any proper documentation for a long journey of this kind an enterprising SIS officer took us to the office of the town major in Klagenfurt (who was fortunately out) and chopped such papers as we had with all the official stamps he could find. Although the town major's authority did not extend outside Klagenfurt, the results if not examined too closely were extremely impressive. Our hosts also gave us what on the British points rationing system would have been about a year's supply of tinned food, but forgot the tin opener. Car tools are a poor substitute, and we were very ready for the dinner provided by OSS in Salzburg, with whom we stayed the night. Next morning we were woken with the news that six years of war were over: this was VJ Day. We decided not to celebrate until we reached Frankfurt that evening; everyone assured us the town would be awash with liquor. Perhaps if we had not had a puncture some thirty miles short of Frankfurt, and then discovered that the driver had failed to bring a spare wheel, we might have arrived in time. When we finally made it to the US Army transit hotel, the whole of Frankfurt had been drunk dry. VJ Day remains in my personal annals, and no doubt in Kim's, as a day totally without alcohol.

From this European visit, and one or two others he made alone in 1945, Kim must have reported to the Russians that for the time being at least, SIS activities were unlikely to bring them many worries. 'After each journey, I concluded, without emotion, that it would take years to lay an effective basis for work against the Soviet Union.'[10] On my side, there was an equally simple conclusion: apart from mopping up the old enemy and redisposing our staff, which might take a few weeks or months, Section V had nothing left to do. But there was still one important question to be settled: should something of the Section V concept and framework at home and overseas be preserved in peacetime and directed towards the new target? In other words, should there be a semi-independent branch of SIS, having its own stations abroad and manned by people spending their whole careers on this work, which would specialise in the investigation of Soviet and satellite espionage and covert communist activities? This is what Felix Cowgill had had in mind. In his book Kim expresses relief that it was eventually decided to wind up the Section V idea. Although he ascribes this decision to the committee – of which he was a member – that was set up to make recommendations for the post-war organisation of SIS, I think it would have happened anyway. There were two main reasons: the need to cut back on post-war expenditure, and the arrival of Major-General John Sinclair, formerly director of military intelligence (DMI) at the War Office, as the new vice-chief.

Sinclair was particularly interested in detailed organisation – a subject for which Sir Stewart Menzies had neither the gift nor the inclination – and brought a military mind to it. To him, a secret intelligence service was something that could be organised as an army could be organised. He was especially keen on tidy chains of command, tier upon tier, with never a loose end. Everything, including statistics of intelligence production, was displayed on charts. There was little prospect that Section V, which had grown away from its titular position as a requirements section into something like a separate service, and whose achievements could not be judged by statistics, would commend itself to him, particularly as the subject of counter-espionage was one in which he as DMI had had little interest and which was now almost in abeyance for lack of material. Sinclair was a strong believer in non-specialisation: with a few obvious exceptions, such as technical experts or people who spoke difficult languages, everyone should be prepared to do anything (an analogous process was going on in the Foreign Office). When soon after his appointment he visited Ryder Street I knew from the first moment that the Section V cause, if it was a cause, was lost. I am not saying he was necessarily wrong in his judgement; there were arguments on either side. Certainly it was important that the espionage and counter-espionage sides of SIS should be closely interlocked, and not allowed to drift apart as they had in the war. But I merely ask myself, why was Kim so pleased that Section V was abolished? I can only imagine that he judged that the lack of a specialist branch would improve his prospects and those of other Soviet agents.

This is not the place to attempt a dispassionate appraisal of Section V's work in the war. Perhaps no proper appraisal can ever be made. Even if the relevant Registry files still exist, they will give a haphazard and fragmented picture of what was achieved, with no clear means of determining relative importance. We never had time to sit back and write our own history, either as we went along or at the end. The nearest we came was in the monthly reports by the subsections, but since these made no attempt to camouflage raw ISOS they would not have gone to Registry, and like much else would presumably have been destroyed. Large areas of activity are now probably little more than memories in the minds of ageing people like myself. But I think a fair verdict would be that Section V was a notable success, especially in the main task of dealing with the enemy on the ground. If I have lent any encouragement in this chapter to the impression that the section was a nest of intrigue, let me hasten to correct it: with the single exception of Kim's anti-Cowgill manoeuvres – which in themselves would have passed as unremarkable in any university college or City boardroom – there was very little intrigue. The other common misconception I would like to correct is that Section V and MI5 were always fighting each other, to the detriment of the general cause; in fact, except for some jousting at the top, working relations were extremely good. I am glad to see that Robert Cecil considers that 'the striking success of British counter-espionage during the war was, in the main, the result of loyal cooperation between SIS and MI5'.

I have said that it was Felix Cowgill who put Section V on the map; but the *quality* of the work probably owed more to Kim Philby than to anyone else. On paper he was admirably concise and clear, and set a standard for us all; he always took the trouble to master the relevant files and correspondence; and above all his judgement on intelligence matters was nearly always sound. In our dealings with MI5 and other departments he, more than anyone, neutralised the possible ill effects of Cowgill's lone battles and established a position of trust from which the rest of us benefited. His achievements for Section V in those three years should not be set aside now that we know his real motives and mainspring.

Towards the end of 1945 our work at Ryder Street was so far

wound down that it was time to look for new jobs. I knew by
now that I could find a place in the post-war service, though I
had no wish to join Section IX. I could also have gone back to
Benson's, once I was demobilised, but lunch with the managing
director showed that the best they could offer me, at that very
uncertain moment for the advertising profession, amounted to
only about two-thirds of my current salary. I therefore turned
the proposal down. Probably I also turned down the one chance
I had in my life of eventually earning first-class money instead
of a fair livelihood.

At the end of December I left Section V for a job in Broadway.[11]
The section carried on at Ryder Street for a short time and then
what little was left was merged into Section IX, or rather its
successor section, under Kim. My new job, if without executive
power, was a fairly central one. There was enough to do but, for
the first time in over four years, not the smallest need to work
late. Meanwhile, for Kim it seems that one or two clouds a good
deal larger than a man's hand had appeared on the horizon.

DECLINE AND FALL

Almost the first lesson I learnt in Section V was that spying is a mug's game. Here were all these German agents, unmasked not through any fault of their own or of the case officers running them but simply because the German cypher was not completely secure. Towards the end of the war German agents were also, and increasingly, given away by *Abwehr* officers who defected to our side or were captured. Indeed, this eventually became an embarrassment to MI5 in their running of double agents: an *Abwehr* officer would say on arrival, 'There's an agent reporting on all your troop movements around Portsmouth. Here are the details – now you can pull him in.'

It was not to be supposed that the same cypher weaknesses would be found in the Soviet intelligence services, still less that we would be capturing any of their officers on the battlefield. But occasionally one of these officers would defect. Already Walter Krivitsky, who came over to the West in 1937, had told MI5 that the Russians had sent a young English journalist to Spain during the Civil War, a lead that apparently was not followed up. Now in the later months of 1945 there were two more danger signs for Kim, one minor, the other a flashing red light. The lesser case was that of Igor Guzenko, a cypher clerk in the Soviet embassy

in Ottawa, who defected and in due course gave away a number
of Soviet agents in Canada. One of them, Gordon Lunan, had
been a colleague of mine in Benson's before he emigrated to
Canada in 1938 or 1939, though he was then a youth of about
nineteen without, as far as I knew, marked political leanings.
Lunan went down for six years. The other and (for Kim) much
more important case was the attempted defection of Konstantin
Volkov in Istanbul. The story has been recounted at length in
the Philby books, especially his own. Assuming Kim's account
is correct, Volkov, nominally a Soviet vice-consul in Istanbul,
secretly approached the British consulate general there in August.
He sought asylum in Britain and offered in return to give much
information about the NKVD, of which he claimed to be an
officer. In particular he offered to identify three Soviet agents
in Britain, namely the head of a counter-espionage organisation in London and two Foreign Office men. But he stipulated
that all communication between Istanbul and London on the
subject should be by diplomatic bag because the Russians had
broken certain British cyphers. Kim had heard nothing of the
case when he was summoned to the chief's office and shown the
letter from Istanbul outlining Volkov's offer. In front of the chief
he had to read what might almost have amounted to his own
death warrant, not to mention that of Guy Burgess and Donald
Maclean. Yet it seems that he showed no sign of shock and
aroused no suspicion. That evening he got word to the Russians,
and the next day persuaded the chief to send him to Istanbul
to investigate. The Russians must have concluded that he had
nerves of steel, and they were able to spirit Volkov out of Turkey.

Neither SIS nor Volkov seem to have thought their positions
through. As Kim points out, SIS observed Volkov's stipulations

about not using cypher telegrams, but only in respect of messages about Volkov himself. Where was the logic in that? Either the cyphers were unsafe and should not have been used for any future messages at all, or they were safe and could have been used for all messages, including those about Volkov. It was also strange that Sir Stewart Menzies, on learning that a Soviet official claimed to be able to name as a Russian spy the head of a counter-espionage organisation in London (admittedly a wide expression that could have covered many people in MI5 and elsewhere), handed over investigation to ... his own counter-espionage head! Volkov for his part was so concerned over cyphers – thereby causing a delay which probably helped to seal his own fate – that he does not seem to have considered the danger that the very man he was talking about might be put in charge of the case, or at least might learn about it. If for his own safety he had mentioned this one name, how different history would have been.

It has been suggested by some writers that Kim deliberately dragged his feet over the Volkov case so as to give the Russians more time to get Volkov away. A close reading of Kim's own account suggests that while he rejoiced inwardly over the fortuitous delays that arose, he did not cause them. It is highly unlikely that at this extremely dangerous moment he would have taken any positive delaying step which could later be remembered against him. At the same time, two aspects of his behaviour could have aroused suspicion and may have done so later: first, that with all his experience of ISOS matters he did not immediately question the validity of obeying Volkov's stipulation about cyphers (in fact he privately spotted the fallacy at once, as he makes clear); and second, that he appears to have accepted with equanimity the delays he encountered in Istanbul, instead of urging utmost speed as most SIS officers would have done. The exact timetable of events in the Volkov case is a little difficult to follow from Kim's account and others, but on one calculation it is possible that Volkov's original approach took place while Kim and I were still on our European travels; in other words, had Volkov not imposed his cypher veto, a telegram might have arrived in London before Kim was available to deal with it.

Kim must have wondered when and where the next blow would fall. A defector might turn up anywhere. He might not defect to the British: it could be to the Americans or any of the large number of other countries. He might spill the beans at once, before there was a chance of Russian counter-action. Kim would have realised more than ever that his future safety depended on events outside his own control and, to a large extent, outside that of his Russian masters. I wonder how he felt on hearing that even the remote Guzenko had put the finger on someone he had happened to know.

Many people have commented on Kim's drinking. I scarcely ever saw him much the worse for drink before 1945. Somewhere around this time there was a perceptible change. I cannot date it exactly, except that it was after he and Aileen and the three children moved to Carlyle Square in, I think, early 1945. One reason for the change could have been that the German war was over, the Russians were no longer (for practical purposes) our allies, and Kim was now nakedly having to work against his own country. But this was a situation he must have long foreseen; a greater factor may have been the Volkov case and all that it implied for his future.

While I knew him, Kim was never an alcoholic, never someone who had to drink, whatever was happening. Both his drinking and his reaction to drink depended on the occasion and the company. He could be sober after a dozen drinks or almost incoherent after two. At this time, 1945–46, he was more likely to get drunk on private, relaxed occasions than in wider company. He was not usually aggressive or unpleasant: just drunk. If his life had ended soon after the war, people would not have remembered him for his drinking.

Number 18 Carlyle Square was much larger than The Spinney or the Grove Court flat. 'They're overhoused,' Dora Philby said to me at the house-warming party. With five in the family plus Nannie Tucker, the health problems of the youngest child, Tommy, and a large house to keep up, Kim could not possibly have managed on his salary. I have no idea whether he received money from the Russians; but if it had been more than pocket money Aileen would surely have known there was another source of income, and others might have wondered. Aileen's mother, Mrs Alleyne, who was very well off, provided the money for the lease and I believe made many other subventions over the years; Kim's parents may possibly also have helped. Wherever the money came from, Carlyle Square was a hospitable place. I remember several informal parties and gatherings and one large and formal cocktail party to which Guy Burgess was going to bring his boss, Hector McNeil,[1] Ernest Bevin's number two at the Foreign Office. In the end McNeil could not come, but his wife did, escorted by Guy, who for once was on his best behaviour. Other friends who were often around included Evelyn Montague of the *Manchester Guardian*, who had been a fellow correspondent of Kim's in the BEF.[2] Kim was very fond of Evelyn. When he fell ill with TB, Kim and Aileen took him in as a lodger for several months. Another likeable friend was John Hackett, the advertising man who had got the SOE job I was interviewed for in 1941. Senior SIS officers, on the other hand, were not often seen at Carlyle Square. Outside office hours Kim preferred to mix with humbler colleagues, with whom he could relax. But his standing in SIS was high – rather higher than one might deduce from the OBE which he, like many others, was awarded at the beginning of 1946. I was given one myself six months later, and received a little note from Kim: 'The Order of the British Empire is to be congratulated on acquiring so distinguished an Officer.' I was also given a medal by the Americans,[3] which under the rules was denied to Kim because he was a civilian. It would have made an interesting addition to his Spanish, British and Russian trio.

Up to the middle of 1946 I was living not far away from Kim, at a point where the Brompton and Fulham Roads join. Sometimes I would go back home with him for a drink, or Marie and I would join the two of them for a bite of supper. Once, he and I and Aileen were walking back to their house from the Cadogan Arms when Kim, in very good humour, announced that his divorce from Lizy was at last going through and he would soon be free. Then he was inspired to propose: 'Darling, will you be the mother of my children?' Aileen, now pregnant with their fourth, giggled all the way back to Number 18.

In the autumn of that year Kim learnt that he was being posted overseas, as head of the SIS station in Istanbul. This was part of the policy of non-specialisation: overseas experience was considered to be a necessary part of an officer's make-up. Kim says in his book that he had already decided he could not reasonably resist a foreign posting without serious loss of standing in the service. Possibly true; but he would be much less use to the Russians abroad than he had been in London. In Istanbul his knowledge would be confined to what his own station was doing, plus such scraps as might come his way from elsewhere, whereas in his key job in London he could probably discover without much difficulty a large part of what not only Istanbul but every other station was doing. I believe that he could have successfully resisted an overseas posting in 1946–47. He had been only two years in the anti-communist section, and most of this time had been spent on preparatory work. It would have made sense to give him another eighteen months or two years. Perhaps finance influenced him; it certainly influenced everyone else. Although the difference may not have been so great at this time as it later became, you were much better off abroad. A cynic once compiled an SIS glossary: the definition of 'home posting' was 'a device calculated to reduce an officer to a state of such penury that he will readily accept a posting to ——' (whatever was currently the most unpopular place). Kim would also have been less than human if he had not contemplated with equanimity a transfer from the rationing and shortages of London in 1946 to the pleasures and summer warmth of Istanbul.

For the last six months of that year I did not see much of him, except occasionally in the office. Marie and I had temporarily left London and rented a cottage near Goudhurst in Kent, and my journey took an hour and three-quarters each way. One Saturday evening Kim and Aileen came through on their way back to London from a visit to Sussex. I think they had been visiting Malcolm Muggeridge. They had supper with us and Kim got drunk. On this as on several other occasions I had the impression that he did so not because he had to but because he wanted to: this was a good moment to do it, with old friends. It must have been a few weeks before his and Aileen's wedding.

Marie and I missed the occasion because we had gone on holiday to St Jean-de-Luz, of Civil War memories, and had then
taken an unscheduled side trip to Madrid with two friends from
Bilbao whom we had run across in St Jean.

From Goudhurst we were forced back to London in January
1947 by the coldest and fiercest winter I had known up to that
time. It became impossible to make the double journey and put
in a day's work. Thus we were in time for Kim's long-drawn-out
departure from London, which lasted about a fortnight. Every
night there was an impromptu farewell party at Carlyle Square;
every morning, unless BOAC telephoned in time, he would leave
in the frozen pre-dawn hours for London airport and wait there
until cancellation was announced. But finally he got off, and not
long afterwards we saw Aileen and the children onto their boat
train to Glasgow at Euston.

I too by then had had my overseas posting orders, though I was
not due to leave England until the end of July. My destination
was the Canal Zone of Egypt, which did not greatly excite me,
but there was some possibility of a transfer to Teheran after a few
months. I had long been interested in Asia, and ever since I read
Robert Byron's *The Road to Oxiana*[4] during the war, Persia had
been at the top of my posting preferences. Before I left England
Marie and I were able to spend a month in Spain, motoring with
our Bilbao friends clockwise from Port-Bou in the north-east via
Gibraltar to San Sebastian in the north-west. The car we were
travelling in, a Mercedes confiscated from the *Abwehr* after the
war, had been allocated to the same FELIPE whom we had such
difficulty in identifying. On the whole, except for a few punctures
in the ersatz tyres, FELIPE did us very well.

My job in the Canal Zone had one advantage: it required me

to visit a number of places in the Middle East. First on the list was Istanbul. I was met by Kim and Aileen at the airport and taken to their house on the water's edge at Beylerbeyi, a village on the Asiatic side of the Bosphorus. Diplomats and Europeans mostly lived on the European side. It has been said that Kim must have chosen this relatively remote area in order to facilitate his contacts with the Russians. (Kim merely says that it was a beautiful place – which was true – and that he saw no reason to follow the accepted wisdom of the old hands.) However, Soviet intelligence officers were liable to be kept under surveillance by the Turkish security service, and I would have thought it easier for two Europeans to make an inconspicuous contact in crowded Pera than among the villages and rough roads of the Asiatic side. Apart from small rowing boats, the only communication between the European and Asiatic sides was by ferry boats, easily watched. However, as Kim had anyway to spend his working day in Europe, living in Asia would at least give him a wider choice of meeting places. It certainly made for pleasurable commuting. Each morning while I was there we would take one of the ferries that plied southward down the Asiatic cost and then across to Galata, and the same in reverse in the evening; one could sip raki and gaze at one of the most beautiful waterways in the world.

Kim's predecessor in Istanbul had been Dick Brooman-White, who spent a year there after leaving Ryder Street. Dick used to enliven official correspondence with London by prefacing it with appropriate quotations. A report on an unsuccessful Balkan operation opened with an eloquent Ottoman proverb, reflecting centuries of imperial frustration: 'All is not lost: God is not an Albanian.' Kim, carrying on the practice, ranged widely for his quotations – German poetry, nineteenth-century Turkish histories, once even Lenin's 'One step forward; two steps back'. When he put up his 'Spyglass' project, an ambitious operation for long-range photography across the Turkish–Soviet frontier, Dick, now at the London desk, headed the official reply:

With a ladder and some glasses
You could see to Hackney Marshes,
If it wasn't for the houses in between.

Life with Kim and Aileen during my week in Istanbul in the late summer of 1947 seemed more relaxed and light hearted than at any time since the days at The Spinney. At the weekend the three of us went off for a camping trip into Anatolia in their rather elderly American car. We had a tent, cooking utensils, plenty of food, including (by some miscalculation) no less than forty-nine hard-boiled eggs, and of course raki, vodka, whisky and beer. In those days when nobody seemed to have accurate information about the state of the Asiatic roads you were expected to take careful notes en route of road surfaces, obstacles, bridges, culverts and so on – especially the culverts, which were considered particularly vulnerable to sabotage. As we drove, we logged culverts busily for a time. We also speculated – for by now we were well into the raki – on the possibility of encountering a bear. Kim propounded a question: which are there more of in the world, culverts or bears? It is when you come to think of it a difficult question, requiring expert knowledge in two unrelated subjects. In western Anatolia, at any rate, there was no contest: it was culverts all the way, and not a bear in sight.

This was my first encounter with Asia, a continent in which I was to spend nearly half of the next twenty years. After returning to Egypt I flew up to Teheran for a week, and came away hoping more than ever to be posted there. But further travels were abruptly halted when Egypt was visited by one of the worst cholera epidemics of recent decades. In the next six months there were more than 20,000 deaths. Neighbouring countries would not accept travellers arriving from Egypt unless they spent several days in an isolation hospital and suffered various medical indignities. Even within Egypt movement was difficult. For a simple visit to Cairo from Ismailia you needed passes for both the car and each of its occupants, obtained forty-eight hours in advance; if you wanted subsequently to vary any of the occupants or even the car you had to start again. Marie arrived on a troopship at the end of September, after doubts had been raised whether she and others would be allowed to land. The only journey abroad I was able to make during this time was a professional but slightly irregular visit to Jerusalem at the beginning of 1948, organised by my excellent secretary, whose wide circle of brass-hat friends included the RAF senior air staff officer. I was flown in a small training plane from the RAF airfield at Ismailia to Kollundia, without passing through any immigration controls, and was thus able to see Jerusalem during the last lurid days of the British mandate.

In February 1948 Kim had occasion to visit Egypt and stayed with us in Ismailia. With the cholera epidemic much diminished but movement controls still in force, he and other visitors had to be brought in by the RAF from Habbaniya in Iraq and out again by the same route. One way or another, Kim's week in Egypt meant an absence of nearly four weeks from Istanbul. He and a second visitor had to share a room in our far from luxurious flat. For baths we had a form of solar heating. This is to say, there was no hot water system, but the cold water tank stood on the roof in full sun. For at least six months of the year this meant steaming hot baths from the cold (and only) bath tap, but in February it was a matter of kettles and saucepans.

Not long before Kim arrived, Marie and I had had two important items of news: we were to be posted to Teheran at the end of March, and Marie was expecting a baby at the beginning of September. From what we then knew of Teheran, it did not for all its other merits seem an ideal place to have a first child. Materially it was still very backward, with no mains water or drainage and primitive electricity. I would need to travel in Persia from time to time, leaving Marie alone. Kim suggested she should have the baby in Istanbul. There were good hospitals, and plenty of room at his house. Although he himself would be out of Istanbul some of the time, Aileen and Nannie Tucker would both be there. So it was arranged. She would fly to Istanbul at the end of June; I would follow in August and spend my annual leave there.

Kim was away in eastern Turkey when she arrived. The family had moved from Beylerbeyi to a rambling, dilapidated but attractive old house at Vaniköy, further up the Asiatic coast. Aileen's mother, Mrs Alleyne, was staying there. Kim came back a week or so later. It had been quite an expedition: over and above their professional tasks, he, his assistant and his secretary had busily collected botanical and other samples and Kim had kept a diary. Travelling was always the happiest part of his life in Turkey. But a few days later there was a disaster. Aileen had set out alone in her car for one of Istanbul's many summer cocktail parties; Kim either could not go or did not wish to go. Shortly afterwards she arrived at the house of nearby friends in a terrible state, badly bruised about the head and covered in dirt, and with a story of having been held up on a narrow road and attacked by a man who hit her on the head with a rock and tried to steal her bag. She was taken to hospital. Several years later she told Marie that she had faked the incident and further that she had prolonged her stay in hospital by reinfecting her wounds. This may or may not be true. When she left the house in the car she seemed perfectly normal and cheerful. It is possible she was genuinely attacked. But the refusal of her injuries to heal over several months in hospital, and other accounts that have been published of her history of self-inflicted and self-aggravated injury, make it likely that part at least of her story to Marie was true. Her illness cast a gloom over the rest of the summer, a gloom that increasingly affected Kim.

Early in August, sometime after Aileen had been taken to hospital, and about a fortnight before I appeared, a new and turbulent visitor arrived at Vaniköy on three weeks' leave: Guy Burgess. Kim describes the visit as professional. It is not clear whether he means professional on the British side or the Soviet, but the context suggests British. It is difficult to think of any possible benefit that could accrue to either the Foreign Service or SIS, but perhaps some gullible person in London was persuaded to approve an official journey. However professional the visit, Guy was in no way inhibited from behaving the way he usually did. He came and went as he pleased. He might be out half the night, or hanging around at home all day. If he was in, he would probably be lolling in a window seat, dirty, unshaven, wearing nothing but an inadequately fastened dressing gown. Often he would sleep there rather than go to bed. As always, he made no secret of his homosexual tastes and exploits. Guy was the masculine type of homosexual: there was nothing of the nancy boy

about him, no mincing speech or giveaway gestures. Indeed he
prided himself on his masculinity. He was strongly built, a good
swimmer and diver. One day – perhaps spurred on by drink
but by no means drunk – he decided to dive into the Bosphorus
from the second-floor balcony at Vaniköy. With no room to stand
upright on the balcony rail, he fluffed his dive and hurt his back.

There was an occasion before I arrived when Guy had
not returned home by about midnight and Kim began to get
extremely worried: perhaps he had had a drunken fight, or
had rashly tried to get off with some pretty Turkish boy already
bespoken. Kim and Marie went out in the jeep to search for him,
driving up and down the Asiatic side for half or three-quarters of
an hour. Probably he had had an assignation with some cadet at
the nearby military academy, which Kim and Marie drove past
several times. But Kim's anxiety was such that it is just conceiv-
able the assignation was with the Russians. Guy turned up the
next day with no explanation, at least none that Marie heard.

I arrived in Vaniköy towards the end of August, after a six-day
overland journey. From Baghdad to Istanbul I took the Taurus
Express, four nights and three days in a little sleeping compart-
ment where the temperature reached 114 degrees. In fiction, the
Taurus is a romantic train, full of international spies (a phrase
I have never understood, indeed it is a contradiction in terms)
and fabulous unattainable women, but I saw nothing more
romantic or sinister than a Turkish officer in a hairnet; probably
I was the nearest thing on the train to an international spy. Kim
and Marie met me at Haydarpaşa. Aileen of course was still in
hospital, but at Vaniköy there were Guy, Nannie Tucker, Kim's
secretary Esther, the four children and the cook-houseboy. Apart
from preoccupations with the impending first-born, I remember

the next few days more for Guy than for Kim. I had met him probably a dozen times in my life, always in Kim's company. He had never been to my home or I to his, except on one occasion when Marie and I dropped him at his flat off Bond Street after a party. Kim was plainly finding him rather a burden. A telegram arrived at the embassy from the Foreign Office, saying that owing to some rearrangement Guy was not needed back immediately and could have another week in Istanbul if he wished. Kim and Esther suppressed the telegram for a time, hoping that Guy would leave as planned, but in the end they had to let him know. He stayed his extra week.

Guy, for all his awfulness, unreliability, malicious tongue and capacity for self-destruction, could be oddly appealing. He let his weaknesses appear, something that Kim seldom did. Indeed he wore almost everything on his sleeve, his celebrity-snobbery and namedropping, his sentimentality, his homosexuality; he never seemed to bother about covering up. One evening he told the story, new to me, of the founder of SIS, Captain Smith-Cumming, who was said, when trapped after a road accident, to have amputated his own leg in order to get to his dying son: at the end Guy burst into tears, to our embarrassment more than his. That same evening the conversation, unusually, turned to basic politics. Guy was talking about the future prospects of conflicting ideologies. Kim suggested that perhaps some 'new synthesis' might emerge – specifically, in the context, of capitalism and communism. No doubt he and Guy were throwing a little dust in the eyes of those present.

Kim, Guy, Marie and I went for one or two countryside drives in the jeep; Guy would sit at the back singing endlessly 'Don't dilly-dally on the way' and a peculiar ditty of his own invention,

'I'm a tired old all-in wrestler, roaming round the old Black Sea'. Always there would be stories about the famous and his encounters with them. 'If I'd had a choice', he would say, 'of meeting either Churchill or Stalin or Roosevelt, but only one of them, I wonder which it would have been. As it is, I've met Churchill...' He was far from being a mere namedropper; he could talk interestingly, often brilliantly, about his celebrities, and indeed about many subjects. But his supposedly great intellectual gifts must, as far as I am concerned, be taken on trust: for what little it is worth, my own opinion would be that he simply did not have the essential application or staying power for intellectual achievement, even on a modest Foreign Office level. Tom Driberg[5] has credited him with political prescience: apparently Guy, in Moscow, tipped Harold Macmillan to succeed Anthony Eden as Prime Minister when all the experts were supposedly saying 'Rab' Butler. Not, I would have thought, a very long shot; and against it can be set a prophecy he made at Istanbul that Hector McNeil would be the next Prime Minister but two.

What did the Russians make of him? If Kim's story is true that Guy had acted as courier for him in Spain in order to replenish his funds, this seems to imply that Guy was in direct touch with the Russians – or at least with a trusted agent of theirs – as early as 1937; in other words, he was not simply a subagent of Kim's, having contact with Soviet intelligence through Kim alone. As personal assistant to McNeil and to some extent in other posts he was in a position to become an important Soviet informant in his own right. Was he so used? Or did the Russians despair of ever getting hard straight intelligence from this mercurial over-subjective contact? He must have been as great a headache to them as he was to his Foreign Office masters. There is a scene in the film *Carry on Spying* where Kenneth Williams, as a preposterous Secret Service agent, has a meeting with the chief and his deputy. As Williams leaves the chief's office – contriving to break the glass-panelled door in the process – the deputy speaks from a full heart: 'If only the other side would make him a decent offer!' In 1951 there must have been many long-suffering people in the Foreign Service and outside who breathed a sigh of relief when Guy finally accepted a decent offer from the other side – or more probably extracted it; characteristically, he seems to have invited himself.

After Aileen, Guy is the most tragic character in this whole story. Almost everything he touched turned to failure in the end. Unlike Kim he did not have the nerve for the role he was called upon to play. I wonder if some hint of this showed itself on his visit to Istanbul, and contributed to Kim's anxiety when Guy failed to return that evening. Poor Guy: banished as it were to Siberia at the age of forty (almost literally so, for the first two or three years of his exile had to be spent in Kuibyshev).[6] Obviously he hated living in Russia, even in Moscow: and when Kim, his friend of thirty years, finally turned up, Guy was already dying.[7]

Our daughter duly arrived, not without minor incident. We were in Asia, the American Hospital was in Europe. Because the ferries stopped early in the evening, Kim had arranged a fallback plan. If things started at night, we would telephone the embassy. A posse consisting of one of the embassy guards and Kim's assistant would then make all speed by road along the European bank to a point opposite Vaniköy. There a fisherman had promised he would row them across the fast-running Bosphorus. There was no possibility, he said, of anything going wrong because he slept in his boat all year round. At midnight

on 1 September this plan had to be put into operation. The boat
was a long time reaching us, and it turned out that the boatman
had chosen that one night to go off on a spree. Kim's resourceful
assistant had seized the first boat he saw, and he and the embassy
guard managed eventually to make landfall at Vaniköy. Kim,
Marie and I piled in; Guy wanted to come but the boat was too
full. Carried southwards by the current, we landed two miles
from where the embassy car was waiting: more delay. Altogether
we took three hours door to door and perhaps it was just as well
it all turned out to be a false alarm. A week later when the real
thing began, we caught the ferry like any commuter. By that time
Guy had gone. We never saw him again.

It had not been a good summer for Kim. For the first time
since I had known him things had begun to get him down. He
was as hospitable and generous as ever, but often rather morose,
more easily given to irritation, even anger. Once I came back
from the hospital at six in the evening to find him almost inco-
herently drunk; he had caught the cook red-handed in some
misdemeanour and had fired him on the spot. It is possible that
during these weeks some new trouble had arisen in his secret life;
Guy might have brought unwelcome information, or there may
have been fears of another knowledgeable defector. But at this
time his domestic troubles seemed quite enough to account for
the change.

Leaving Marie and the baby to come on by air, I returned overland to Teheran: three nights in a Turkish sleeper to Erzurum,
then by road with a friend who had brought his car from Tabriz.
We passed below Ararat, which with its lesser partner dominates
the surrounding countryside as does Fuji in Japan. This was one
of Kim's favourite parts of Turkey. Though I preferred in general

the more uncompromising terrain of northern Persia, I had to concede him Ararat. I would like to have travelled with him in eastern Turkey, or for that matter in Persia, but it was not to be.

I saw Kim only once in the next three years. In the late summer of 1949 he was selected for the exacting post of SIS representative in Washington, with responsibility for liaison with CIA and FBI headquarters. It was an important upward step in his career. His period of preparatory briefing in London partly coincided with my own home leave from Teheran, and we ran into one another in Head Office. He took me off for lunch at Mrs Alleyne's flat in Cadogan Gardens, where the family were staying. Soon afterwards he left for America and for the time being passed out of my life. I had no direct news of him after returning to Teheran, and the only item that reached me indirectly was that Guy had also been posted to Washington and was believed to be staying with Kim.

Early in June 1951, some three months before I was due to be posted home – Marie and my daughter had already flown back – I was having a drink at the house of some embassy friends. They happened to turn on the BBC short-wave news. Reception was poor, but through the crackles we caught a few words of an announcement about two missing Foreign Office officials. The name of Guy Burgess came through, though Maclean's was lost. So unaware was I of possible implications that I was merely intrigued and rather amused; I thought he'd turn up under a table in Paris or somewhere. As the days went on I learnt a little more from *The Times* but not much. Telegrams from the Foreign Office gave news of possible sightings: one such had them on their way to Turkey or Persia. Once all this had died down, I thought little of the matter. It had not crossed my mind that

Kim might be seriously involved. In the Teheran embassy we too were caught up in a crisis of a different kind: the Anglo-Iranian Oil Company had been nationalised, the Prime Minister had been murdered, Mohammed Musaddiq had taken his place, and there were riots and anti-British demonstrations.

An old friend of mine, Robin Zaehner,[8] who had worked in Teheran for SOE during the war and usually turned up there when anything interesting was happening, arrived in July. His first words to me were, 'Your friend Kim Philby's in trouble.' I was surprised and asked why. 'Well, Burgess was a friend of his and was actually staying with him.' This did not strike me as an adequate reason, but Zaehner had no other information, and I soon put it out of my mind. It was not until September, on my way back to England, that I heard things were serious. Finally in Rome I learnt that Kim had resigned. Even then the general office belief was that he'd had to go simply to preserve good relations with the Americans. It was said that CIA and FBI officials had been displeased to find, when they came along to Kim's house for a confidential chat, that Guy always seemed to be around. It was also alleged that Kim had more than once caused embarrassment by being drunk on semi-official occasions. I think now that people were trying to find excuses for what was still unbelievable. There were very few people in the service who had inspired so much trust and respect as Kim, and so much affection among those who had worked closely with him. It seemed impossible that he had done anything worse than act a little unwisely.

I finally arrived back in London in October, after staying with friends and relatives in Istanbul, Athens and Geneva as well as Rome. No one had asked me to speed my journey, although my friendship with Kim was very well known. Not indeed that I would have had any very important information to give even if I had been summoned home at once. By the time I reached London his politics at Cambridge and many other matters must have been gone over in the greatest detail.

Soon after we arrived, Marie and I had dinner with Kim and Aileen at the home of mutual friends. It was the first time we had seen him for two years. As he came in he grinned at me half-sheepishly, half-naughtily; I was reminded of Churchill's words, 'I've been in rather a scrape'. He obviously did not want to talk about what had happened, and I did not try to probe. I had the impression that he felt deeply humiliated. Nor did I learn much more from my office colleagues. Most were reluctant to talk about the affair, already several months old, or about Kim himself: he had become largely an unperson. As an old friend I felt somewhat inhibited about asking questions. But it was comforting to find that at least there did not appear to be a witch-hunt against everyone who had known him well; and my work was unaffected.

As it happened I spent very little time in England. In Rome I had been told that before I took up my expected London job I was to spend a few months in Germany. We had time to go out to Hertfordshire to see the house at Rickmansworth that Kim and Aileen had rented but were not yet living in, and help them pull down some of the obscuring ivy and other lush growth. But in truth Kim was now in the wilderness, and was to remain there for the next five years.

OVER AND OUT

Most people go through a bad patch or two in their lives, but the ordeal Kim now went through was of a different order. His world seemed to have collapsed about him. The brilliant career, the high hopes had vanished and he was now an outcast, under serious suspicion. Aileen told Marie later that for several weeks their Rickmansworth house, The Sun Box, was under surveillance by a team of workmen not very convincingly engaged in digging up the road. Perhaps so, or perhaps they were simply rather lazy workmen; once you think you are being watched or followed everything becomes sinister. Kim, according to Aileen, was in a state almost of shock, and hated to be left alone; at the same time he would not stir from the house if he could help it.

This was the period of the main MI5 interrogation, that is to say the 'judicial inquiry' of November 1951 conducted by H. P. Milmo, previously of MI5 and by this time a KC, and the subsequent sessions Kim had with the expert interrogator Jim Skardon. In Germany I heard little of what went on except for one or two scraps, not necessarily reliable. It was said for instance that when Kim tried to light a cigarette Milmo snatched it angrily from his mouth and hurled it to the floor. I also heard – this may have come later from Aileen – that Kim was personally distressed by

having to face interrogation at the hands of old MI5 colleagues
like Dick White and Milmo who had once thought so highly
of him. It may seem strange that the attitude of SIS and MI5
friends should have mattered so much to him, but I am sure that
one part of Kim was fully and genuinely involved in his SIS life,
and as much interested in his work and in the company and good
opinion of his colleagues as any other SIS officer. I do not think
this is necessarily true of any spy in Kim's position; for instance
I doubt if it altogether applies to George Blake, although as I
never knew Blake well – or at all outside the office – this is only
an impression.

By the time Marie and I came back to England in August
1952 Kim's interrogation was over, with evidently inconclusive
results, and the heat had been taken off. But the hopelessness
remained. All official or semi-official jobs were, of course, closed
to him. It was some time before he was able to find, through
Jack Ivens, a place in a trading firm, where he stayed for several
months. Kim had no gift for minor commerce. It was sad to see
him reduced to a dreary job which was both beneath his abilities
and, in a sense, above them; like watching a Czech professor
forced to sweep the streets, and not doing it very well. It may
have been difficult for Kim, a natural elitist, to come to terms
with humdrum uncongenial work. But I suppose he would have
buckled down to it if he had had to; one now sees that he had
his eyes on something else, a chance to serve the Russians again.

For the next three years, until we were posted abroad in
October 1955, Marie and I saw either the whole family or Kim
by himself quite frequently, usually at intervals of a few weeks at
most. I had no instructions from my employers not to see him;
equally, I had no instructions to see and report on him, though

Kim may possibly have wondered whether I had. Most of his old friends in SIS and other official departments thought it wiser not to know him; indeed I can remember only one other person still so employed who continued to see him at all regularly. One or two who had left, like Dick Brooman-White (by then a Conservative MP) and Jack Ivens, remained faithful. Jack and his Greek wife Nina in particular, intensely warm-hearted people whose politics were probably the opposite of Kim's, tried to help him. Kim was very genuinely grateful – 'They're pure gold,' he said. Of his and Aileen's other friends at this time I remember especially Douglas Collins, who had founded the Goya perfume firm, and his wife Patsy, who had been a school friend of Aileen's. But Tommy and Hilda Harris had retired to Majorca, and seldom came to England: I never saw them after about 1946.

Many people in SIS who, like me, knew very little of the case against Kim clung to the belief that he was innocent of any serious offence, although we recognised we were in no real position to judge. One important thing we did not know – and I only know it now having read *My Silent War* – was that among the evidence brought against him in the MI5 interrogation were two very sinister little items. Two days after the Volkov information reached London in 1945 there had been a 'spectacular' rise in the volume of NKVD telegraphic traffic between London and Moscow, followed by a parallel rise in the traffic between Moscow and Istanbul; and in September 1949, shortly after Kim had learnt that the British and Americans were investigating a suspected leakage from the British embassy in Washington some years earlier, there had been a similar rise in NKVD traffic. Kim does not say whether MI5 showed him any statistics to support these statements or merely left him to take them on trust. If the latter, one cannot exclude that MI5 may have been bluffing a little, and exaggerating lesser rises of a kind that must have occurred frequently. But either way Kim's reply probably helped to confirm their belief in his guilt: asked if he could explain the jumps in traffic, he replied simply that he could not. This is hardly the reaction of an innocent man. Kim's line hitherto had been to argue that the reason why Donald Maclean had been alerted to danger was that he had observed both that he was being followed and that certain categories of secret papers had been withdrawn from him; in other words, there was no need to postulate a Third Man. But here was new and independent evidence to suggest that the Russians might have indeed been tipped off, at least about Volkov. One would have expected an innocent man, after very little thought, to have pointed out to his interrogators that, if the figures meant anything at all, then MI5 ought to be looking for someone who was still at large.

I think that if the facts about the NKVD traffic had been generally known in SIS there would have been a much greater tendency to believe Kim guilty. One also wonders to what extent those who briefed Harold Macmillan before his statement in the House of Commons in November 1955 were aware of this particular evidence, on the face of it fairly damning.

The line that Kim took after the disappearance of Maclean and Guy Burgess, as related in his book, contains a further inconsistency. Before he was summoned back from Washington, Kim had several post-mortem discussions with Geoffrey Paterson, the local MI5 representative, and Bobby Mackenzie, the embassy security officer. Kim put forward a theory of how events might have gone. Maclean, he suggested, had discovered he was under suspicion and being followed. But this would make it extremely difficult for him to attempt any contact with the Russians, without which his chances of escape were greatly reduced. The fortuitous arrival of Burgess offered a way out, because Burgess could make the necessary arrangements through his own Soviet contact. The reason why Burgess also fled, Kim suggested, was because he was near the end of his tether and his Russian friends thought it safest to remove him from the scene. In Washington Kim stuck to this reconstruction of events, and was able to use it to good effect with the FBI. It assumed, of course, that Burgess had been a Soviet agent. Yet three pages and a few days later we find Kim back in London, telling Dick White of MI5 that it was almost inconceivable that anyone as notoriously indiscreet as Burgess could have been a secret agent of any kind, let alone a Soviet agent. If anyone ever taxed him with this inconsistency, he does not mention it.

In conversation with me – or other friends as far as I know – Kim never referred to the ordeal he had been through. Nor did he try to refute, or even mention, the evidence that had been brought against him. Only once did he discuss any part of the matter with me. One evening after he had been having supper with us he began to talk a little about Guy Burgess. Life for Guy, he said, had evidently become absolutely hopeless by 1951, and if he was indeed a Russian spy the strain on him must have been intolerable. Kim went on to say that he had been searching in his memory for any evidence which might point to the truth about Guy, and had remembered one possibly significant thing: during the war Guy had for a time assiduously sought the company of a lady of illustrious family who was working at Bletchley. Conceivably, Kim surmised, Guy had been hoping she would eventually talk indiscreetly to him about her work. Taken somewhat aback, I asked whether he was expecting me to pass this on to the security people. 'Why yes,' said Kim in surprise, 'that's why I mentioned it.'

The more I thought of it afterwards the more puzzling I found this incident. Two things seemed absolutely obvious. First, if Guy really had been cultivating this lady's company so busily, the fact was sure by now to be well known. Second, the reason why he had done so was much more likely to be connected with her famous name than with anything else. Guy could never resist a celebrity; as Denis Greenhill put it in a *Times* article, 'I have never heard a name-dropper in the same class'. When I mentioned this story in the appropriate quarter it aroused no interest at all, presumably for the reasons I have suggested.

During the winter of 1952–53 we had several other evening visits from Kim at our small flat in Chancery Lane. His export–import job was in the City, not far away, and often he preferred to spend the night at his mother's flat in Drayton Gardens rather than get back to Rickmansworth. Together we all listened to the American Presidential election results, Kim ardently supporting Adlai Stevenson against Eisenhower. Another evening he insisted on cooking us a superb lobster paella, taking everything upon himself from buying and killing the lobster to finally serving up. Once he got very drunk. It so happened that we had been painting the bathroom. Kim lurched in, leant heavily on the window ledge and left a permanent impression of his hand, like the footprints of the famous in the wet cement outside Grauman's Chinese Theatre in Hollywood. If by any chance some later occupant of the first-floor flat at Chancery Lane ever found that the bathroom window ledge still bore faint traces of a hand that is how it came about.

Another of his visits also had enduring results, of a very

different kind. Not long after he arrived, an old friend of Marie's and mine from Benson days, Connie,[1] happened to drop in. Although we had known her for sixteen years she and Kim had apparently not met before. They got on well from the start. Connie too was working in a commercial office and it seemed that she might be able to put him in the way of some business. Before she left they had arranged to meet again. Quite soon Connie's flat in Highgate had replaced Drayton Gardens as Kim's *pied-à-terre* in London. The affair lasted, in one degree or another, until he left for Beirut in 1956.

Kim was still spending much of his time at The Sun Box with Aileen and the five children. The marriage had been in difficulties since Istanbul and if he had not met Connie he would no doubt have met someone else. This did not alter the fact that, however unintentionally, Marie and I had been the means of introducing them, and a note of falseness had been brought into our relations with Aileen, whom we had always liked. The occasional weekends or Sundays we spent at Rickmansworth were rather sad occasions. The casual friendly take-it-or-leave-it hospitality was still there, we still had to climb into bed over kiddie-cars and collapsible paddling pools, but there was now much less to laugh at. There was also less to talk about, now that shop was ruled out. I could not discuss SIS matters with Kim – not even what was happening to his former friends in the service – and he was careful never to ask questions. For ten years, while we had been together in SIS, there had always been so much to talk about: not only the endlessly fascinating work itself, but our richly assorted colleagues and contacts and the many parts of the world that the work might take us to. The fact that we did not have very many private interests in common had not mattered.

I have read that during this period he was drinking heavily, but that was not my impression. For one thing money was too short. The dominant memory I retain of visits to the Philby family in these years is that of young children: five of theirs, one of ours and sometimes neighbourly additions. There was a permanent fairly well-behaved hullabaloo. With all their troubles, Kim and Aileen were good parents. Kim's children meant an enormous amount to him. I have a strong feeling that, if it had not been for the five of them, he might well have been tempted to defect during this period. This would not have presented great operational difficulties. He was not debarred from travelling abroad. According to his book, he visited Madrid as a freelance journalist in 1952 (I do not remember this but I was probably still in Germany). Later, if my memory is correct, he flew to Tripoli in Libya on export–import business, and in 1954 he took Connie to Majorca to stay with Tommy and Hilda. He speaks in his book of having considered escape several times during this period, and mentions an escape plan, designed originally for America, but requiring only minor modifications to adapt it to Europe. I cannot see that much planning was necessary. He could simply have travelled on his existing British passport to some Western country having air communications with the Soviet bloc, from where, after visiting the Soviet embassy or possibly the Aeroflot office and obtaining a visa, he could have flown on to Moscow, Prague or elsewhere. All that would have needed arranging beforehand was a means of identifying himself to the embassy for what he was. Who would – or could – have stopped him at any point?

His export–import job folded up after some months, and for two years or more he had no real employment outside desultory journalism. At one moment he had hopes of being engaged to do some work on the script of a film, an ambitious project about the life of primitive man. 'It's got one thing going for it,' said Kim. 'I don't believe there's ever before been a film showing men and women completely naked.' One fairly well-known actor was said to be interested, and Kim attended a few meetings, but nothing came of the idea.

Kim began to spend less and less time at The Sun Box, and our own visits there became rarer. We continued to see Aileen occasionally, however, partly because our daughter had gone to a kindergarten attended also at different times by three of the Philby children, Tommy, Miranda and the youngest boy, Harry: the third generation of Philbys and Milnes to be at school together. But we also saw Connie and Kim in London. Some kind of rift arose between us and the two of them. The immediate cause was never clear at the time and now escapes me altogether, but the underlying reason must have been that we were seeing both Kim and Aileen, sometimes together but usually separately, and were finding ourselves in an ever-falser position. Before long, the rift was patched up and Kim and I had a drink together. Exceptionally, he talked of personal matters and his estrangement from Aileen. I asked whether the Burgess–Maclean affair had made matters worse. On the contrary, said Kim, it had helped to bring them together for a time.

In about 1954 the family moved from Rickmansworth to a house near Crowborough, Sussex, which we visited once or twice. My London stint was now nearing its end, and we were preparing for a move to Berne. In the summer of 1955 we gave a farewell party to which we invited Kim and Connie. It was rather a disastrous affair. Not only Kim but, surprisingly, Connie got tight. For once in my life I lost my temper with Kim and bawled him out. They came round the next day, disarmingly contrite, and we all laughed it off.

The worst of his bad time was now nearly over, but first the suspicions which had lain dormant for so long were to come into the open. The change began with an article in *The People* in September 1955 in which Vladimir Petrov, a Soviet defector of the previous year, asserted that Burgess and Maclean had been Soviet agents ever since their Cambridge days and had defected to avoid arrest. The government was forced to issue a long-promised but not very informative White Paper on the two men. Fleet Street was full of rumours about a Third Man who had warned them. These culminated in Marcus Lipton's question in the House on 25 October, naming Kim openly for the first time. Marie and I were now on the point of leaving for Switzerland. We had a farewell dinner with Kim at a restaurant and drove him back to his mother's flat at Drayton Gardens, which had been under siege by reporters for some days. Kim asked us to drop him at the back of the building so that he could climb up the fire escape. For a man facing a supreme crisis in his life, he was remarkably calm and cheerful. We were already in Berne by the time Harold Macmillan made his statement in the Commons: 'I have no reason to conclude that Mr Philby has at any time betrayed the interests of this country.'

At first I did not regard the statement as making a radical difference, except that the press hunt was now called off. Nothing, as far as I knew, had come to light to remove any suspicions that MI5 or SIS might have entertained for the last four years; whatever evidence they had, for or against him, remained exactly the same. The government, forced to make a statement, had followed the principle of 'innocent till proved guilty'. But before long it appeared that the atmosphere had changed after the parliamentary statement, and that Kim, while certainly not restored to official trust and favour, was no longer considered a total outcast. In July, shortly after Colonel Nasser had nationalised the Suez Canal, I received an elated postcard from Kim: he was back in journalism and about to take off for Beirut as *The Observer*'s correspondent.[2] 'What's the betting I'll be a war reporter again within six months?' And so he was, in half that time.

It was not until July 1957 that I saw him again. At the beginning of that year I had been brought back to a London post which involved much travelling. Fairly soon I found myself visiting Beirut. Kim and I had a pleasant and rather mellow evening together, slightly marred at the end by my speaking of Connie. Though I did not know it, and indeed had never heard of her, he was already in love with Eleanor Brewer. Reminders of discarded lives were not welcome.

In December Aileen died. Marie and I had last seen her only a month or so earlier, when the three of us took an assortment of children to the zoo. Kim came back for the funeral. Characteristically, he insisted that the youngest children should not be told of her death before he arrived, as he wished to tell them himself; he was never one to shirk an unpleasant duty. He stayed in England a few weeks, clearing up family affairs. Marie and I went down for a final weekend at Crowborough, not more than a fortnight after Aileen's death. It could hardly be described as a happy occasion, but the atmosphere was in a way almost light hearted. This was nearly the last time we were to see any of the children. Jo was growing up to be a very pretty girl. The two elder boys, John and Tommy, just turned fifteen and fourteen, were learning to drive. Kim and I took them out in the old car Aileen had been using, and Kim made each of them take the wheel for a mile or two on the public road. The boys drove just as well as any learners of legal age, but the incident surprised me – it was so out of keeping with the law-abiding Kim I had known.

He returned to Beirut, leaving the children in the care of a sister of Aileen's and other relatives. After twenty years I was once again following his career from the press, that is to say his despatches in *The Observer*. But one story came through on the grapevine which in its first bald presentation was most alarming. Kim, it was said, had tried to commit suicide by jumping off a high balcony, and had been restrained just in time. A later version was less dramatic: he had got very drunk at a party in a fifth-floor flat and had been seen with one leg over the balcony railing, saying he was sick of this bloody party and was getting out. Somebody pulled him back. Probably, if the story is true, he was too drunk to realise what floor he was on.

I had occasion to visit Beirut again in October 1958. This time Kim said, 'There's someone I want you to meet,' and presented Eleanor as his fiancée. That he should be marrying again was quite to be expected, but that it should be an American was not; however, Eleanor, if not *déracinée*, was at least somewhat internationalised by the travelling life she had led for many years. Whereas I had quickly got on terms with Aileen – and Lizy for that matter – I cannot say that I ever came to know Eleanor. She gave the impression that she lacked personality, that her life was shaped for her by others; she seemed something of a lame duck. And yet her book on Kim reveals her as a sensitive, intelligent and sympathetic person. Obviously I missed most of this.

The two of them came to London in December of that year, but after an initial evening together Marie and I did not see or hear from them for some weeks. Then out of the blue Kim telephoned me at my office one Friday evening to ask me to be a witness the next morning at their wedding. I do not know why he left it so late. I had a slight feeling that he thought I would be reluctant to take it on. Anyway, at eleven the next morning Jack Ivens and I, together with Nina and Marie, were at the register office in Russell Square to see them on their way, for better or worse. I think there were no other guests at the ceremony, but a few dropped in at the Ivens house afterwards.

Douglas and Patsy Collins had lent the couple their London flat, a very smart place in Hertford Street where we were invited for a farewell drink before they left for Beirut. We arrived at about half past six to be met at the door by an extremely shaken Eleanor. Kim had passed out and was supine on his bed. Eleanor, Marie and I and the only other guests, the Ivenses, sat around talking uneasily for an hour or two until Kim finally made a brief and groggy appearance. I had scarcely ever known him get drunk in this way, without benefit of outside company. He and Eleanor had apparently had an alcoholic lunch and then gone on drinking.

This was the last time I was to see him for nearly three years. At the end of 1959 I was transferred to Tokyo. When I arrived back in London on leave in November 1961 it so happened that Kim and Eleanor were there on a short visit. The four of us met at our wartime favourite, the Unicorn in Jermyn Street. Kim mentioned – though I never heard more of this – that he might later be visiting Tokyo with Eleanor on journalistic business. They had planned to return to Beirut the following Sunday, overland

as far as Paris, and we arranged to have a last drink on the morning of that day at a pub in Strand-on-the-Green, near where
we were staying with Kim's sister Pat. Regrettably we turned up
very late, and the rest of the party – Kim, Eleanor, Pat, Jo and
her fiancé – were already on their way back from the pub when
we arrived. Kim was a little annoyed. 'We'd given you up and
written you a note,' he said, and handed me one of his visiting
cards, on the back of which he had inscribed in his unforgettable
handwriting a message which ran like this: 'Nothing can excuse
defection. God rot you all – but look after Jo.' Unaccountably the
signature, still in Kim's writing, was 'Eleanor Philby'. Fussed at
being late, we took little note of the message – which incidentally
did not appear to be in any way private, even though Jo was
there – and would no doubt have thrown the card away if we
had not used it to take down Pat and Jo's telephone numbers.
We came across it nearly two years later when packing up before
leaving Tokyo. By that time Kim had indeed defected. It is easy
now to read all sorts of meanings into this card, but the only
one I read into the first four words at the time was that we had
let him down by being too late to say goodbye. It was natural,
among people accustomed to intelligence jargon, to use a term
like defection light-heartedly to mean some minor social derelic-
tion. In any case 'Nothing can excuse defection', in the ordinary
sense of the word, makes no sense in the context of his life. It
is clear from his book that he had had an escape plan for many
years. One might as well say 'Nothing can excuse a lifeboat' on
an ocean liner.

After we had been a few minutes in Pat's house, the taxi arrived
to take Kim and Eleanor to Victoria. The rest of us stood outside
in the weak November sunlight to say goodbye. With a last genial

touch of *schadenfreude*, Kim exclaimed, 'Why Tim, you're going grey!' A moment later they were off. I never saw or heard from him again.

Early in March 1963 I was having a quick lunch at home in Tokyo before going back to the embassy. Marie, glancing through the *Japan Times*, came across a four-line news agency item on an inside page which I had missed at breakfast. The Foreign Office had asked the Lebanese government for information about Harold Philby, a British journalist in Beirut, who had disappeared towards the end of January. No more than that; but it did not take much thought to realise that if he had been missing for several weeks without trace, he had almost certainly vanished deliberately. Behind the Iron Curtain? With all that had happened before, it seemed likely enough. But why? I knew nothing at all of his life since he had returned to Beirut – the new suspicions that had fallen on him, the confrontations with an investigator from London and the growing mental strain.[3] One or two improbable scenarios went through my mind in the next few days. Even then I was looking for less disastrous explanations than the obvious.

Some weeks later came the news that Kim was in Russia, and had been a Soviet agent for many years. In the world civil war we were now on opposite sides for ever.

10

'THE KGB OFFICER'

In his introduction to *My Silent War* Kim repeatedly makes a remarkable claim: that he became an officer of Soviet intelligence as early as the 1930s. Let me summarise what he says of his secret career. He began with 'nearly a year of illegal activity' in central Europe (1933–34). Returning to England, he seems to have undergone a period of training which involved weekly clandestine meetings with the Russians in the 'remoter open spaces' of London; at this time he was a 'sort of intelligence probationer'. His first 'challenges' came in Germany (1936) and fascist Spain (1937–39). During the Spanish war he learnt that his probationary period was at an end, and he emerged from the conflict as a 'fully fledged officer of the Soviet service'. When his years of underground work ended in the Lebanon in January 1963 'only then was I able to emerge in my true colours, the colours of a Soviet intelligence officer'. In 1968 he was able to claim that he had been a Soviet intelligence officer for some thirty-odd years.

A great gulf normally separates the functions of an intelligence officer from those of an agent. The officer is not a promoted agent, but something different in kind – a difference usually ignored or blurred in the media, which tend to call everyone an agent or a spy. Intelligence officers are basically government officials; that is to say an SIS officer is a British government official, a CIA officer an American official, and a KGB officer a Soviet official. Usually the officer works in one of the intelligence service's offices or establishments, at home or abroad, or at least has access to them. His task is to conceive and direct intelligence and other operations; to organise, and often to carry out, the recruitment and running of agents; to perform functions within the office, such as handling the intelligence received, or providing administrative, technical or other support services; to deal with other government departments; to liaise, where appropriate, with the intelligence services of friendly countries. Almost invariably he is a citizen of the country of whose intelligence service he is an officer. He will know, and need to know, many secrets. He will therefore seldom be put in a position (in peacetime at any rate) where he might be arrested and interrogated, though he may have to risk being declared *persona non grata* by a foreign country and expelled. Whether at home or abroad, he will need some kind of cover, usually in one of his country's official establishments. Sometimes the cover is not difficult to see through, and is intended to protect the decencies, and (abroad) the ambassador's feelings, rather than the security of the officer or his activities.

The agent is an entirely different creature. He may be of any nationality or background. His *raison d'être* arises from the fact that he is (or can be put in) a position, often deriving from his job, that gives him access, direct or through subsources, to needed information, or that enables him to perform other services for the intelligence service employing him. Usually he is required, in some degree, to betray a trust placed in him by his firm or

department or other associates – often indeed to spy against his
own country. His personal freedom, even his life, may be at risk.
Two particular questions will be of concern to his intelligence
masters. Is he secretly a double agent, working against them?
Alternatively, is he in danger of being arrested and interrogated?
It stands to reason that an agent should not be allowed to know
more about the service he is working for than is necessary for
that work.

In SIS, of course, Kim was an officer until he had to resign
in 1951. By all the normal criteria one would have thought
that in the Soviet service he was an agent, at least until he finally
defected. Indeed he allows that most of his work lay in fields
'normally covered, in British and American practice, by agents';
and he refers to himself as a penetration agent. It can be argued
that Kim's claim to have been an officer is merely false, and
designed to serve some KGB purpose such as encouraging other
potential spies, or perhaps, as Hugh Trevor-Roper hints, as part
of the Soviet policy to glorify its spies but never to admit that
they actually were spies.[1]

There is some independent evidence that Kim very early
achieved unusual status in Soviet eyes. Walter Krivitsky, who
defected in October 1937, was later able to tell British investigators that Soviet intelligence had sent a young English journalist
to Spain. Krivitsky knew of this although Kim had been sent
there only a few months earlier and Krivitsky was apparently not
concerned in running him. The story of Alexander Orlov, who
defected in 1938, may provide further evidence. According to
Gordon Brook-Shepherd in *The Storm Petrels*,[2] Orlov claimed
to have had occasion in about 1937 to discuss with Kislov, of the
NKVD Paris station, the possibility of finding a Russian agent

in Spain who could make radio voice contact in an emergency.
Kislov said he had a first-class man, a British journalist, but there
was no possibility of using him because he had a stammer. Since
Orlov did not come out with this until about 1970, by which time
Kim was a public character, its value is uncertain. But if the story is
true, it means that Kim's repute, though not his name, was already
known by 1937 to two of the relatively few pre-war defectors.

What had he done up to then to get himself talked about among
the security-conscious Russians? Let us try to assess the record.
According to Elizabeth Monroe, writing from documentary
evidence, Kim had applied to take the Civil Service examination
at this time.[3] Of the three referees he named, two, both Cambridge
dons, felt unable to recommend him for administrative work in
view of his strong political feelings. Kim, apparently just back
from Vienna, rushed to Cambridge to discuss the problem. It was
agreed that he should withdraw from the examination, and thus
the doubts of his referees were never officially recorded. St John
Philby was furious and wanted to fight the issue, but Kim would
have none of it. It appears that from the moment difficulties arose
he was anxious only to erase the whole matter, so that it would
not later be remembered against him. The likely conclusion
is that a change had arisen in Kim's life which made it important
that his record should remain as clean as possible.

This was the period of working for the *Review of Reviews*, and
also of being trained by the Russians at clandestine meetings
in the 'remoter open spaces' of London. His personal access to
useful non-public information at this time was surely minimal,
scarcely more than my own as I toiled away at slogans for Bovril
or parodies for Guinness.

In his introduction Kim makes an odd claim relating to this

period: 'In the first year or two, I penetrated very little, though I did beat Gordon Lonsdale to the London School of Oriental Studies by ten years.' I do not know why in the mid-1930s Kim should have had any dealings with this school (renamed the School of Oriental and African Studies in 1938, though the old title continued to be commonly used), and can only suppose that he needed information on the Middle East or some other area in connection with his *Review of Reviews* work. Lonsdale's period at SOAS was not until 1955–57. Presumably Kim simply meant to say 'twenty years': it is quite clear that in referring to his 'penetration' of the school he is speaking of the 1930s. Strangely, however, he *could* have gone to SOAS in 1946–47 in order to take Turkish lessons in preparation for his posting to Istanbul; this was a common practice in the Foreign Service.

In 1936 came Kim's involvement in the Anglo-German Fellowship and the abortive trade journal. Although this is said to have involved visits to the Propaganda Ministry in Berlin and some acquaintance with Ribbentrop, and although Kim says that overt and covert links between Britain and Germany at that time were of serious concern to the Russians, I would have thought it unlikely that important inside information resulted. Overt links between Britain and Germany would hardly need to be reported on by a trained secret agent of high potential (and high vulnerability). Could any of the cavortings of the Anglo-German Fellowship be described as covert links? Most of it was rather public stuff, of the kind that a good journalist usually reports far better than a secret agent. There may have been a few intelligence dividends, but probably the Russians looked on Kim's participation partly as an aid to removing the taint of left-ism, and partly as a training exercise.

From early in 1937 to the summer of 1939, except for brief
periods, Kim was in Spain. Here at last he had something worth
reporting on. True, his job gave him no access to British secret
information, and possibly no formal access to that of the Spanish
Nationalists; but a war reporter attached to the headquarters
of one of the combatants inevitably learns much of value to
the other. What we do not know is how many other sources the
Russians and Spanish Republicans had among the Nationalists.
A civil war – or any arbitrary division of a single country into two
halves, as for so many years in West and East Germany – gives
ample opportunity for the recruitment of agents, because there
are so many family and other links transcending the division.
Kim's value to the Russians may have lain not so much in any
unique access to information as in the cool analytical mind he
brought to his reporting and in the detachment and objectivity
he derived from not being Spanish.

Even at this early stage, Kim must have impressed his Russian
masters as a case officer's dream. Agents are always exaggerating their access, wanting more money, reporting what they think
you want to hear, getting into scrapes, missing their rendezvous
(except on payday), intruding their personal problems, talking
indiscreetly and getting cold feet. Relatively few can produce
a really literate report. Training, if practicable, can do something to improve performance, but it cannot give a man either
brains or background education, nor is it likely to change his
character. In Kim the Russians must have found themselves
presented with an agent who not only was remarkably free
of the faults I have mentioned but could absorb complicated
briefing and express himself with unusual clarity and concise-
ness both verbally and on paper. On top of this he was

ideologically devoted to the cause and, apparently, required little or no payment.

So far I have spoken of Kim's pre-war value to the Russians in terms only of his own intelligence reporting. But he may have rendered other services. At some point before he went to Spain in February 1937 he claims to have suggested Guy Burgess as a possible agent. (Whether this turned out to be a service or disservice to the Russians, not to mention Guy and Kim himself, is of course another matter.) Not only was Guy used as a courier to replenish Kim's funds in Spain in 1937, but his access to intelligence in this pre-war period, though nothing much, may have been more than Kim's.

Up to this point it is quite possible that Kim had broken no British law, or at least had done nothing which could possibly have led to a successful prosecution in British courts. As far as I know, he had not had access to confidential British information. But as a *Times* correspondent with the BEF at Arras he was in an altogether different position. Though still not employed by His Majesty's Government, he would doubtless have come within the Official Secrets Act. The Soviet Union had a pact with Germany. If it had been discovered that Kim was passing information about British military movements and plans, in wartime, I imagine he could have faced a capital charge. He would have known much about the capabilities, dispositions, defences and weapons of British forces in France, and of some French units as well. He may have had some insight into Allied military plans, such as they were. But the much more important subject of German plans presumably lay hidden. Once the hectic fighting began he can have had little if any opportunity to report to the Russians, and whatever he said would be out of date before it got to Moscow.

But Arras, like the phoney war itself, was only an interlude. Kim had already been told 'in pressing terms' by the Russians that his first priority must be the British secret service. He relates that after he returned to England in the summer of 1940 he had an interview with Frank Birch at Bletchley, arranged through a mutual friend, but was turned down because GC&CS thought the salary was not worth his while. (Conceivably, the friend was Dilly Knox, of whom Aileen sometimes spoke in familiar terms.[4]) How different his history might have been if Birch had been able to lay hands on another £100 a year.

When Kim finally joined Section D of SIS in July 1940, with Guy Burgess's help, he was still some way from what the Russians had in mind. The training schools at Brickendonbury and Beaulieu must have yielded interesting rather than vital information. Probably Kim's greatest usefulness to Soviet intelligence at this time arose from his visits to London and such access as this gave him to senior officers in SOE and elsewhere; no doubt, too, it was these visits that allowed an opportunity for occasional contact with the Russians. But although his reports may not have been of great moment, he had two important things going for him: his own obvious ability and a now increasing circle of friends in the intelligence world. Through Burgess and SOE he met Tommy Harris; through Harris he came to know Dick Brooman-White and others in MI5; and thence came the introduction to Section V in August 1941. Now he was inside the citadel.

In spite of his faith in the Soviet Union, Kim must have had some anxious moments as the Germans drove rapidly towards Moscow. The Red Army might be defeated, an anti-communist government installed. And even if the worst did not happen,

Kim's own role might become known to the Germans through captured NKVD records or staff. The German propaganda machine could have made a good deal of the Kim story. Probably it was not until after Stalingrad that this particular danger could safely be discounted.

Kim's three years in Section V, 1941 to 1944, gave him access to abundant secret information, and not only on Section V's own work. Here, not necessarily in order of priority, are a few of the subjects he could have reported on:

1. The past work of SIS and MI5 against the Soviet Union and communism generally, and future plans in this field. Kim was able, as he relates, to do some delving into the first in SIS files, and was well placed to cover the second.

2. The Axis intelligence services. His information on these was obviously extensive, but would relate mainly to the western European and western Mediterranean area, in which the Russians may not have been closely interested. If he had tried to find out in detail what was known in the east European and Middle East subsection about *Abwehr* and SD work against the USSR, he would have run the risk of making himself conspicuous. Probably he picked up items here and there, and perhaps an occasional monthly summary, but did not have the opportunity to probe thoroughly.

3. Axis military movements and plans. In Section V we saw very little of the vast Bletchley output on this subject, or of the intelligence appreciations made there and in the War Office, Admiralty and Air Ministry. SIS agent reports, filed in Central Registry, might in theory have been accessible to Kim, but in practice he would not have had the necessary time or

background knowledge to assess and deal with them. Nor could he have got hold of them in quantity without drawing attention to himself. Probably he was told to give this whole subject a miss.

4. Allied war plans. Kim could have told the Russians something about Torch, Overlord and other major operations several months in advance; but, of course, the Russians were given much of this information officially.

5. SIS organisation, operations, agents, capabilities and plans; and details of SIS staff at home and abroad. He could have covered this subject fairly extensively, though not exhaustively. Likewise for MI5, and to a much smaller extent SOE.

6. American and other Allied intelligence services, especially on the counter-espionage side. After OSS and FBI, the information Kim could have produced on the French and the Poles might have been of much interest.

7. Political information. Here the spin-off from counter-espionage work was considerable. Enemy peace feelers, for example, would have been of special importance. Our work also gave us insight into the political position and intentions of Spain, Portugal and other countries. The Russians had no diplomatic representation in the Iberian area and probably few sources of information. In addition we saw many diplomatic intercepts and some Foreign Office telegrams.

8. GC&CS. Kim could have told the Russians in detail which *Abwehr* and SD cyphers were being read, but his information about GC&CS work on diplomatic cyphers might have been more valuable. I doubt if he knew much about enemy military cyphers.

9. The X Factor – the information a person in Kim's position

could have picked up outside his own field, if he were so minded. It is always far more than one expects.

It is a formidable list. But there were two extremely stringent limiting factors: first, the extent to which Kim and the Russians would have judged it safe to meet, and second, the time he could spare from his fairly exacting Section V work to prepare written or verbal reports for Moscow, or to carry out other risky and time-consuming tasks such as extracting papers and later getting them back to the office. The Russians would have calculated that Kim's real fulfilment would come after the war, when anti-communist work would be resumed, and that his first wartime priority must be to improve his own position and reputation in SIS and avoid all serious risks. I would judge that the Russians had to exercise fierce self-denial over Kim at this time. The section of the NKVD that controlled him may have had to resist many demands from other sections and departments for information on this or that pet subject.

Paradoxically, a case can be made that in these years, mid-1941 to mid-1944, Kim's position as a Russian spy may actually have brought the British greater advantage than disadvantage, irrespective of the merits of his work for Section V. Consider the balance sheet. We and the Russians were fighting on the same side. To give them our information about enemy intelligence activities or armed forces could not do us much harm provided that the information was not put at risk by Russian insecurity or by enemy capture. Details of British and Allied intelligence services and their work, though obviously relevant to their post-war capabilities, might not be of great practical value to the Russians unless and until updated after the war. On the other side of the balance sheet, Kim was in a position to render an unusual service to the British. During the war we and the Americans were constantly giving assurances to the Russians on a number of matters. The Russian attitude was often sceptical, even when our assurances were genuine and accurate. But where Churchill, Eden and Roosevelt might not be believed, Kim probably would be. For example, he could have told them, if he reported accurately, that the Allies were broadly trustworthy in their refusal to consider any kind of anti-Soviet deal either with the German government or with anti-Nazi plotters. Whether he did so report, of course I cannot say. Certainly the Russians in their propaganda often accused the Allies of such deals – I remember particularly seeing as part of my post-war diplomatic duties a shamefully menda-cious Soviet film, *The Fall of Berlin*, in which Churchill was shown in collusion with a German arms dealer while the Russians were fighting for their lives – but if they really believed such nonsense then they must have been bigger political fools than I take them for. With Kim (and Donald Maclean and perhaps others) to advise them, can they truly have feared the totally unreal pros-pect that the British and American governments might make a political anti-Soviet arrangement with any Germans? Churchill's account of the approach by General Wolff, commander of the SS in Italy, to Allen Dulles in Switzerland in 1945 makes it clear that what the Russians chiefly feared was rather different: that German forces on one or other of the western fronts might make a military surrender which would allow Allied troops to proceed unopposed and eventually make contact with Soviet troops a good deal further east than had been anticipated. The Russians complained bitterly that they had done most of the fighting, and now the Germans were surrendering ground everywhere in the west while disputing it inch by inch in the east. Stalin's violent reaction to the meetings in Switzerland and his imputation of British and American political deals with the Germans, on the basis of information from what he calls 'conscientious and well-informed Soviet agents', admittedly suggest that if Kim was indeed in a position to report on this affair he did nothing to allay Soviet suspicions. He might even have been one of the conscientious Soviet agents. But he was now in Section IX and may not have been closely concerned.

One assurance he could have given the Russians – as no politician could have done – was that during these years the British were not conducting significant secret intelligence operations against the USSR. Presumably he did so report, and may even have done something thereby to improve trust between the two countries; how ironical that only a Soviet agent could have performed this particular service to Britain! But one needs to remember that Kim was in a delicate position. As in any secret service, there must surely have been some doubters at NKVD headquarters ready to question the genuineness of this agent whom so few people had ever seen. Kim – or his London masters – may not have liked to send reports to Moscow couched in terms too favourable to the British. In any case, his book gives the impression that he saw many things through Soviet eyes. One cannot be certain how he may have seen and reported German peace feelers, or SIS policy vis-à-vis the Russians.

With his move to Section IX the whole picture changed. It is on those remaining seven years in SIS, 1944 to 1951, that his fame or notoriety rests. No longer is there any question of a balance between benefit and harm to SIS and Britain: it was all harm, so much so that myths have begun to form. Take this sentence from his own publisher's blurb: 'Throughout the tense and perilous years of the Cold War, every British intelligence activity was jeopardised – because the head of anti-Soviet operations was a Russian spy!' Kim was head of Section IX and its successor section only from September 1944 to the end of 1946, before the Cold War really got going. Post-war intelligence had yet to move out of low gear. Probably his greatest service to the Russians at this time was the purely defensive one of stifling Konstantin Volkov. In Istanbul, between 1947 and 1949, his access to intelligence on SIS, though complete in his own territory, was geographically limited. It was not until he reached Washington in September 1949 that something like his full post-war potential to the Russians began to be realised. In the next twenty-one months he would presumably have been privy to all SIS, MI5, CIA and FBI matters that required high-level Anglo-American consultation; he was well placed to report on several other aspects of the American intelligence world; and there would have been important visitors to keep him up to date on London gossip. He would also have had some access to the ordinary political correspondence between his embassy and the Foreign Office. But he would not necessarily have been made aware of matters of Anglo-American intelligence interest that could be dealt with by contact in London or at the stations; still less of SIS operations and policies that did not need to be discussed with the Americans at all.

Even in the many things that came to his knowledge in these seven years, there were major limitations on his effectiveness. In the first place Kim was only one among a large number of SIS officers. Most of his actions, such as reports to his superiors, instructions to subordinates or comments on proposals and other papers, would be known to several people. If he had shown, say, a marked disinclination to follow up a promising idea, or had tried to steer policy away from what had commended itself to his colleagues or Whitehall, this would have been noticed. Kim had a high reputation in SIS. One often finds duds in senior posts whose actions seem calculated only to help the other side, but one knows they are duds, not traitors, and one tries to bypass them. Not so with Kim; he was good, and had to be seen to be good. I would judge that in his general conduct of office affairs he could afford to differ very little from expectations. It is absurd to say, as has been said, that under Kim the anti-communist section of SIS became an extension of the corresponding NKVD section. He simply did not have that freedom of action. For 99 per cent of the time the only safe way he could help the Russians was to tell them what was happening, give advice where he could and leave the rest to them.

But the Russians too were far from able to act freely on his information. The trouble with a really good secret source is that you have to be so careful not to blow him. I can think of at least one large-scale intelligence operation – not connected with Kim – which in my opinion survived for several months simply *because* the other side learnt about it at an early stage from a highly delicate source.[5] Probably they soon happened on it by other less delicate means as well, but dared not take action in case it drew attention to their original source. It is the old ISOS dilemma. I suspect that there were long arguments in the NKVD over the elaborate SIS/CIA plans for landing parties of agents in Albania and the Ukraine, on which Kim had presumably kept them informed. Was it safe to give those perverse and unreliable Albanian authorities the dates and times and map references of expected landings? Might it not be wiser to wait and see if the infiltrators got caught anyway? After Volkov, the Russians must have been intensely aware that Kim was living dangerously and that precipitate action on his information might put someone on his track.

A further factor was that from 1949 onwards Kim had to devote more and more of his attention to negative defensive work, trying to shield Maclean (and by extension himself) from discovery. Among other things, Kim was a lookout man for Soviet intelligence, charged with warning them when SIS and MI5 were getting suspicious of a Russian agent. He seems also to have played something of the same role in relation to the FBI, once Judith Coplon had been arrested;[6] until then she had apparently been able to keep the Russians informed of certain FBI investigations, but thereafter they looked to Kim.

Finally, one of the greatest limitations on his work for the Russians in these seven years must have lain simply in the short-ness of the day. A stream of interesting paper passed through his in-tray, containing far more than he could possibly even read, let alone memorise or condense. Conferences and discussions would have yielded much further information. His legitimate work for SIS was quite enough to occupy a full working day, even if there had been no Russians to bother about. His value as a reporting agent would have been enormously increased if he or an accomplice were in a position to photocopy useful papers on a large scale. Did this happen? He describes how, on hearing that Burgess had fled with Maclean, he went down to the base-ment of his house in Washington, collected camera, tripod and accessories and buried them in the nearby woods. Somehow I can't see Kim finding a way to photograph papers night after night, at home, with Aileen and all the children around, not to mention Guy and the whisky bottle. Aileen once told my wife that in Washington she came across Tommy Philby, then aged about seven, playing with some expensive-looking photographic equipment which he had pulled out of a cupboard or drawer in Guy's room and which she had not seen before. Was Guy the photographer? He had plenty of time on his hands and was possibly better placed than Kim himself to claim a little privacy from time to time. But 'Brigadier Brilliant', as Cyril Connolly called Guy, is difficult to visualise in this tedious and unspectacular role. Perhaps photography of documents was no more than an occasional luxury. Perhaps too it is relevant to quote a comment made by Kim in the context of his Beirut period: 'Documentary intelligence, to be really valuable, must come as a steady stream, embellished with an awful lot of explanatory annotation. An hour's serious discussion with a trustworthy informant is often more valuable than any number of original documents. Of course, it is best to have both.' Kim is speaking here of the kind of documents a journalist might get hold of, but I think he intends his remarks to have a wider application. Is he defending his own style of espionage against that of George Blake or Oleg Penkovsky, who both handed over so much paper? The fact remains that many types of document are crammed with detail impossible to memorise. If one regards Kim simply as a reporting agent, his Soviet espionage career cried out for regular photocopying of papers, but how far it took place remains a matter for conjecture. It may well be that the Russians – and he – preferred to concentrate on other things.

The basic pattern of his work for the Russians throughout his decade in SIS can only have been: to do as good a job for SIS as possible and thus advance his career; to keep the Russians informed of all important matters; to give them advice; and, within SIS, never to act in a way inappropriate to a loyal officer of the service unless either the need was imperative or there was no risk whatsoever. He mentions four occasions when trouble or near-trouble resulted from his sticking his neck out. The first, at St Albans, was relatively trivial: he managed, irregularly, to get hold of the old files relating to SIS agents in Soviet Russia, but even this nearly landed him in difficulties because of a mix-up. Second, in order to secure the Section IX post for himself; while this did not put him under suspicion, the affair evidently left a bad taste. Third, the Volkov affair: again he escaped suspicion at the time, but the incident was later to contribute strongly to the case against him. Finally, the operation to get Maclean to safety: and with it the end of Kim's career as an SIS officer. These four cases occurred in ascending order of necessity, and of damage to himself. It is hardly likely that there would not have been other crises if he had survived the Maclean affair.

People usually think that the higher he rose in SIS the more valuable he could be to the Russians, and the more he could influence and twist SIS actions in the Soviet interest; what a disaster, they say, if he had eventually become chief! I believe this to be a fallacy. By 1951 Kim had probably already reached his optimum level in SIS, the level at which he could serve the Russians most effectively. Perhaps I can illustrate this best by supposing, entirely for argument's sake, that he had eventually become chief of SIS. He would no longer be in very close touch with detail. Unless he made special and probably conspicuous efforts to find out, he would seldom know the closely identifying particulars of an agent, and his knowledge of current or future operations would be broad rather than detailed. He would have surprisingly little freedom to influence events in favour of the Russians; in everything he did he would in effect be highly accountable, both to Whitehall and to his subordinates, through whom he would nearly always have to act. On their side, the Russians would have enormous difficulties in running him as an agent. How do you arrange frequent clandestine meetings with a person of this stature? You really cannot have a chief of the Secret Service taking numerous zigzag bus and Tube journeys to get from A to B; although he would not be a well-known public figure, his face would be familiar to a large number of people – for instance, junior staff, many of whom he himself would not know. The perpetual problem of how to handle and act on the information produced by a delicately placed agent would be more acute than ever with someone so eminent. There would also be the difficulty of restricting knowledge of his identity to the fewest possible KGB staff. Even the KGB consists of human beings. The fact that one of their agents was chief of the British secret service would be almost irresistible gossip material among the better informed, and useful political capital for the KGB in the corridors of power. How long before a defector or informant would be able to point the finger?

Of course, there could be other ways of exploiting the situation. Hugh Trevor-Roper suggests that after the war the Russians, hopeful of carrying the revolution to western Europe, would have looked on Kim primarily as a likely future head of the Secret Service who could play a vital part in a communist takeover; this would be far more important than having him produce current secret information. Even without postulating such a takeover, it is known that the Russians are especially interested in establishing 'agents of influence' in high political and government places; such agents probably make contact relatively rarely and do not pass regular information, but are relied on, without the need for instruction, to give a subtle pro-Russian twist to things – or to pull their anti-Russian punches – when they can safely do so. But after Volkov, and still more after the Russians learnt of the danger to Maclean, I doubt whether long-term hopes of this kind played much part in their plans for Kim: better to get all the current use they could out of him, while the going was good. His career suggests that he was constantly immersed in problems of the moment, not that he was being kept on ice for a greater future.

Nobody in any case will ever know whether Kim could have made it to the top. Several other SIS officers of about his age were in the running, not to mention candidates who might come in from outside. In 1951 he still had a long way to go, and the strain of his double life must have been telling on him. If he ever set his sights on becoming chief, I think he had probably begun to abandon the prospect by 1950 or 1951, realising that his years as an SIS officer might be numbered. Otherwise he would surely have been more strongly impelled to find a way of keeping the raffish Guy Burgess out of his Washington household; the effect on his reputation as a solid reliable man, destined for high places, was likely to be damaging. Patrick Seale claims that even before Burgess and Maclean fled adverse reports on Kim's behaviour in Washington had spoilt his chances of becoming chief. Things had probably not gone as far as this, but his reputation may have begun to suffer; I heard stories to that effect afterwards, but it was difficult to judge how far people were merely being wise after the event.

Aware though the Russians may have been that time was running out for their Cambridge trio, even they can hardly have expected, in May–June 1951, to lose the effective services of all three at a single blow. Though Maclean and Burgess, safe in Russia, could still be used as consultants and advisers on diplomatic and political matters, the fact that they were packed off to remote Kuibyshev for the next two years, while their knowledge was at its freshest, suggests that their usefulness in Russia was never seen as more than marginal. (Kim says more or less the same thing: 'It was essential to rescue Maclean ... No question was raised about his future potential to the Soviet Union.' It was enough that he was an old comrade.) Kim himself, out of his SIS job yet still in England, fell between two stools. He had lost his access and could no longer report on current intelligence matters; nor, probably, could he be used as a background consultant, because it was now surely unsafe to make regular contact with him. Indeed, it appears from his account that he and the Russians had to break off relations for much of the next five years. If he had been able to continue serving them at this time, I think he would have said so in his book.

His loss was no doubt mitigated for the Russians by the acquisition of George Blake. I know too little of Blake to be able to compare his seven fat years, 1953–60, with Kim's 1944–51. Blake's time coincided with a more interesting period in the intelligence world, but he was not so close to the centre of things. A statement made by him and quoted at his trial included the sentence: 'There was not an official document on any matter to which I had access which was not passed to my Soviet contact.' This admission, or claim, can hardly be taken literally unless Blake's in-tray was unlike any other I have known; it would be

quite impossible to photograph or take away all the pages of all
the documents and files that pass across one's desk in the course
of a day. But it does seem that Blake had a capacity for producing
papers for the Russians which puts him very high in the league
table of agents.

Kim's great value to the Russians during his years in SIS
had been that he was there. Within and to some extent outside
his own wide field, nothing of importance could happen that
would not be disclosed to the Russians at the next contact. Now,
abruptly, he was gone. His usefulness in the period mid-1951
to mid-1956 must have been either nil or vestigial. Would he
have done better to escape to Moscow as soon as possible after
Burgess and Maclean? He would have arrived there at the age of
thirty-nine or forty, with his knowledge of SIS and CIA still fresh
and many years of active service before him. Instead, his worth
to the Russians for the whole of the period between his resignation from SIS in 1951 and his defection in 1963 must hang on his
performance in Beirut, where he arrived in August 1956.

Kim writes: 'While the British and American special services
can reconstruct pretty accurately my activities up to 1955, there
is positive and negative evidence that they know nothing about
my subsequent career in the Soviet service.' This suggests that,
although reporting on SIS would undoubtedly have been one of
his activities in the Middle East, it was not the main one, since
SIS would afterwards be able to work out fairly closely what
information he had been in a position to pass. The subject of
greatest interest to the Soviet Union in the Middle East, according to Kim himself, was that of American and British intentions
in the area, for an assessment of which he was 'not too badly
placed'. He implies that he went about this target by exploiting

his journalistic access to British, American and other officials. In other words, it was Spain and the BEF all over again, in a different setting. But Kim by this time was the highly experienced product of two major intelligence services, capable of playing a much more important part than previously. The Soviet Union at that time did not have diplomatic representation everywhere in the Middle East, the Arabian peninsula being particularly blank. Here, even as a straight journalist, he would have been able to fill in gaps in Moscow's knowledge. But he had one other advantage which he may have exploited for intelligence purposes: he was British. It is likely that some of his Arab contacts passed him information in the belief that it was destined for the British government. He may even have recruited some of them as agents, ostensibly on behalf of SIS, but actually, though they did not know it, for the KGB. This technique, quite common among intelligence services, would have enabled him to tap a reservoir of informants who would otherwise be unwilling to help. It seems unlikely, at all events, that he would have taken the risk of revealing his hand as a *Soviet* agent to Arab contacts.

Some have interpreted his Beirut years as a complicated chess game between British and Soviet intelligence. Maybe; I do not know the inside story. But espionage is usually a much more straightforward affair than one would imagine from novels and TV – or even from some allegedly factual accounts. It is great fun in theory to work out double, triple, quadruple bluffs, with the other side going most of the way but missing the final step. In practice, the law of diminishing returns begins to operate almost at once. Every step away from the simple and straightforward means that you are using more brain-power and time to produce less certain results. An intelligence operation is not much use unless you can interpret the results with confidence. Even a complicated deception project like Operation Mincemeat – described by Ewen Montagu in *The Man Who Never Was*[7] – was at bottom quite simple, with clear-cut aims and fairly solid means of determining whether they were being achieved. The shadowy exchanges of espionage, counter-espionage, counter-counter-espionage that fill so many novels would in the real world be a shocking waste of time and effort, like trying to play table tennis in the dark. *The Spy Who Came in from the Cold*[8] is a man who never was.

'So, after seven years, I left Beirut and turned up in the Soviet Union. Why? Maybe I was tipped off by a Fourth Man. Maybe someone had blundered. It is even possible that I was just tired.' Kim wrote this before the *Sunday Times* authors and Patrick Seale and others had published their accounts of the last months in Beirut. I know no more about the questioning he underwent there than I have read in these accounts, but it is obvious that Kim was not tipped off by an unauthorised person, even though he inevitably learnt, from being questioned, that the British now believed he was a spy. 'Someone had blundered': yes, in the sense that the final exposure apparently came from a defector, reinforced by other evidence. 'It's possible that I was just tired.' One side of Kim was undoubtedly relieved when the long struggle was over and he could sleep peacefully at night. But another side surely did not want to break finally with the West. He went when he did because the game was up. Incidentally, as far as one can judge from his own book and any other evidence, it does not seem that the relative value of the work he was doing for the KGB in Beirut, by comparison with what he might do for them in Moscow, was much of a factor one way or the other.

We can be sure of one thing. His full value to Soviet intelligence in 1941–51 was not to be measured in reporting statistics; it would not have shown up in the equivalent of General Sinclair's charts. The Russians probably sacrificed much immediate reporting in order not to overload Kim; the important thing was to keep him in place. The extremely unusual situation called for great judgement and skill from the Soviet service as well as from Kim; and it is worth asking, in the next chapter, whether they always made the wisest possible use of him, and in particular what we can deduce from the extraordinary affair of Burgess and Maclean.

THE ELITE FORCE

SIS has come in for harsh criticism over the Philby affair, some of it undeserved. What about the other side, the 'elite force' that he joined in the 1930s? In the period up to 1944, there are four episodes in his underground career which on present evidence the KGB and its predecessors may be thought to have handled with less than their usual judgement and professionalism. A much bigger question mark hangs over the events that led up to the debacle of 1951. Let us start with a glance at the earlier episodes, already touched on in previous chapters.

First, Vienna. If indeed Soviet intelligence recruited him before he went there, or soon after, then to use him on 'activist' work was the opposite of far sighted: it might have damaged him forever. That is why I have suggested the recruitment did not come till near the end of his time in Vienna, or even later.

Second, the pro-German phase of 1936: on the face of it a crass idea. I imagine that he had to play it well down in order not to strain the credulity of his friends. If he were really instructed to behave as heavy-handedly as we have been given to understand, the only way one can make sense of it is to assume that the Russians, victims of their own propaganda, were expecting or at least allowing for an eventual Anglo-German line-up against themselves. Kim's Spanish interlude would fit into this picture.

Third, the recruitment of Guy Burgess. I have read somewhere that Kim, probably in a newspaper interview after the publication of his book, admitted that he had made mistakes and invited readers to spot them. The introduction of Burgess, if that is what he did, seems by far the most obvious one. But some of the blame would have to fall on the Russians for taking him on.

Fourth, the pressure that the Russians put on Kim in 1944 to elbow his way through in order to become head of Section IX. Kim says he made an attempt to demur, and not surprisingly. He would probably have been just as useful to his masters if events had simply been allowed to take their course. With Cowgill's tendency to dig holes for himself Kim might well have become head of the anti-Soviet section before long; and if not he would almost certainly have been its number two, with comparable access to information. The only question is whether he would then have been told about Volkov. (I feel fairly sure he would.)

There may have been good reason for any or all of these four episodes, but hindsight suggests that if the Russians – and Kim – had their time over again they might have arranged things differently. One notes that the first three had all occurred by 1937, before the pattern of his career become plain, and even the fourth took place before his seven most important years began. But now we come to the event that terminated his career as an SIS officer. Much remains obscure about the interplay between the careers of Kim, Guy and Maclean, but we do know the ending: the need to rescue Maclean brought down all three. Why was the highly experienced Soviet service unable to prevent this?

Writing of the situation in 1950–51, Kim makes two ambiguous references to his earlier acquaintance with Maclean: 'I had only seen Maclean twice, and briefly, in fourteen years' and 'I had only met him twice, for about half an hour in all and both times on a conspiratorial basis, since 1937.' This seems to mean that he had met him only twice in his life, one of the occasions probably being in 1937 or 1938 and the other later; but, linguistically, another interpretation is not excluded, that he had met Maclean (perhaps on several occasions) in the years up to 1937 and only twice since then. The ambiguity could be intentional.[†] What does seem certain is that their *public* acquaintance was either nil or extremely small, otherwise Kim would not have dared to tell Dick White in 1951, and his press conference in 1955, that he could not clearly remember having met Maclean. (I never heard Kim mention him. Before 1951 I knew of Maclean's existence only because his sister was posted to the office in Egypt where I was working in early 1948, and people spoke of her having a brilliant brother in the Foreign Office.) 'On a conspiratorial basis' can only mean that Kim and Maclean were each aware that the other was working for the Russians. By all the normal principles of espionage, the Russians ought to have made every effort to ensure that two such dangerously exposed agents should never become 'interconscious'. Yet apparently that is what they were, from at least 1937–38. Why?

One can guess at several possible explanations. For example,

---

†   *Editor's note:* Philby claimed in his 1963 confession to have recruited Burgess or Maclean as agents. This was not the case. But shortly after his own recruitment in 1934, he supplied his handler with a list of seven potential recruits he had known while a member of the Cambridge Socialist Union. Maclean's was the first name on the list, Burgess's the last.

Kim might have been involved in Maclean's recruitment in about 1935; but it is difficult to see why, if the two were not well acquainted. Or problems might have arisen over contacting arrangements between the Russians and one of the two men, and the other had to be brought in to help. Here the dates may be significant. Kim was out of England almost continuously from early 1937 to mid-1940. While he was reporting the Spanish war his contacts with the Russians presumably took place in France; moreover Lizy had a flat in Paris in 1938–39. Again, during his time with the BEF in 1939–40 he says that he spent most of his weekends in Paris, 'not only for the obvious purpose of philandering'. Maclean was working in the Paris embassy from 1938 to mid-1940. Possibly one or both of the conspiratorial meetings took place in Paris. A third possible explanation might be that from time to time agents like Kim and Maclean must desperately need the company of others in the know; the Russians may have found it more important to improve morale – especially Maclean's – than to stick to the rules of security. And, fourthly, wherever we find something getting out of line, Guy Burgess comes to mind. Little things like rules on interconsciousness would be difficult to maintain in the vicinity of Guy, who knew everybody and liked to be in on everything. No doubt he knew Maclean at Cambridge. There is some evidence, referred to below, that at least by the time Guy was posted to Washington in 1950 he was aware that Maclean was a Soviet agent. Perhaps the Russians found it impossible to keep Kim and Guy on the one hand and Maclean on the other in complete mutual ignorance, and decided instead to extract whatever advantage they could from interconsciousness.

One apparent advantage was that in 1949 Kim was able to

warn the Russians that Maclean was in danger. Already Kim had
been asked by his Soviet contact in Istanbul if he could discover
what the British were doing about a case under FBI investigation
involving the British embassy in Washington. At that time he
was unable to help. But during his briefing at SIS headquarters
in September 1949, before his departure for Washington, he was
given details of a serious leakage of information to the Russians
from the Washington embassy in 1944–45, which the British and
Americans were still investigating though they had not yet identified the culprit. (He does not mention that what had alerted them
was an NKVD coding error which had allowed certain messages
to be deciphered by the British and Americans,[1] although he does
speak of the 'documents' and the use of the code-name HOMER
for Maclean. It is interesting that Kim, who was head of Section
IX in 1944–46, was apparently not told of this development at
the time. Perhaps the information was not clearly established till
later.) A check of the relevant Foreign Office list left Kim in little
doubt that the source of the leakage must be Maclean. Moscow
confirmed to him that this investigation and the one he had been
asked about in Istanbul were the same. But even if Kim had
known nothing at all about Maclean it would have made little
difference; once he had passed on the information obtained at his
briefing, the Russians would soon realise it referred to Maclean.
In Washington Kim was able to keep his Soviet contact closely
informed on the investigations, but he would equally have done
so without his previous knowledge.

By this time Maclean himself was already launched on his
spectacular downhill course in Cairo. One supposes that the
Russians had had to give him some sort of warning about
the investigation, and that this contributed to his crack-up of

May 1950 and recall to London. They would surely have been wiser to pull him out there and then. His subsequent usefulness must have been limited. Not until November was he sufficiently recovered to begin work as head of the American Department in the Foreign Office. At some point between then and his defection six months later he came under suspicion, and eventually under Special Branch surveillance. Contact with Russians was evidently broken off. For the sake of a few months' reporting – admittedly at an important time in the Korean War – the Russians eventually lost three agents instead of one. It appears that Maclean's rescue operation was delayed until it was too late to arrange it without bringing in someone else.

In Washington Kim had been drawn ever further into the case. So too was Burgess, who had arrived there in August 1950. Kim says that he discussed with the Russians the question whether Guy should be let into the secret of the British embassy source. The Russians subsequently decided that the balance of opinion was that Guy's special knowledge of the problem might be helpful. Whatever this obscure sentence may mean – it reads as if it had passed through more than one KGB in-tray – it does suggest previous knowledge on Guy's part of what Maclean had been doing. (If Guy was also being used to photocopy SIS documents on Kim's behalf, this could have been a further reason for bringing him in.) Guy was briefed by Kim in great detail.

Kim's account of what followed leaves much unexplained. He speaks of the high-grade intelligence to which Maclean, now in charge of the American Department, had access and the need for him to remain there as long as possible. Suspicions had not yet begun to crystallise in the investigators' minds; they were still chasing embassy charladies and the like. However it seemed unlikely to Kim and the Russians that this situation could last, and it was eventually decided to extract Maclean by mid-1951 at the latest. Kim does not explain why the Russians did not thereupon go about things in the obvious way: that is, plan the thing fully with Maclean while they were still in contact. Indeed, they could have done this much earlier; they had known since at least September 1949 that an investigation was going on which could lead to him. As in the case of Kim himself after 1951, no elaborate plan would have been necessary, especially since surveillance did not begin until fairly soon before the escape took place: a flight to somewhere in western Europe on a Friday night or Saturday morning, and then on to Prague or elsewhere in the Soviet bloc. He would have been clean away by Monday morning.

It is possible that by the winter of 1950–51 Maclean, for security reasons, was no longer seeing his Soviet contacts in London directly and was reporting by some other means such as 'dead letterboxes'. Even so, one might have expected the Russians to be able to get messages to him by the same means in reverse. But no: of all people, Guy Burgess had to be brought in to 'set the ball rolling for the rescue operation'. Apart from his other shortcomings, Guy was far from readily available; even his own return from Washington to London required a sort of escape plan. Three times in a day he contrived to get himself booked for speeding, so that the ambassador was forced to send him home. I have never found this part of the story convincing. Kim's account gives the impression that the speeding was followed almost immediately by Guy's recall; and indeed the escape plan would seem to require this, for there was no knowing when suspicion might suddenly fall on Maclean. Yet the *Sunday Times* authors, who presumably checked the facts, say that the speeding took place as early as February, whereas Guy did not leave for England until the beginning of May; and even then he went by sea.

The choice of Burgess is all the more remarkable since it was made in the full knowledge that it could endanger Kim. In the hope that if need should arise it might help to divert suspicion from himself, Kim now chose deliberately to point the investigators in the right direction. He wrote to London suggesting that they should look again at statements Krivitsky had made about a young Foreign Office official recruited by Soviet intelligence in the mid-1930s, and compare these with records of British diplomats stationed in Washington at the time of the leakage.

This is really very odd. Burgess was still in Washington and there was obviously much to be done before the rescue could take place; yet here was Kim intentionally and unpredictably speeding up the investigation. The effect, according to his own account, was that MI5 homed in fairly rapidly on Maclean as the chief suspect; what is more, they put him under surveillance, thereby making rescue more difficult. Kim admits that he was alarmed at the speed of developments. (It is possible that he was unaware of one piece of evidence mentioned by Patrick Seale as thrown up by the intercepts, namely that HOMER used to visit New York twice a week; this fitted Maclean and may have been a deciding factor.) Another oddity is that he should have drawn attention to the evidence of the very man who had spoken of a young English journalist in Spain. In the event his initiative seems to have done nothing to improve his position after Maclean's escape. I find it all so peculiar that I have sometimes toyed with the idea that the real purpose was quite different – perhaps to divert suspicion away from someone important onto the now burnt-out Maclean – but it simply does not fit the known evidence.

On arrival in London (Kim continues) Guy was to meet a Soviet contact and give him a full briefing. He would then pay an official call on Maclean at the Foreign Office, as head of the American Department. During the meeting he would slip a piece of paper across Maclean's desk giving the time and place of a rendezvous. There he would put Maclean fully in the picture. From then on the matter would be out of Kim's hands.

There are one or two obscurities here. Why was it Burgess who had to give the Soviet contact a full briefing and not the other way around? Who was in charge? The Russians in Washington had been kept fully informed. They would have passed their information to the Russians in London, who indeed would have been more up to date than the leisurely Guy. Again, did Maclean have any idea that Burgess would be approaching him? If he did not – and bearing in mind that by May he was near a breakdown – the whole thing must have come as a shock. Alternatively, if the Russians were sufficiently in touch with him to be able to prepare him for the approach, then why was the intervention of Burgess necessary at all? And why, with Maclean in dire peril, did this 'tired old all-in wrestler' dilly-dally on the way so casually? Kim had to find a pretext for writing to him and telling him to get a move on. Presumably Guy had failed even to make the initial contact with the Russians, otherwise *they* could have given him the necessary push.

In the end of course the plan succeeded, in the limited sense that Maclean got away. But even in 1951 it was easy for anyone to leave England provided that he had a passport and there were no legal grounds for detaining him. We are left with the question: why was anyone else brought in and particularly why Burgess?

One of the answers obviously lay in the personality and
mental state of Maclean. Significantly, Kim's story says nothing
at all about this. Nor are we told whether Maclean was consulted
about or even made aware of the escape plan being hatched
in Washington; he is purely a lay figure. In reality his mental
state must have been as important a factor as the investigation
into HOMER. The evidence suggests that the Russians had long
made up their minds that Maclean could not be relied on to
effect his own escape. Is it possible that he was actually refusing
to see them? I recall being told by someone closely concerned
that, after his return from Cairo, Maclean utterly refused to have
anything to do with the Foreign Office and eventually had to be
coaxed along to a Soho restaurant by a sympathetic colleague
who finally prevailed on him to come back. The Russians may
well have decided that Maclean needed to be pushed into escape
– and preferably by a sympathetic colleague.

How well Burgess and Maclean knew one another personally
and overtly never seems to have been satisfactorily established.
But the introduction of Burgess into the plan makes much better
sense if one assumes that he was already known to Maclean as a
Soviet agent. Since there was no guarantee that Maclean would
not be pulled in and interrogated before his escape, the advantage
of using Guy was that it did not materially add to the information Maclean could give away. Again, if Maclean knew Guy as
a long-time fellow agent – perhaps the only one he knew apart
from Kim – this might be a valuable psychological aid.

One can accept that Guy was not intended all along to defect
with Maclean, and that Kim's account of his consternation at the
news is genuine; otherwise the whole plan becomes unbelievably
suicidal.[2] (Moreover, if Kim had known Guy was going he would

surely have buried the camera much earlier, rather than leave it until attention was beginning to be focused upon himself.) But we are never told at what point Guy, having helped Maclean to get started, was intended to break off and return to London. If the reason for Guy's participation was that Maclean could not be relied on to go it alone, the obvious guess is that Guy was meant to stay until he could hand him over to the Russians in France or elsewhere on the Continent. It has usually been assumed – certainly by me – that Guy then lost his nerve, insisted on coming too and was accepted by the Russians because otherwise he was likely to give the whole game away. This remains the most probable theory, particularly since Guy showed signs of wavering even before he left Washington. 'Don't you go too' were Kim's farewell words to him. But it is also possible that something happened at the last moment which persuaded the Russians that if Guy went back he could not avoid coming under suspicion.

The *Sunday Times* authors, writing before Kim's book appeared, consider that up to the morning of Friday 25 May Burgess was planning a genuine weekend holiday abroad, but that not later than 10.30 a.m. he changed direction abruptly and put the escape plan into effect. The authors suggest that the reason was the decision taken by the Foreign Office, MI5 and SIS the previous evening to seek the Foreign Secretary's approval for Maclean to be interrogated on the following Monday. The theory requires that this news should have been telegraphed by SIS to Kim on Thursday night for passing to CIA; that would have enabled Kim to warn the Russians, and the Russians to get a message to Burgess on the Friday morning. All this is just possible, although the timing is very tight; but if London had indeed sent such a telegram one might have expected it to be mentioned in Kim's book, especially since its existence would be known to SIS and MI5, and probably CIA and FBI. (Might one also have expected a sharp surge of NKVD traffic between Washington, Moscow and London? It would have made useful further ammunition at Kim's interrogation by Milmo.) Kim's account of the final days, which can hardly be far out of line since several people would have known the truth, indicates that he had been told two or three weeks earlier that Maclean would probably be interrogated when the case against him was complete; but it appears that he and Geoffrey Paterson, the MI5 man, were by no means waiting on tenterhooks for the long urgent telegram that reached Washington after Burgess and Maclean had fled, as they might have been if they had known exactly when Maclean was to be pulled in. Perhaps the Russians simply decided for some reason unknown to us that the escape plan – which obviously needed to be carried out over a weekend – could not safely wait another seven days, and instructed Burgess on the Friday morning to go ahead. They do not seem to have kept Kim informed of developments – possibly they judged it too risky to contact him.

To sum up, the whole bizarre and convoluted rescue plan becomes slightly easier to explain and justify if we make three assumptions: first, that the Russians decided, not later than January 1951 and perhaps much earlier, that Maclean was in no state to manage his exit alone; second, that Burgess was chosen to help because he and Maclean were already fully interconscious; and third, that Burgess was neither intended nor expected to go too. Nevertheless, the affair leaves an impression of amateurishness quite untypical of the highly professional Soviet intelligence service; nor does anything fully explain Guy's leisurely behaviour. There may well be some major factors not yet revealed.

I have suggested that the Russians used Burgess because he was already blown to Maclean. But it could also be that they didn't have anyone else they could call on. It has often been surmised that Kim, Burgess and Maclean were merely three of many young men at Cambridge and elsewhere who were recruited into Soviet intelligence in the 1930s. We cannot deduce much about this from the events of 1951, but perhaps one small conclusion may be attempted: that there was no one else who was both known to Maclean for what he was and available to be used as an intermediary. Otherwise the Russians might well have called on him in preference to Guy, who was bound to endanger Kim.

We can possibly deduce a little more about Soviet penetration in the 1930s from the extent to which known evidence from defectors and other sources so often seems to come back to just three people – Kim, Maclean and Burgess. Walter Krivitsky mentioned a young English journalist in Spain, and a young man of good family and education who had joined the Foreign Office. Alexander Orlov, if his evidence is valid, spoke of an English journalist in Spain who stammered. Konstantin Volkov claimed to be able to name a British head of counter-espionage in London and two Foreign Office officials. The Washington embassy leakage was ultimately narrowed down to Maclean. It has to be admitted that we do not know for certain that Krivitsky was referring to Kim and Maclean, or Volkov to Kim, Maclean and Burgess. Kim himself – who, of course, has an interest in keeping us all guessing – points out that there is still no basis for supposing that Krivitsky, Volkov and the HOMER information all

referred to the same Foreign Office official. The details Krivitsky
is supposed to have given of his Foreign Office man vary from
book to book, and in at least one respect (the reference to Eton
and Oxford) are actually untrue of Maclean; but this was apparently discounted by MI5 and it seems a fair assumption that
Maclean was meant. Volkov appears to have given no details
of his two Foreign Office officials, but if indeed he could name
only two that fact could be significant in itself. So we come to
this: if during the 1930s – when pro-Soviet 'idealism' was at its
strongest – the Russians did succeed in recruiting a number of up-
and-coming young men in Britain and getting them established
in the official world, then one would have expected others besides
the Cambridge Three to have been named or indicated by one
or more of the sources I have mentioned above, and possibly by
others. Perhaps they were; but if so, the facts have not come out
and no one in this category – unless one includes Alan Nunn
May[†] – appears to have been brought to book. To press the point
too far would be to beg the question, but it is worth considering.
Put briefly: if there were a lot more just like these three, why
haven't we heard of any of them?[‡]

One other KGB activity – or rather inactivity – deserves attention, though I am not suggesting that it represents inefficiency or
wrong judgement. The Russians have never seriously exploited
the public propaganda value of the Maclean, Burgess, Philby
and Blake affairs, or tried to extract the maximum political

---

†   *Editor's note:* Alan Nunn May was a British scientist who passed details of
the Anglo-US atomic weapons programme to Moscow in the 1940s.

‡   *Editor's note:* Milne was writing in the 1970s before the public exposure of
the other members of the so-called Cambridge Spy Ring, Anthony Blunt
and John Cairncross.

embarrassment for Britain out of either the fact of their treachery or the information they provided. It is true that for a period in the 1960s there was a policy of glorifying important Soviet agents like Kim, Blake, Sorge and Lonsdale, and the Soviet intelligence apparatus in general. But, over the last quarter of a century, this is nothing to what the Russians could have done – for example with Blake's voluminous documentary intelligence while it still had some relevance. Nor for that matter was it Moscow that made a cause célèbre out of the Profumo–Keeler–Ivanov affair. Obviously the Russians have had other political priorities. Even the publication of Kim's own book was indefinitely shelved by the KGB, until the *Sunday Times* and *Observer* articles of 1967 changed the situation, and the further writings foreshadowed in his preface of 1968 have not yet appeared.

Kim Philby's career ought to tell us more about the Soviet intelligence service than we can learn from dozens of other individual cases because he has written a book which in spite of his omissions says a great deal. Professionally, one of the features of his Soviet espionage career seems to have been the rapport established at an early stage between service and agent, and maintained throughout; they appear to have been speaking the same language. I base this not on the rosy picture Kim paints of the KGB and its predecessors, as a band of high-minded philanthropic equals with never a cross word among them, but on the facts of the affair so far as they can be judged. How much of the credit for the relationship should go to one party and how much to the other is hard to say, as in a successful marriage. I suspect, however, that Kim often called the shots. Indeed it would be foolish to try to run an agent in his position without constantly deferring to his better judgement. With the exception of the Section IX job, the Russians generally seem to have left it to him to fashion his own SIS career – for example, to decide whether to accept or resist a posting. Even the intervention from Washington which helped to put London on Maclean's track is represented as his own idea and made on his responsibility, although no doubt he cleared it with the Russians.

I have tried in this book to correct some of the wilder estimates of Kim's achievements for the Russians and damage to British interests, and to emphasise the difficulties and realities of running an agent in his position. But I do not seek, as some have, to make him out as less important and dangerous than he was. His place in the pantheon or rogues' gallery of secret intelligence is secure.

RETROSPECT

'…The greatest treason: To do the right deed for the wrong reason.'
– *T. S. Eliot*

Eliot's kind of treason will not fit Kim. Some might argue that he did the wrong deed for the right reason, that he was a misguided idealist; others, again, that the deed was so wrong that no reason for it could be right. But Kim regarded himself in a different light: not as an SIS officer who treasonably handed over its secrets to a foreign power, but as someone who boldly infiltrated the British secret service because it was the target he was best equipped to penetrate. Yet he must always have been perfectly aware that in doing so he had continually to betray a trust placed in him by his country, service, friends and family, and it is clear that at least in respect of the last two the conflict distressed him. How did it happen that this man of strong loyalties, especially personal ones, was prepared to put one alien abstract loyalty above all others? No one has convincingly answered this question, nor do I pretend to be able to do so, only to offer one or two personal impressions.

I do not believe in the theory of Kim's father as the dominating influence. The important thing about St John Philby in Kim's life was not his presence but his absence. They were seldom under the same roof. While his father was in the Middle East, Kim was brought up in England by his grandmother and mother, by his prep school and public school, and by himself. As far as I know, apart from a visit when he was eleven Kim never saw the Middle East until after World War II, and his father usually spent no longer in England than he could help. Undoubtedly St John helped to implant in him a strong non-conformism and unwillingness to accept the accepted; but from there they each took quite different paths. Even at school Kim was very much his own master.

Nor do I believe that his career should be seen as a lifelong expression of revenge, a means of working out a deep resentment against authority or the Establishment, however defined. Kim had no love for the values of his class, but though he might be contemptuous of them he was not embittered. The best way I can describe him at the time he went up to Cambridge is to fall back on a cliché: a rebel looking for a cause.

His four years at university were spent in the search. He eventually found his cause in communism. It was not a merely emotional conversion, or it could not possibly have gone so deep or lasted so long. In oversimplified terms, it was a matter of the head, not the heart. I believe now that he was *intellectually* convinced, over a long period of reading and discussion, by the Marxian analysis of history and class struggle. (He says something like this in his book, but it should not be rejected on that account.) Whatever he may have said later for public consumption, he was not driven to communism by compassion for the sufferings of the poor and unemployed in Britain, or of Jews in Berlin or socialists in Vienna. Not that he was particularly lacking in compassion; rather he would always prefer to look at things in terms of historical process and analysis and political solution. This intellectual acceptance of communism was the turning point in his life.

To become a communist is one thing; to remain a communist is quite another. He describes it thus:

> It cannot be so very surprising that I adopted a Communist viewpoint in the 1930s; so many of my contemporaries made the same choice. But many of those who made that choice in those days changed sides when some of the worst features of Stalinism became apparent. I stayed the course.

He decided 'to stick it out, in the confident faith that the principles of the Revolution would outlive the aberrations of individuals, however enormous.'[1] If we are to be convinced we need to know much more about this mental struggle, which he firmly places in the Baldwin–Chamberlain era. Was he really shaken at the time by what Stalin was doing? The period 1937–38 was one of the worst of the purge. Yet it was then that Kim unhesitatingly accepted the invitation to become an NKVD agent. Historically it has usually been some dramatic Soviet intervention in foreign affairs – the Nazi–Soviet pact, the invasion of Finland 1939, Czechoslovakia 1948, Hungary 1956, Czechoslovakia 1968 – that has caused wholesale desertions among the Western communist intelligentsia, rather than what has been going on inside the USSR. Many others have changed sides not because a god has failed them but because their own values and outlook have gradually altered. Kim's brief account of this political development does not suggest that the foreign interventions had much if any effect on him, or that his personal values radically changed at any time after his acceptance of communism.

The publishers of *My Silent War* have claimed that it tells why Kim became a Soviet agent. Unfortunately this is just what it does not do. The book touches on his reasons for becoming and remaining a communist, but contains no word to show why he chose to become a spy rather than pursue the aims of communism in any of a dozen legitimate ways. Perhaps the choice was less remarkable in the mid-1930s than it would be today. Communism had a long conspiratorial history. While Kim may have been an intellectual convert, his study of that history had probably left him with a romantic admiration for the leaders of the Revolution and the secret lives they had led. The urgent task was to work against Nazism and fascism, and here was an immediate way of doing so. His escapades in Vienna would have given him a taste for the exciting underground life. And Kim possessed one useful psychological qualification for the life of a spy: from boyhood he had been accustomed to keeping his secrets to himself, and to shutting off the world from the inner keep.

Once a man has been recruited as a Soviet agent he is usually reckoned to have entered a one-way street down which he must travel as long as the Russians wish. He is not allowed the luxury of changing his mind; he knows too much, his masters need his reports and he can easily be blackmailed by them. Was this unspoken threat, ultimately, what kept Kim a faithful Soviet spy?

It is most unlikely. Kim had probably been an agent for a long time before he broke any British law. If during his first five years he had strongly wished to pull out it would have been difficult for the NKVD to exert really serious pressure on him (provided, of course, that he did not try to do so while in Germany or Spain, where they could readily have arranged trouble). The same is not true, I take it, of Maclean, who seems to have become a Soviet agent at about the time he joined the Foreign Office, and was probably spying against his country from the beginning. Kim had several years to reflect both on his career of espionage and on the political faith he had embraced. There is no real evidence that he ever chafed under either, or that Soviet pressure, however muted, had to be exercised on him. I think it more likely that, if he had any doubts, most of the drive to continue came from within himself. He had crossed two very broad Rubicons by his intellectual acceptance of communism and his choice of a conspiratorial career. A man of Kim's pride and (to quote Graham Greene) 'chilling certainty'[2] of his own rightness could not recross either of these Rubicons without destroying something in himself.

In that sense he was certainly an egotist. He now had a convinced purpose in life and must be allowed to pursue it regardless of the inconvenience or worse that it might bring to other people. To elevate one's own principles above all other considerations can be a very strong form of egotism. But I do not think it correct to describe him, in Professor Trevor-Roper's words, as totally, blindly egocentric, or to cite as evidence of this the fact that he never thought it necessary to offer Eleanor in Moscow any justification for landing her in such a situation. He could reasonably argue that she was fully aware before she married him that he had recently been accused, and officially cleared, of being the Third Man; and she had agreed to follow him to Moscow after the truth had been exposed. Kim, like thousands of other men, could certainly be ruthless with women. But what struck me most in Eleanor's story was the unexpected weakness and indecision he showed over breaking with her.[3] Although he was having an affair with Melinda Maclean, and although his marriage to Eleanor must by now have become a serious embarrassment in his relations with the KGB, he seemed unable to say the decisive words. Kim, the egotist, the admirer of 'ruthless common sense', was behaving like a human being who found it difficult to hurt other people.

The idea of power was very important in Kim's life, but I do not believe he had an overriding interest in power for himself. Dora Philby remarked bluntly to me in about 1936, 'The trouble with you and Kim is that neither of you has any ambition.' Whether she was right about me does not matter; anyway, she did not know me well. But Kim was her son. While her remark may have been partly directed at his apparent lack of success or purpose since leaving Cambridge, she was speaking of what she saw as an inborn characteristic. Kim's life suggests that he was prepared to accept anything for the cause, from maximum subordination to maximum responsibility. Of course he would have enjoyed such measure of power as this gave him, as anyone might, but I do not see this as a mainspring. On the other hand, he was deeply impressed by the *concept* of power as a necessary basis for action or policy, on the largest or smallest scale. He had only contempt for a politician – or an intelligence officer – whose pretensions exceeded the power or resources available to him.

What was Kim *like*, as a person? It is interesting that whereas the character sketches we have of Burgess and Maclean are detailed, convincing and reasonably consistent, nobody seems able to pin down Kim himself. Even those who knew him best probably all have different pictures. Most who have written about him tend to omit the rumbustiousness, the engaging irreverence towards established authority, the casual Bohemianism, the sociability, the preference for mildly earthy company and conversation. This was not usually the face he showed to his superiors in SIS or the ambassadors and counsellors of the Foreign Service. In more formal company there was a gravitas, combined with a certain diffidence and shyness to which his stammer no doubt contributed.

I think those who knew him well were hardly aware of this stammer except when strangers were present, and one can only guess at the distress it must have caused him. Everyone who suffers from a handicap has a right to turn it to occasional advantage, and Kim consciously or unconsciously did so now and then, especially at conferences and committee meetings. Because it could be painful for him to speak, his interventions were rare and invariably short, well considered and received with respect: a lesson there for all of us committee men.

Hugh Trevor-Roper puts his finger on an important point when he expresses doubts whether Kim ever engaged in intellectual discussion.[4] It is true that he did not often talk about ideology, philosophy, history, literary appreciation, art and several other subjects. I am not sure, however, that it is correct to put this down to an atrophying of the mind imposed by acceptance of the communist dialectic. In some respects it preceded his conversion. Even as a schoolboy or undergraduate he had begun to lose interest in discussing a number of things including much of literature and art, though not music. He was easily bored by other people's views. But as long as I knew him, he would come out with remarks which showed that if he had wanted he could perfectly easily have engaged in well-informed conversation on

many things. It might, however, be true to say that one reason
he avoided discussion was that there were so many subjects on
which he could not express his real views.

Trevor-Roper quotes a description of Kim in Istanbul after
the war, as a voluptuary living a self-indulgent life of lotus-eating
ease, and adds that in America his opulent way of life excited
comment. Kim liked good food and drink, but most of the time
he ate simple fare. Physical comfort never seemed to matter to
him. I can testify that his life in Istanbul was a long way from
sybaritic, and anyway he preferred roughing it in eastern Turkey.
In the years just after the war, people coming out from rationed
England and seeing plenty of meat and duty-free drink were
often inclined to speak of self-indulgence in the Foreign Service.
Trevor-Roper also describes Kim in Rickmansworth as living
far above his retirement income of a few hundred a year, and
implies that he was dependent on Russian subvention. I doubt
this. It would have been extremely dangerous for him to accept
much from the Russians – if indeed he had contact with them
at the time – and I know that Aileen's mother was giving help;
he also had a job for part of the period. There was no luxury at
all and not too much comfort at Rickmansworth; nor it seems
in Beirut. In Moscow, to judge from Eleanor, he was plunged
back into a life at least as austere as that of wartime St Albans,
but I doubt if that particular change in his fortunes greatly
bothered him.

Kim kept much of himself to himself, but outside this
protected inner sanctum he had a great need for company. He
liked to have round him a small familiar circle of friends. Some
might almost be described as cronies, one or two were there to
be ribbed and joshed in a friendly way. But he also liked the

stimulation provided, in their different styles, by such companions as Dick Brooman-White and Tommy Harris. Friendship
was always important to him. When he went to Moscow he gave
up many things, but I should be surprised if he regretted any
of his deprivations except that of his family and the people he
knew best. He was sentimental about and very loyal to friends,
even Guy, whom he didn't really like. The relationship with
Guy was equivocal: Kim was intrigued by his peculiar mentality
and character, but I had the impression even from early days
that Guy was a mysterious cross he had to bear. I put this down
to the undoubted fact that Kim could never refuse anything to
an old friend. This was certainly part of the reason, but one
now sees that he could not completely get away from Guy, for
whose introduction into Soviet intelligence he had apparently
been responsible, a situation which Guy was probably not
above exploiting.

Kim has said in an interview that if he had his time over again
he would do the same thing. I wish that were not true, but I do not
doubt he meant it. But I do not regret knowing him. He enriched
my world for many years and I owed a lot to him. Certainly my
association with him caused many difficulties for me but I do
not feel bitterness towards him, only sadness. '*Corruptis optimis
pessima.*'[†] Let me leave it at that.

[†]   'The corruption of that which is best is the worst tragedy.'

EPILOGUE†

Finally, I must turn to what happened to me after Kim Philby's defection to Moscow in January 1963.

Initially, nothing whatsoever: I had ten months to go in my Tokyo posting and saw them out without interference or correspondence of any kind. After I returned to London in November 1963 (taking a week's leave in Hong Kong en route) I was fully questioned, as, of course, was everyone closely connected with Kim. I wrote a long account of our association (which, incidentally, although I did not keep a copy, has formed the skeleton of much of this book). Eventually I appeared before an MI5 officer, who revealed what Kim was supposed to have said about me to Nicholas Elliott in Beirut before defecting. Kim apparently said that he had mentioned me (among others) to the Russians as someone they might find it worth approaching. However, he went on to say that they had turned the idea down. Kim did not suggest, according to what I was told, that I had any knowledge of all this.

I was horrified. I think my immediate reaction was to say something like 'How dare he? He never said anything to me!' I

---

† *Editor's note*: The Epilogue was written in the 1980s, after the exposure of Anthony Blunt as the so-called Fourth Man.

went on to ask when this 'recommendation' could have occurred. Probably sometime in the war, I was told. This made a little more sense. Kim must certainly have said something about me to the Russians when I was taken on by SIS in 1941. Kim never sought to find out what my true views were. One might also point out that at this meeting in Beirut – for which he may have been briefed by the KGB – Kim is said to have cleared Anthony Blunt.

According to one author,[1] Kim named me at the Beirut meeting as a 'fellow conspirator'. The same author goes on to say that I came under suspicion and was for a while suspended from duty; eventually, he says, I was cleared but had to resign because of American pressure.

This could hardly be further from the truth. First, I was never aware of being 'suspended from duty' at any time. I was not even sure at first what period the author was referring to, but I imagine now that it must have been the few weeks after I returned from Tokyo, as described above. I was on normal leave during that time, and returned to take up a new post in the London office when my leave was up. During my leave, I visited the office on several occasions.

I have pointed out to various writers who have sought information the following facts:

1. Kim Philby defected in January 1963. I did not retire from SIS until October 1968.
2. About halfway between these two dates I received the CMG.[2]
3. Throughout the period I was in close and candid touch with CIA, as and when needed; and I visited Washington and Langley, Virginia (CIA headquarters) in 1966.

4. Subsequently I worked for seven years in the House of
   Commons as clerk to various select committees.

I obviously cannot prove that I visited CIA in Washington,[3]
except that I see from an old passport that I entered New York
on 23 August 1966; but the rest is a matter of public record.
There was not the slightest reason why SIS or the House of
Commons should have employed me, or continued to employ
me, if my loyalty were in doubt. And indeed, when I left SIS I
was told in writing that I was not under any suspicion. This, of
course, is implicit in my subsequent employment in the House
of Commons.

It is clear that if Kim had named me as a 'fellow conspirator'
in January 1963, events would have taken a very different course.
First, he would have been pressed at once to give details: when
did I begin to conspire, what did I actually do, and so on. It is
inconceivable that I would have been left to carry on in Tokyo
for nearly a year as though nothing had happened. (Incidentally,
the same author says I had only one overseas posting; I had six.[4])

But I have to say that after the *Sunday Times* articles of October
1967 I had become a less desirable SIS property. The articles,
while not fully naming me, pointed to me (by clear identification)
as a long-time friend and associate of Kim's.

An SIS officer who is publicly named or identified, particularly
if he is serving abroad (I was in Hong Kong at the time, with the
Cultural Revolution in full swing in China, and all sorts of local
trouble), loses his value. I was already past the official retiring
age, and it was thought wise a few months later that I should
retire. The Americans, of course, never came into it.

APPENDICES

INTRODUCTION

The three appendices which follow reveal the depth of the confusion and denial which continued within SIS even after Philby's defection in January 1963. The first is a summary of the affair prepared for Harold Macmillan, the then Prime Minister. It details how in 1951, in the wake of the defections of Donald Maclean and Guy Burgess, Philby was suspected of being the 'Third Man' who had warned them of Maclean's imminent arrest. Philby was interrogated by Helenus Milmo, a distinguished barrister and former member of MI5, who concluded that although there was insufficient evidence to secure a conviction, 'I find myself unable to avoid the conclusion that Philby is and has for many years been a Soviet agent.' Giving its verdict on Philby, MI5 said it accepted Milmo's conclusions 'without qualification' and that 'for all practical purposes it should be assumed that Philby was a Soviet agent throughout his service with SIS'.

The rest of the document describes the sustained campaign by SIS to have Philby declared innocent. This began immediately after the MI5 judgement with the insistence of Sir Stewart Menzies, then SIS 'chief', that the case against Philby was 'capable of a less sinister interpretation than is implied by the bare evidence'. In 1955, amid press speculation that Philby was the 'Third Man', the new chief of SIS, Sir John Sinclair, insisted that new evidence threw even more doubt on his guilt and came close to accusing Milmo of having concocted the case against him. Sinclair's intensive lobbying of the Foreign Office led Harold Macmillan, then Foreign Secretary, to tell Parliament that he had 'no reason to conclude that Mr Philby has at any time betrayed the interests of his country, or to identify him with the so-called "Third Man", if indeed there was one'.

The second document is a record of the meeting in February 1963 when Sinclair's successor, Sir Dick White[†], had to tell Macmillan, by now Prime Minister, that Philby had admitted spying for Moscow and disappeared, having defected to the Soviet Union. The emergence of new evidence against Philby had led White to send the senior SIS officer Nicholas Elliott to Beirut, where Philby was working as a journalist for *The Observer*, to obtain a confession. Elliott was a surprising choice. He had a poor reputation within SIS, having botched a number of high-profile operations, and as head of station in Beirut had continued to use Philby as an agent − despite the MI5 health warning − so had an interest in playing down the extent of any betrayal. Elliott nevertheless persuaded White that he was the best person to interview Philby since they were 'close friends'. He was, of course, unaware that in his assessment for Moscow Centre, Philby had described him as 'ugly and rather pig-like to look at' albeit crediting him, perhaps surprisingly, with a 'good brain'.

The third document is a briefing paper prepared for Macmillan

---

† White, a wartime friend of Philby, was Director General of MI5 (1953–6) before taking charge of MI6.

so he could inform Harold Wilson, the leader of the Labour Party, of Philby's defection. It is notable for the continuing SIS attempts, even now, to cover up the relationship which both SIS and the Russians maintained with Philby during his period in Beirut and the extent to which Elliott botched the interview. If Philby was right about Elliott's 'good brain', it was not much in evidence. Philby ran rings round Elliott, who accepted that he had not spied for Moscow beyond 1946, allowed him to compose and type up his own very brief confession and, to the evident embarrassment of SIS, didn't even get him to sign it. This only became clear after the Macmillan briefing paper was typed up, when the word 'signed' had to be crossed out. Elliott had recorded his conversations with Philby, but had left the window open and the noise from the busy street below ensured that very little of what they said could be heard. It was evidently a shock to SIS when Philby left Beirut bound for Moscow. Despite the document's claims that Philby cleared up the truth of seven different security issues, it is impossible to see how anyone could have believed a word he said. If, as seems inevitable, he was asked about Anthony Blunt and John Cairncross, the two other members of the so-called 'Cambridge Five', both of whom had been under suspicion because of their links to Burgess, Philby would certainly have downplayed any suggestion that they were KGB agents. Equally, he threw suspicion on Milne, arguably his closest and oldest friend, who was subsequently shown to have done nothing wrong at all.

Michael Smith

These documents were released at the beginning of 2014 as a result of a Freedom of Information request. They are contained in the UK National Archives file PREM 11/4457.

APPENDIX 1

NOTES ON THE EARLY STAGES OF THE PHILBY CASE

1. Maclean and Burgess disappeared from the UK on May 25, 1951. Philby was seen by the Security Service but not for formal investigation, on June 12, 14 and 16, 1951. About the end of October, the Foreign Office were told by the Security Service that Philby was under suspicion. On December 8, 1951, the Prime Minister approved a proposal that Philby should be interrogated by Mr H Milmo KC on behalf of the Security Service. The interrogation took place on December 12. The results of this interrogation were discussed at a meeting with the Secretary of State (Sir Anthony Eden) and Sir William Strang (the Permanent Under-Secretary)[1] on December 14. It was also known at the time of that meeting that the Director of Public Prosecutions had advised that there was no legal evidence on which Philby could be prosecuted. As a result, the Secretary of State agreed that Philby's passport should be returned to him and not cancelled and that if the Security Service wished to cease surveillance on him they could do so. This was conveyed by Sir W Strang to Sir P Sillitoe, then Head of the Security Service, with the recommendation that he should inform the Prime Minister.

2. On January 14, 1952, Sir P Sillitoe[2] sent to Sir W Strang a final version of Mr Milmo's report of his interrogation of Philby

incorporating certain amendments proposed by 'C' (General Sinclair).[3] Mr Milmo's report contains a report of 'findings' in the following words:-

> 'There is no room for doubt that it was as a result of a leakage of information that Burgess and Maclean disappeared from this country on 25th May 1951. There is no evidence in law to prove the source of the leakage or to establish the identity of the person or persons responsible for the leakage. Subject to this important qualification, I find myself unable to avoid the conclusion that Philby is and has for many years been a Soviet agent and that he was directly and deliberately responsible for the leakage which in fact occurred.'

3. In comment on Mr Milmo's report the Security Service said among other things:-

> 'It is not for the Security Service to pass judgment on a case which it cannot prove. Investigation will continue and one day final proof of guilt or innocence may be obtained. Advice must be given now however on the urgent practical issues which arise and on this aspect the Security Service accepts without qualification the independent judgment formed by Mr Milmo; it must recommend that for all practical purposes it should be assumed that Philby was a Soviet agent throughout his service with SIS.'

4. The SIS commented on the report:-
>'We feel that the case against Philby is not proved and
>moreover is capable of a less sinister interpretation than
>is implied by the bare evidence.'

5. 'C' wrote to Sir W Strang on January 17, 1952, commenting further on Mr Milmo's report that it presented the case for the prosecution against Philby but that there was no comparably full case for the defence. Correspondence about how much of these papers should be shown to the Americans continued.

6. In a letter to Sir Patrick Dean on September 23, 1955,[4] 'C' (General Sinclair) referred to a current reassessment by the Security Service and SIS of the suspicions surrounding Philby and gave further views which in his opinion 'reduced very considerably the suspicion that Philby was a Soviet agent'.

7. In a reply on September 30 Sir P Dean told 'C' that the Foreign Office had always understood that the case against Philby was not conclusive but that all the relevant considerations would have to be put before Ministers in advising them on what was to be said in the House of Commons.

8. On October 24, 1955 (a fortnight before the debate), 'C' wrote to Sir I Kirkpatrick[5] enclosing a draft submission for what the Secretary of State should say in the debate about Philby. This

submission was agreed by the Director General of the Security Service (Sir Dick White), and with small amendments formed the basis of what the Secretary of State said in the debate on November 7, 1955, i.e. that there was no evidence to show that Philby was responsible for warning Burgess or Maclean or that he had betrayed the interests of his country.

9. A letter to Sir I Kirkpatrick from 'C' on December 21, 1955, enclosed a statement of the considerations 'for the defence' of the Philby case which enabled the Director General of the Security Service and 'C' to review the existing case 'for the prosecution' and to recommend to the Secretary of State the line which he in fact took on the subject of Philby during the debate on Burgess and Maclean. The concluding paragraph of this paper reads as follows:-

> 'The Milmo Report, which produces no single piece of direct evidence to show that Philby was a Soviet agent or that he was the 'Third Man' is therefore a case for the prosecution inadmissible at law and unsuccessful in security intelligence. It is constructed of suppositions and circumstantial evidence, summing up in a circular argument everything the ingenuity of a prosecutor could devise against a subject. It seems likely to remain as a permanently accusing finger pointed at Philby unless some at least of the arguments which were not included in it are given their due weight. Philby was in

fact convicted of nothing by the investigation in 1951 and despite four years of subsequent investigation is still convicted of nothing. It is entirely contrary to the English tradition for a man to have to prove his innocence even when the prosecution is in possession of hard facts. In a case where the prosecution has nothing but suspicion to go upon there is even less reason for him, even if he were able to do so, to prove his innocence. But if documents summarising the suspicions are permanently to play a part in our assessment it is only just that others which offset those suspicions should lie beside them. The case set out in this recent paper was sufficient to lead to agreement between the Directors of SIS and the Security Service as to what should be submitted for the Secretary of State's speech. It is submitted that the argument of this paper should be considered as balancing, for reasons of justice, the material in the Foreign Office's possession.'

10. In sending this paper 'C' quotes a comment by the Director General of the Security Service on it as follows:-

'I regard the memorandum as a paper worth putting alongside others in the case. I think it brings out a number of points which are fair to Philby and that the effect of it is decidedly to reduce the case of his being the "third man". At the same time I cannot but note that

<u>**TOP SECRET**</u>

the memorandum neglects to deal with his early record
and consequently does not purport to contain a full intelligence assessment of the case.'

APPENDIX 2

<u>TOP SECRET</u>

Sir Dick White came to see the Prime Minister on February 14 in order to report about a former employee of M.I.6, a Mr. Philby. Mr. Philby was mentioned at the time of the Burgess and Maclean defections. He was at the time the M.I.6 representative in Washington. No evidence was then available against Mr. Philby but he was asked to leave the Service and has since been working as a journalist in Beirut in the employ of *The Observer* and *The Economist*. Sir Dick White said that a few days ago Mr. Philby had confessed to a member of M.I.6 that he had in fact been working for the Russians from 1934 to 1946 and had recruited both Maclean and Burgess into the Soviet network at Cambridge before the war. Mr. Philby had signed this confession but had subsequently disappeared and no-one knew where he was. It might be that he was still in the Lebanon, he might have gone to Egypt or elsewhere in the Middle East, or he might be in the Soviet Union.

Sir Dick explained that it would not have been possible to extradite Mr. Philby from the Lebanon or to prosecute him if he had come to England because the evidence was not sufficiently strong for a Court of Law.

It was agreed that Sir Dick White should prepare the necessary material in case Press enquiries became embarrassing.

<u>February 15, 1963</u>

APPENDIX 3

CASE OF H. A. R. PHILBY

AIDE MEMOIRE FOR THE PRIME MINISTER'S TALK WITH MR. HAROLD WILSON

1. Philby's Government service from 1940 to 1951 was as a member of the British Secret Service (M.I.6). His appointments as First Secretary at H.M. Embassies in Turkey and in the U.S.A. gave him the cover for his M.I.6 functions in these countries. In America he acted as liaison officer between M.I.6, C.I.A. and the F.B.I.

2. In May, 1951, Maclean fled to Russia with Burgess, after apparently becoming aware that he was under suspicion. Enquiries were immediately made into the possibility that Maclean had been alerted by some person in the Foreign Office, M.I.6 or the Security Service.

3. Philby was included in these enquiries by reason of his friendship with Burgess, who had been sharing Philby's home in Washington. Philby protested that since Burgess had been considered fit for employment in H.M. Embassy there seemed no reason why they should not have lived together. Nevertheless, it was felt by the then Head of M.I.6 that in view of Philby's friendship with Burgess he could not continue his employment. He was accordingly asked to resign in July 1951 and he was paid the sum of £5,000 with no pension in compensation for the loss of his career. (He had only 8 ½ years reckonable service, and not 10 − the minimum for a pension).

4. It was after Philby's resignation that enquiries by the Security Service produced the first evidence of early Communist sympathies. The possibility that he might have been working for the Russians also now came under close investigation. No direct evidence of this could be obtained and it was decided at the highest level to put the matter to the test by severe interrogation. This was undertaken by the experienced barrister, Mr. H. P. Milmo, then by the Security Service and finally by M.I.6. Throughout these cross examinations Philby refused to admit more than youthful Marxist interests and strenuously denied all charges of disloyalty. Nevertheless, the circumstantial case against him seemed strong. Enquiries into the case, therefore, continued both in the Security Service and M.I.6 from 1952 to 1955. These failed to develop anything further against him. On the M.I.6 side certain things were discovered in his favour, in particular that he had himself provided an important clue to the detection of Maclean. It also had to be taken into account that he had had prior knowledge of certain espionage cases which had been successfully completed, e.g. in the U.K., Nunn May and Fuchs;[6] and in the U.S.A., Greenglass, Gold and the Rosenbergs.[7] In these circumstances the Security Service and M.I.6 agreed that Philby must be given the benefit of the doubt. It was upon this joint report that the Foreign Secretary made his statement in the House of Commons on the 7th November, 1955.

5. After his resignation in 1951 Philby had found no worthwhile permanent employment. He had no private means and a wife and five children to support. The then Head of M.I.6 considered it bad security for a former member of the Secret Service to be destitute and, bearing in mind that an

injustice might have been done him, agreed to give him help in finding a journalistic appointment on the 'Observer'. The approach to the Editor was made by an officer of M.I.6. The Editor undertook to consider an application from Philby if he applied in the normal manner and could obtain the job on his journalistic merits.

6. Philby took up his new assignment as the 'Observer's' Middle East correspondent in 1956, resident in Beirut. He was similarly employed by the 'Economist', who were however unaware of any M.I.6 connection. While Philby was in the Lebanon M.I.6 maintained contact with him under strict security precautions. [*Editor's note:* There are then just over two lines redacted which almost certainly informed Macmillan that Philby continued to work for MI6 during his period in Beirut.] ... He had no access to official information. The arrangement whereby a connection was preserved with Philby seemed right to those who felt that one day further evidence might come to light requiring new investigation. [A final passage of this paragraph is also redacted.]

7. Philby's continuous residence in the Lebanon from 1956 to 1963 was broken by a few visits to the U.K. on vacation and for consultation with his newspapers. On one of these visits he also remarried. As these were visits by a British subject, they were not recorded by the Immigration Authorities and are, therefore, not on the files of the Security Service. In 1962, certain new information, including the first direct allegation by someone who knew of his activities before the Second World War, came into our hands. The case was therefore re-examined by the Security Services and the conclusion reached that we now had a better

chance to induce Philby's confession, if he were tackled on neutral ground, since without this there was insufficient evidence to warrant a prosecution. An M.I.6 officer, with intimate knowledge of his character, was accordingly sent to the Lebanon in January 1963 where he managed at last to secure from Philby admissions of his guilt, including a ~~signed~~ statement which he typed himself.

8. As background to [one line of text redacted] it must be appreciated that since 1945 evidence had been accumulating of the extent to which Soviet Intelligence had successfully penetrated the British Intelligence Services during the war-time period of alliance. In all there were seven separate indications. The significance of the information recently obtained from Philby may be judged by the fact that it has resolved with certainty these causes of anxiety. It has also resulted in the removal of suspicion from several innocent people.

9. Philby's disappearance was unexpected. The probable reason was his realisation that, as a result of his confession, it was impossible for him to continue his life in the West. To the best of our knowledge his wife was unaware of his treachery and intentions and she has given us all possible help in our enquiries into his whereabouts. We believe he left Beirut for Odessa clandestinely by a Russian ship on the night of the 23rd January.

SOURCE NOTES

[*Editor's note:* These notes were compiled (not by the author) some time after the book was written.]

Foreword (pages vii–x)
1. From childhood and for the rest of his life, Milne was known to his family and friends as 'Tim'.
2. Phillip Knightley, Bruce Page and David Leitch, *Philby: The Spy Who Betrayed a Generation*, André Deutsch, London, 1968.
3. A lengthy obituary was published in *The Times* on 8 April 2010.
4. For an excellent account of the life of A. A. Milne and the close relationship with Kenneth (who died in 1929) and Kenneth's widow and children, see Anne Thwaite, *A. A. Milne: His Life*, Faber, London, 1990.
5. Phillip Knightley, *Philby: The Life and Views of the KGB Masterspy*, André Deutsch, London, 1988, p. 219.
6. Rufina Philby, interview with the *Sunday Times*, June 2003.
7. Gordon Corera, *The Art of Betrayal: Life and Death in the British Secret Service*, Weidenfeld & Nicolson, London, 2011, p. 92.

Introduction (pages xv–xvii)
1. Kim Philby, *My Silent War*, MacGibbon & Kee, London, 1968.

Chapter 1: The Public Schoolboy (pages 1–11)
1. The Westminster School uniform for scholars was tails, a white bow tie and a top hat.
2. A noted Arabist and explorer.
3. St John Philby, *Arabian Days: An Autobiography*, Robert Hale, London, 1948.
4. Lizy (née Friedman), Philby's first wife.

5.   Later Sir John Winnifrith, Permanent Under-Secretary at the Ministry of Agriculture.

Chapter 2: New Frontiers (pages 13–40)

1.   Now part of District VII in Budapest.
2.   Elizabeth Monroe, *Philby of Arabia*, Faber, London, 1973.
3.   An English classical scholar and academic, later Sir Cecil Maurice Bowra. Warden of Wadham College, Oxford 1938–70 and vice-chancellor of Oxford University 1951–54.
4.   See Phillip Knightley, Bruce Page and David Leitch, *Philby: The Spy Who Betrayed a Generation*, André Deutsch, London, 1968, p. 169.
5.   Monroe, *Philby of Arabia*.
6.   Lizy was a friend of Edith Tudor-Hart, née Suschitzky, an Austrian-British photographer and an ardent communist. Tudor-Hart introduced Philby to Arnold Deutsch, who would act as the first Soviet controller of the Cambridge spies. Philby in turn recommended that Deutsch approach seven potential agents, including Donald Maclean and Guy Burgess.
7.   According to his entry in the *Dictionary of National Biography*, Gedye, who helped Philby in Vienna, was 'the greatest British correspondent of the inter-war years'. Gedye was extremely prescient in his views about the reasons for the rise of the Nazis. The great mistake made by the Allies, in his view, was not to give more support to the moderate German Social Democratic government which came to power at the end of the First World War, after the Kaiser abdicated and German sailors and soldiers mutinied, creating revolutionary conditions in many parts of the country. By imposing harsh conditions in the Treaty of Versailles, supporting separatist movements in the Rhineland and taking advantage of their superior military power in the occupied areas to rule by force, rather than in strict accordance with the law, the Allies fatally weakened the moderate Social Democratic government, set the example of rule by force and paved the way for a revival of national-ism which was to lead to the Nazi seizure of power in 1933. According to Gedye, 'Fascism, Hitlerism, dreamers of revanche and of a new-born militarism – those are the plants which the Allies nurtured in German soil. Democracy, pacifism, international understanding – those are the plants, which springing up after the Revolution, found themselves faced with the withering lack of sympathy and encouragement from the victorious Allies, who had it in their power for several vital years to encourage their growth by moderation and understanding. All the world knows today that British and American statesmanship at Paris [during the negotiations which led to the Treaty of Versailles] tried to stand out for more reasonable treatment for Germany, but was out-manoeuvred by the implacable determination

of France to be revenged on her enemy and to push the disruption of the German State to the extreme limit. Month after month we watched the spontaneous efforts of the German people ... to secure and consolidate the ground which had been won for democracy being foiled by Allied severity and distrust.' (G. E. R. Gedye, *The Revolver Republic: France's Bid for the Rhine*, Arrowsmith, London, 1930.)

8.   Patrick Seale and Maureen McConville, *Philby: The Long Road to Moscow*, Hamish Hamilton, London, 1973.

9.   Founded in 1893, the largest and most prestigious British advertising agency pre-war, and famous for creating the 'Guinness is good for you' campaign. When Milne joined the company, the copywriting team was known as the 'Literary Department'. In 1971, Benson's, by then a publicly listed company, was acquired by Ogilvy & Mather, becoming Ogilvy, Benson & Mather in the UK. Within a decade the 'Benson' name had been quietly dropped.

Chapter 3: Change of Life (pages 41–56)

1.   At the time deputy director general of MI5, subsequently director general 1953–56 and chief of SIS 1956–68. Retired as chief in March 1968, some six months before Milne's retirement.

2.   A 1977 Granada TV drama-documentary.

3.   Frances ('Bunny') Doble was the divorced Canadian-born wife of Sir Anthony Lindsay-Hogg, an English baronet. As Lady Lindsay-Hogg she had achieved some fame on the London stage.

Chapter 4: Own Trumpet (pages 57–64)

1.   Phillip Knightley, Bruce Page and David Leitch, *Philby: The Spy Who Betrayed a Generation*, André Deutsch, London, 1968, p. 177.

Chapter 5: Section V (pages 65–91)

1.   A British physicist and scientific military intelligence expert attached to SIS during the war. In 1946, Jones was appointed to the Chair of Natural Philosophy at the University of Aberdeen, which he held until his retirement in 1981. He did not want to stay in intelligence under the proposed post-war reorganisation.

2.   Known as Operation Biting. One of the most daring raids of the war, it was carried out in February 1942 by units of the newly formed British 1st Airborne Division, who seized the German radar station at Bruneval in northern France, and brought back to England vital components of the German 'Würzburg' radar installation.

3.   See Patrick Seale and Maureen McConville, *Philby: The Long Road to Moscow*, Hamish Hamilton, London, 1973.

4. BJ stood for 'Blue Jacket', denoting the colour of the files in which they were circulated. They were the product of material produced by the Government Code and Cypher School (GC&CS), later GCHQ

Chapter 6: On the Map (pages 93–121)

1. Patrick Seale and Maureen McConville, *Philby: The Long Road to Moscow*, Hamish Hamilton, London, 1973, pp. 167–8.
2. Dick Brooman-White was MP for Rutherglen 1951–64 and Under-Secretary of State for Scotland 1960–63. He died in 1964.
3. Tomás Harris was an expert on El Greco and Goya, and settled in Spain soon after the war. A brilliant intuitive agent handler who ran GARBO (see note 4), he had a theory as to why elaborate deception operations against the Germans could work so well and why the British were never taken in by similar German attempts. From his point of view the Germans were culturally and institutionally handicapped when it came to deception, 'because they had closed their minds to the irrational'. Quoted from Stephen Talty, *Agent Garbo: The Brilliant, Eccentric Secret Agent Who Tricked Hitler and saved D-Day*, Houghton Mifflin Harcourt, New York, 2012.
4. Operation Garbo. Juan Pujol García, a Spaniard, was known by the British code-name GARBO and to the Germans as Agent ARABEL. He was one of the few people to receive decorations from both sides, an MBE from the British and an Iron Cross from the Germans. Initially from Lisbon and later from London, GARBO built a fictional network of agents feeding disinformation to the Germans and played a key role in the success of Operation Fortitude, the deception operation to mislead the Germans about the timing and location of the Normandy landings in 1944. For the full story of his life, Pujol's own account makes compelling reading: *Operation Garbo*, Dialogue, London, 2011.
5. Arthur George Trevor-Wilson was raised in France from an early age and pre war worked in Paris and north Africa in finance and trading, even at one time as an Abyssinian skunk exporter. He joined the British army at the outbreak of hostilities and served as a liaison officer with the British 2nd Division until his evacuation from Dunkirk. Because of his fluent French, Trevor-Wilson joined SOE and later transferred to SIS, specialising in north African affairs. Towards the end of the war and fresh from a posting in Algiers, he was dispatched to Hanoi, where he was to spend much of the next ten years. He formed a close friendship with Ho Chi Minh, whom he met on a weekly basis. Historians sifting back through the morass of reports generated by the many different intelligence agencies during this complex period in the history of Indochina have singled out Trevor-Wilson's reports as the most perceptive and

objective. A great friend of the novelist Graham Greene and a fellow Catholic, Trevor-Wilson was subsequently ordered out of Vietnam by General de Lattre de Tassigny (the overall commander of French forces in Indochina from 1950). Greene, in his autobiography, wrote, 'De Lattre reported to the Foreign Office that Trevor-Wilson, who had been decorated for his services to France during the Second World War, was no longer *persona grata*. Trevor was thrown out of Indo-China, and the Foreign Office lost a remarkable Consul and the French a great friend of their country.' De Lattre justified his decision by telling the head of the Sureté, 'All these English, they're too much! It isn't sufficient to have a Consul who's in the Secret Service; they even send me their novelists as agents, and Catholic novelists into the bargain.' After de Lattre left Vietnam, Trevor-Wilson returned, but this time under commercial cover as a leather goods distributor. He continued to do work for SIS, largely in Asia, until his retirement in the 1960s. Malcolm Muggeridge, a wartime colleague in Section V, described Trevor-Wilson as the ablest intelligence officer he had come across during the war. (Richard J. Aldrich, 'Britain's Secret Intelligence Service in Asia during the Second World War', *Modern Asian Studies* (1998), vol. 32, no. 1, pp. 179–227; Graham Greene, *Ways of Escape* p. 154, Bodley Head, London, 1980.) For a fuller account of Trevor-Wilson's time in Vietnam and the particular incident that earned de Lattre's displeasure, see Norman Sherry, *The Life of Graham Greene, Volume Two: 1939–1955*, Jonathan Cape, London, 1994, pp. 481–7.

6. Alan Williams, *Gentleman Traitor*, Blond & Briggs, London, 1975.

7. A rising star of the Foreign Office who died tragically in 1945.

8. An influential Zionist and long-time Philby family friend. In 1937 Kim had told her that he was doing 'dangerous work for the communists'. She subsequently introduced him to Aileen. In 1962, when Philby was the correspondent of *The Observer* in Beirut, Solomon objected to what she perceived to be the anti-Israeli tone of his articles and related the details of her earlier conversation with Philby to Victor Rothschild, who in turn introduced her to MI5. This was the first hard evidence MI5 had obtained on Philby and led to his interrogation in Beirut.

9. Henry Desmond Vernon Pakenham CBE. A schoolteacher before the war, he joined the Foreign Office in 1946, serving in Madrid, Djakarta, Havana, Singapore, Tel Aviv, Buenos Aires and Australia before his retirement in 1971.

10. The distinguished Russian author and playwright Genrikh Borovik was allowed to interview Philby at length in the years 1985–8 and after Philby's death was granted unprecedented access to KGB archives including the entire KGB case files on their master spy. In his subsequent book, Borovik

quotes Philby's Soviet controller's report to Moscow Centre on 10 March 1943, which read, 'Meetings with [KP] take place in London once every ten to twelve days, in the customary way, as with other agents. Sometimes, when the opportunity arises, he brings separate files to photograph (only when we ask him). In these instances we meet him in the morning and return the material in the evening. This, of course is inconvenient and incorrect according to operational procedures, but it's the only way to get the documentary files that [KP] can't copy, because they are too large. Earlier, as far as we know, he used to have a "Minox" but his photographs weren't very good, and at your instruction we took the camera from him.' (Genrikh Borovik, *The Philby Files: The Secret Life of Master Spy Kim Philby*, Little, Brown, Boston, 1994, p. 206.)

11. Eleanor Philby, *Kim Philby: The Spy I Loved*, Hamish Hamilton, London, 1968.

Chapter 7: Ryder Street and Broadway (pages 123–158)

1. A classical scholar and Greek papyrologist who later became director of Oxford University Press. He published *The Codex* in 1954, subsequently expanded into *The Birth of the Codex*, which examined the process by which the codex – the traditional form of the Western book – replaced the scroll as the primary vehicle for literature. (Colin H. Roberts and T. C. Skeat, *The Birth of the Codex*, Oxford University Press, 1983.)

2. A German commando and specialist in unconventional warfare. Apart from his successful mission to free Mussolini, Skorzeny was the leader of Operation Greif in late 1944, where German soldiers fluent in English and wearing Allied uniforms infiltrated American lines. At the end of the war he was involved in the *Werwolf* stay-behind guerrilla network as well as the Odessa line, which helped fugitive Nazis escape to South America and the Middle East.

3. WOOD was Fritz Kolbe, a German diplomat who became America's most important spy against the Nazis. In 1943 he became a diplomatic courier and on a visit to Berne, he offered secret documents to the British, who rebuffed his approach. He then went to the Americans, who realised that in Kolbe they had an agent of the highest quality. He was given the code-name GEORGE WOOD and Allen Dulles wrote of him, 'George Wood was not only our best source on Germany but undoubtedly one of the best secret agents any intelligence service has ever had.' (James Srodes, *Alan Dulles: Master of Spies*, Regnery, Washington DC, 1999.) After the war, Kolbe unsuccessfully applied to rejoin the German Foreign Office.

4. The first head of Germany's post-war domestic intelligence agency. In 1954, he sensationally disappeared to East Berlin and was subsequently

interrogated by the KGB in Moscow. Eighteen months later, he reappeared in West Berlin claiming he had been kidnapped by the Russians. He was tried for treason, found guilty and sentenced to four years' imprisonment.

5. Patrick Seale and Maureen McConville, *Philby: The Long Road to Moscow*, Hamish Hamilton, London, 1973.

6. The Foreign Office official assigned as PA to the chief of SIS from 1943 to 1945. In 1994 he contributed a scholarly article to the journal *Intelligence and National Security* entitled 'Five of Six at War: Section V of MI6' (vol. 9, no. 2, pp. 345–53). For this article, Cecil had corresponded at some length with Felix Cowgill. Cecil makes the point that ISOS and ISK were vital sources and Cowgill, very conscious of the 'need-to-know' principle, was determined to restrict its circulation. When Trevor-Roper defied the restriction, Cowgill recommended to the chief that he be sacked. Cowgill's wish to restrict circulation was neither arbitrary nor frivolous as another traitor, Anthony Blunt, then working in MI5, was one of the recipients of the ISOS and ISK material, but he went too far, restricting its availability to members of the Double Cross Committee in a way that hampered its operations. Regarding Philby, Cowgill commented that he 'was recruited at a time when MI5 records were still in chaos. An MI5 trace was therefore of little value and Vivian may be excused for relying on his own judgement.'

7. Phillip Knightley, Bruce Page and David Leitch, *Philby: The Spy Who Betrayed a Generation*, André Deutsch, London, 1968.

8. Thomas Argyll Robertson, always known as 'Tar'. After a short stint as a professional soldier, Robertson joined MI5 in 1933. During the war he ran one of the cleverest deception and disinformation operations, Operation Mincemeat, revealed for the first time in Ewen Montagu's book *The Man Who Never Was*, Evans Brothers, London, 1953. For an account of Robertson's remarkable life, see Geoffrey Elliott, *Gentleman Spymaster: How Lt Col. Tommy 'Tar' Robertson Double-crossed the Nazis*, Methuen, London, 2011.

9. James Malcolm Mackintosh CMG. He read Russian at Glasgow University and joined SOE in 1942, later parachuting behind German lines to join the British mission with Tito's Partisans. He subsequently transferred to Section V, where he was posted to Bulgaria (Sofia) and then to Berlin at the end of hostilities. Post war, Mackintosh achieved wide renown as an intelligence analyst, Sovietologist and adviser to successive Prime Ministers and Cabinets. Retired from the Cabinet Office in 1987.

10. Kim Philby, *My Silent War*, MacGibbon & Kee, London, 1968.

11. Milne's new job was as Staff Officer to the new Assistant Chief of the Secret Service, Jack Easton.

Chapter 8: Decline and Fall (pages 159–179)

1. A Scottish Labour politician and junior minister of state at the Foreign Office. Burgess was his private secretary before the Washington posting.
2. The British Expeditionary Force in France, evacuated from Dunkirk in 1940.
3. Officer of the Legion of Merit, an award for 'exceptionally meritorious conduct in the performance of outstanding services and achievement'. Only awarded to those in uniform.
4. The book, published by Macmillan in 1937, recounts the voyage Robert Byron undertook in the company of the author Christopher Sykes between August 1933 and July 1934 to the legendary Oxiana, the region surrounding the Amu River, whose flow effectively delineates the northern border of Afghanistan with Tajikistan and Uzbekistan. Their adventurous expedition took them across Palestine (Israel and Lebanon today), Syria, Iraq, Persia (Iran) and Afghanistan, to end in British-ruled Pakistan.
5. Tom Driberg (later Baron Bradwell of Bradwell) was a British journalist, politician and member of Parliament for twenty-eight years. An open communist for twenty years and a close friend of Guy Burgess, he was later to visit him in Moscow, after which he wrote the book *Guy Burgess: A Portrait with Background*, Weidenfeld & Nicholson, London, 1956.
6. Renamed Samara in 1991.
7. Although Philby arrived in Moscow in late January 1963, he did not get to meet Burgess before the latter's death on 30 August that year in a Moscow hospital. As Philby related to Phillip Knightley in Moscow in 1988, 'They kept us apart when I arrived, to avoid recriminations. I didn't get to see him before he died.' (Quoted in Phillip Knightley, *Philby: The Life and Views of the KGB Masterspy*, André Deutsch, London, 1988, p. 223.)
8. An intelligence officer with an exceptional knowledge of Iran, and a noted linguist and scholar. He was elected Spalding Professor of Eastern Religions and Ethics at Oxford University and a fellow of All Souls.

Chapter 9: Over and Out (pages 181–195)

1. Constance Ashley-Jones, later Stobo.
2. He was also the correspondent for *The Economist*; his employment with *The Observer* was arranged by SIS, who had taken him back on their payroll as an agent.
3. The investigator was Nicholas Elliott, who was a friend of Philby's and had directly arranged his appointment as Middle East correspondent of *The Observer* in 1956 with Lord Astor, the proprietor, after Philby's clearance by Harold Macmillan. Station chief in Beirut from 1960 to

1962, Elliott's selection (by Sir Dick White) as the person chosen by SIS to confront Philby was to cause controversy within his own service as well as within MI5 where the 'molehunters' had long been convinced of Philby's guilt and now wanted to carry out an aggressive and professional interrogation. Flora Solomon's statement and those of the KGB officer Anatoli Golitsyn, who defected to the Americans in 1961 and provided the first confirmation of a 'Ring of Five' spy ring all recruited from Cambridge University in the early 1930s, were the final pieces of evidence needed to confront Philby, who was to be offered immunity against prosecution in return for a full confession. SIS, however, wanted to keep the interrogation an in-house affair and White felt that Elliott as a friend and previous defender of Philby could appeal to the latter's 'sense of decency'. Elliott, at the time in charge of SIS operations in Africa, arrived in Beirut and rather bungled the confrontation by managing to leave open the windows of the apartment where the taped interrogation took place. As a result, traffic noise drowned out a good part of the audio recording and only about 80 per cent was able to be successfully transcribed by MI5. Elliott was considered somewhat 'accident prone' by a number of his colleagues: in 1956 as the then head of the SIS London station, he had personally approved the choice of the unfortunate frogman Lionel 'Buster' Crabb to carry out a risky operation in Portsmouth Harbour to inspect the hull of the Russian cruiser *Ordzhonikidze*, which had brought Nikita Khrushchev and Nikolai Bulganin to Britain on a visit to improve Anglo-Soviet relations. Crabb, who smoked sixty cigarettes a day, had a drink problem, suffered from depression and had been to a party the night before the operation, was clearly not in the greatest of shape for such a delicate mission. Unsurprisingly, he never returned from it and his headless body was found washed up on a nearby beach some fourteen months later (according to recent accounts, Crabb had his throat cut by a Russian frogman from the cruiser who was sent down to investigate the flow of air bubbles that were surfacing). The net result was a major diplomatic incident and the dismissal of Sir John Sinclair, the chief of SIS (who was replaced by White), as well as the demotion of the Foreign Office adviser to the service. Elliott, however, managed to keep his job. Part of the *ancien régime* and a 'robber baron', one of a small number of senior SIS officers who were regarded as having virtual carte blanche to do what they wanted on behalf of their country, Elliott had joined SIS before the war. (Peter Wright, *Spycatcher: The Candid Autobiography of a Senior Intelligence Officer*, Viking , New York, 1987, pp. 72–5, 194; Gordon Corera, *MI6: Life and Death in the British Secret Service*, Phoenix, London, p. 77.)

Chapter 10: 'The KGB Officer' (pages 197–221)

1. The author was correct in his assumption that Philby was run purely as an
    agent by the KGB, a fact that was to cause Philby himself much distress
    after his arrival in Moscow in 1963 when he discovered this fact. Indeed,
    following the initial lengthy debriefing he was then effectively retired with
    a pension, a situation that continued until the early 1970s when he was
    partly rehabilitated by the KGB and used as a consultant. The first seven
    or eight years after his flight to Moscow were, from later published Russian
    accounts, extremely unhappy ones for him. Largely abandoned by the
    KGB, Philby's life at this time consisted of drinking binges and even a
    failed attempt at suicide in the late 1960s, such was his despair. Indeed his
    one and only visit to KGB headquarters came many years later. However,
    there was a strong belief in Western intelligence circles that Philby,
    in the ten year period 1963–73, was masterminding all offensive KGB
    operations against the West. This was the position of James Angleton, the
    legendary and powerful head of counter-intelligence for the CIA for two
    decades, who had been completely hoodwinked by Philby in Washington.
    Angleton developed paranoid tendencies in his search for 'moles' within
    the CIA and other friendly intelligence services, notably MI5. Offensive
    CIA operations against the Soviets in the decade after Philby's defection
    largely ground to a halt as Angleton and his disciples on both sides of the
    Atlantic were of the belief that all Soviet bloc defectors during this period
    were dispatched to peddle disinformation. Angleton's theories were later
    ridiculed and he was fired by the CIA in late 1974.

    For a detailed account of Angleton's career and stewardship of CIA
    counterintelligence see Tom Mangold, *Cold Warrior: James Jesus Angleton –
    the CIA's Master Spy Hunter*, London, Simon & Schuster, 1991.
2. Gordon Brook-Shepherd, *The Storm Petrels: The First Soviet Defectors, 1928–
    1938*, Collins, London, 1977.
3. Elizabeth Monroe, *Philby of Arabia*, Faber, London, 1973.
4. Alfred Dillwyn Knox CMG. Knox was a leading codebreaker during
    both world wars and throughout the inter-war period, breaking a
    number of important codes and ciphers, including the cipher used in the
    Zimmerman telegram, the exposure of which brought the US into
    the First World War. He was the leading codebreaker working on the
    Enigma cipher, breaking a number of different variants, including those
    used by Spain and Italy during the Spanish Civil War, and leading the
    initial breaks into the German armed forces Enigma ciphers at Bletchley
    Park. Knox broke the *Abwehr* Enigma, probably the most complex Enigma
    cipher broken by the Allies, to produce the ISK material, without which

the Double Cross deception, which ensured the safety of the D-Day landings, could not have taken place.

5. The author is referring to Operation Gold, the code-name for the Berlin Tunnel, which involved tapping the telephone cables in East Berlin. 'Gold' was a joint SIS–CIA operation and betrayed from the start by George Blake, who was stationed in Berlin at the time and was secretary to the joint planning committee and thus keeping the minutes.

6. Judith Coplon was allegedly recruited by the KGB in 1944 when she was working at the US Department of Justice. Arrested in 1949, she was convicted in two separate trials with both verdicts being overturned on appeal, not because of insufficient evidence but largely because the FBI had engaged in wiretapping and had bugged her telephone without having a warrant to do so. The Justice Department finally dropped the charges against her in 1967.

7. Ewen Montagu, *The Man Who Never Was*, Evans Brothers, London, 1953.

8. John le Carré, *The Spy Who Came In from the Cold*, Victor Gollancz, London, 1963.

Chapter 11: The Elite Force (pages 223–238)

1. The one-time pad cipher systems used by the KGB had been duplicated, defeating the purpose of the one-time pad, which, as the name suggests, should be used only once to encipher a message. When used properly, a one-time pad system cannot be deciphered. The duplication allowed US and British codebreakers to decipher KGB messages which indicated that the KGB had an agent in Washington code-named HOMER who had access to the secret messages between US President Harry S. Truman and British Prime Minister Winston Churchill. One message revealed that HOMER was able to visit his KGB contact in New York because his American-born wife was pregnant and staying with her mother in the city. That message confirmed the growing US and British suspicions that the KGB agent HOMER was Donald Maclean.

2. This is particularly true since Burgess knew both of the two other members of the Cambridge Spy Ring, Anthony Blunt and John Cairncross, and both fell under suspicion as a direct result of his defection.

Chapter 12: Retrospect (pages 239–247)

1. Kim Philby, *My Silent War*, MacGibbon & Kee, London, 1968, pp. 15–16.

2. Graham Greene, Foreword, in Philby, *My Silent War*.

3. Eleanor Philby, *Kim Philby: The Spy I Loved*, Hamish Hamilton, London, 1968.

4. Hugh Trevor-Roper, *The Philby Affair: Espionage, Treason, and Secret Services*, William Kimber, London, 1968.

Epilogue (pages 249–251)
1. Nigel West, *The Friends: Britain's Post-war Secret Intelligence Operations*, Weidenfeld & Nicolson, London, 1987, p. 145.
2. Milne was appointed a CMG on 12 June 1965.
3. Milne was controller for all SIS operations in the Middle East at the time of his visit to Washington.
4. The six overseas postings in order of service were Egypt (Ismailiya), Iran (Tehran), West Germany (Cologne), Switzerland (Berne), Japan (Tokyo) and finally Hong Kong. In the last three posts, Milne was head of station.

Appendices (pages 253–266)
1. Sir William Strang, Permanent Under-Secretary of State at the Foreign Office 1949–53.
2. Sir Percy Sillitoe, Director General of the Security Service (MI5) 1946–53.
3. In fact, Major-General Sir John Sinclair did not become Chief of the SIS, or 'C', until 1953. At this stage, and at the time of the reference in paragraph 5 of this document to 17 January 1952, the Chief of the SIS was Sir Stewart Menzies, who served as 'C' from 1939 to 1953.
4. Sir Patrick Dean, chairman of the Joint Intelligence Committee 1953–60.
5. Sir Ivone Kirkpatrick, Permanent Under-Secretary at the Foreign Office 1953–57.
6. Klaus Fuchs, German scientist who worked on the Manhattan Project, the Anglo-US nuclear weapons programme, and betrayed its secrets to the Russians.
7. David Greenglass and Julius and Ethel Rosenberg were American communists who worked on the Manhattan Project and were among the Soviet 'atom spies'; Harry Gold, another American communist, was a courier for the 'atom spies'. The Rosenbergs were the only 'atom spies' to be executed, even though in Ethel's case there was no evidence that she had done anything more than support her husband. Their execution while others served only relatively short prison sentences or went free altogether remains highly controversial.

INDEX

Abwehr 70, 72, 73, 74, 75, 77, 79–80,
  89, 100, 108–10, 111–12, 114, 128,
  129, 133
Albania
  Kim Philby and Tim Milne in
  24–7, 29–30
Anglo-German Fellowship 41, 42,
  201
Arabia of the Wahhabis (Philby) 10
Arnold-Forster, Christopher 137
Axel (TM's dog) 106
Azores 114–15

Bankhead, Tallulah 7
Barsley, Michael 61
Beck, Ludwig 130
Birch, Frank 204
Bishop, Adrian 23, 24
Blake, George 217–18
Bletchley Park 113–14
Blunt, Anthony 250, 255
Bodden operation 79–81
Bowra, Maurice 23–4, 33
Brackenbury, Buz 47–8
Brewer, Eleanor (KP's third wife)
  191, 192, 193–4, 244

Brewer, Sam 106
Brook-Shepherd, Gordon 199
Brooman-White, Dick 99, 105, 136,
  146–7, 167, 168, 183, 204, 247
Budapest
  Kim Philby and Tim Milne
  travel to 13–18
Burgess, Guy 203, 213
  Tim Milne meets 33, 44, 55
  at The Spinney 106
  visits Kim Philby in Turkey
  171–2, 173–4
  concerns over behaviour 174–5
  disappearance of 175–6, 177–8,
  184, 230, 232–4
  Kim Philby talks about 185–6
  loses usefulness to Soviet Union
  216–17
  recruitment of 224
  and Donald Maclean 226, 228,
  231–2
  contact with Soviet Union 229–30
  relationship with Kim Philby 247

Cairncross, John 255
Canaris, Admiral 129

Cecil, Robert 140
Christ Church, Oxford
Tim Milne at 18–19, 60
Churchill, Winston 119, 208
CICERO 127
Collins, Douglas 183
Collins, Patsy 183
Coplon, Judith 212
Cowgill, Felix 54, 65, 72, 80, 93–9, 100–102, 110–111, 120, 124, 125, 128, 138, 138, 139–40, 141, 157
Cowgill, Mary 101

Dansey, Claude 96
Dawson, Geoffrey 49
Doble, Frances 49
Dollfuss, Chancellor 37, 39
Driberg, Tom 174
Dulles, Allen 127–8, 208

Eden, Anthony 174
Egypt
Tim Milne posted to 166–7, 169
Elliott, Nicholas 249, 254, 25
Engleheart, Jock 7–8

FELIPE 78–9, 166
Franco, General 81, 82, 83
Friedmann, Lizy (KP's first wife) 38, 43–6, 50–51, 117–18, 164
Furse, Aileen (KP's second wife) 53, 54, 67–9, 87–9, 103, 105, 121, 163, 164, 165–6, 170–171, 187, 188, 191, 213

Gaynor, Janet 7
Gedye, Eric 39, 40
Gentleman Traitor (Philby) 104

Germany
Kim Philby and Tim Milne holiday in 21–2, 34–7
Section V works on 128–34
Kim Philby and Tim Milne at end of war 150–155
Gisevius, Hans Bernd 130
Goerdeler, Carl Friedrich 130
Gort, General 61
Greene, Graham 123–4, 138–9, 243
Greenhill, Denis 186
Guzenko, Igor 159–60

Hackett, John 163–4
Hammond, Wally 7
Hardy, Harold 19
Harris, Hilda 54, 183, 188
Harris, Tommy 54, 99–100, 183, 188, 204, 247
Haw-Haw, Lord 73
Healey, Denis 142
Hitler, Adolf
heard by Kim Philby and Tim Milne 21
becomes Chancellor 34
assassination attempt on 132
Hoover, J. Edgar 140
Hugenberg, Alfred 21

Iran
Tim Milne posted to 176, 177–8
ISOS messages 73–9, 81–2, 89, 90–91, 97–8, 107–8, 114, 125, 147
Italy
Kim Philby and Tim Milne in 22–3
Section V work on 125–6
Ivens, Jack 148, 182, 183

Japan
  Section V work on 149–50
John, Otto 130
Jones, R. V. 80, 94

Knox, Dilly 204
Koestler, Arthur 153
Krivitsky, Walter 159, 199, 230, 235–6
Kunz, Charlie 73

Lipton, Marcus 190
Lonsdale, Gordon 201
Loxley, Peter 104–5
Luce, Kenneth 4
Lunan, Gordon 160
Lyall, Archibald 24

Mackenzie, Bobby 184
Maclean, Donald 184–5, 216, 224–9, 230–3, 234, 243
Maclean, Melinda 244
Macmillan, Harold 174, 190, 253, 254–5
McNeil, Hector 163, 174
May, Alan Nunn 236
Menzies, Sir Stewart 144–5, 253–4
MI5
  and Section V 72–3, 98
  and double-agent operations 107–8
  and War Room 145–6
  investigates Kim Philby 183–4
Midgley, John 33, 36
Milmo, Helenus 181–2, 234, 253, 254
Milne, A. A. (TM's uncle) 13, 58
Milne, Angela (TM's sister) 42, 64, 113–14

Milne, J. V. (TM's grandfather) 2
Milne, Janet (TM's sister) 64
Milne, Marie (TM's wife) 46, 53, 55, 64, 125, 148, 165, 166, 170, 189, 190
Milne, Tim
  press interest in viii
  death of viii
  at Westminster School 1–2, 7, 10–11, 58–60
  first trip to Continent with Kim Philby 13–18
  at Christ Church, Oxford 18–19, 60
  second trip to Continent with Kim Philby 20–33
  witnesses rise of Nazis 21–2
  trip to Germany with Kim Philby 34–7
  travels to Vienna to see Kim Philby 38–40
  works for S. H. Benson 40, 60–61
  joins SIS 46
  travels to Spain to see Kim Philby 46–7
  works for Section V 54–6, 64, 73–81, 110–111, 117, 123–5, 128, 130–132, 135, 137–8, 143–9, 150–155
  early childhood 57–8
  at start of Second World War 61
  political views of 62–3
  visit to Bletchley Park 113
  move to London 121
  made head of Section V 138
  fails to report Kim Philby's communist views 142–3

Milne, Tim *cont.*
  in Germany for Section V
    150–155
  posted to Egypt 166–7
  visits Turkey 166–8, 172–4,
    175–6
  posted to Iran 176, 177–8
  last meeting with Kim Philby
    193–5
  named by Kim Philby as 'fellow
    conspirator' 249–51
Milne, Tony (TM's brother) 64
Monroe, Elizabeth 19, 37, 200
Montague, Evelyn 163
Muggeridge, Malcolm 124, 147,
  165
Murder Must Advertise (Sayers) 60
Musaddiq, Mohammed 178
Mussolini, Benito 125, 126
My Silent War (Philby) 183, 197, 242

'ORKI companions' incident
  89–91
Orlov, Alexander 199–200, 235
OSS/X2 95–6, 127, 135–6, 145–6,
  147–8

Page, Denys 98, 113
Pakenham, Desmond 114, 125, 130
Palmer, Leonard 98, 113
Papen, Franz von 127
PASCAL 78
Paterson, Geoffrey 184
Pearson, Norman 147–9
Petrov, Vladimir 190
Philby, Burgess and Maclean (TV film)
  46
Philby, Diana (KP's sister) 18, 51

Philby, Dora (KP's mother) 17–18,
  19, 38, 40, 51, 121, 163, 244
Philby, Harry (KP's son) 189
Philby, Helena (KP's sister) 18,
  51–2, 106–7
Philby, Josephine (KP's daughter)
  54–5, 68, 191
Philby, Kim
  Sunday Times reports on viii, xv,
    42, 57
  at Westminster School 1–2, 3–11
  sexuality of 5, 6, 21
  relationship with father 9–10,
    19–20, 239–40
  at Trinity College, Cambridge
    13, 33–4
  first trip to Continent with Tim
    Milne 13–18
  political views of 18, 22, 33–4,
    35–6, 42–3, 240–242
  trip to Yugoslavia 20
  second trip to Continent with
    Tim Milne 20–33
  witnesses rise of Nazis 21–2
  trip to Germany with Tim
    Milne 34–7
  moves to Vienna 37–9, 223
  marriage to Lizy Friedmann 38,
    43–5, 50–51
  works for *Review of Reviews* 40,
    200–201
  fakes sympathy for Nazism
    41–2, 43, 223–4
  as journalist in Spain 45–50,
    202
  first approached by SIS 50
  work during Second World War
    52–5

Philby, Kim *cont.*

political influence on Tim
Milne 62–3

works for Section V 66–7, 69–70,
76, 77, 81, 82, 84, 87–8, 94, 96,
104–5, 108, 110, 114, 116–18, 124,
125, 127–8, 130–131, 132–3, 135

relationship with Aileen Furse
67–9, 105, 164

home life 88–9, 1056, 163–4

and 'ORKI companions' incident 89–91

personality of 116–20, 243–7

move to London 121

works for Section IX 137–8,
139–41, 150–155

communist views not reported
142–3

in Germany for Section IX
150–155

and Konstantin Volkov 160–162

drinking habits 162–3

posted to Turkey 164–5, 167–8

marriage to Aileen Furse 165–6,
187, 188

visits Egypt 169–70

suspicions over 178–9, 183–5,
190–191

talks about Guy Burgess 185–6

affair with Connie 187, 188,
189–90

work as freelance journalist
187–8, 191, 192

relationship with Eleanor
Brewer 191, 192

marriage to Eleanor Brewer 193

last meeting with Tim Milne
193–5

defects to Soviet Union 195

starts as spy for NKVD 197,
199

access to Section V information
205–9

access to Section IX information 209–10

limitations on as spy 210–215

usefulness of to Soviet Union
216–21

and Donald Maclean 224–9

propaganda value of 236–7

reasons for becoming a Soviet
agent 242–3

relationship with Guy Burgess 247

names Tim Milne as 'fellow
conspirator' 249–51

Philby, Miranda (KP's daughter)
189

Philby, Patricia (KP's sister) 18, 51

Philby, St John (KP's father) 2,
6, 9–10, 17, 19–20, 51, 58, 200,
239–40

Philby, Tommy (KP's son) 100, 163,
192, 213

Philby of Arabia (Monroe) 19

Radio Security Service (RSS) 100

Reilly, Patrick 82, 140

Review of Reviews 40, 200–201

Roberts, Colin 125–6, 146

Robertson, 'Tar' 146

Rothschild, Victor 106

Ryle, Gilbert 101

S. H. Benson (advertising agency)
40

Sammy (dog at Section 5) 103–4

Sandham, Andrew 7

Sandys, Duncan 136, 146

Sayers, Dorothy L. 60

SD 70–71, 73, 77, 100, 127, 128,
129–30, 131, 133

Seale, Patrick 40, 86, 98, 216–17,
220, 230

Section V
   Tim Milne works for 54–6, 64,
   73–81, 110–111, 117, 123–5, 128,
   130–132, 135, 137–8, 143–9,
   150–155
   description of 65–7, 71–2
   Kim Philby works for 66–7,
   69–70, 76, 77, 81, 82, 84, 87–8,
   94, 96, 104–5, 108, 110, 114,
   116–18, 124, 125, 127–8, 130–131,
   132–3, 135
   and MI5 72–3, 98
   and ISOS messages 73–9, 81–2,
   89, 90–91, 97–8, 107–8, 114
   under Felix Cowgill 93–102
   links to OSS/X2 95–6, 135–6,
   147–8
   and German sabotage attempts
   109–11
   work on Azores 114–15
   moves to London 120–121
   work on Italy 125–6
   work on Germany 128–34
   and V-weapons 136
   Tim Milne made head of 138
   and War Room 145–6
   work on Japan 149–50
   at end of Second World War 156
   appraisal of 156–8
   information on given to Soviet
      Union 205–9

Section IX
   Kim Philby works for 137–8,
   139–41, 150–155
   kept secret from OSS 148–9
   information on given to Soviet
   Union 209–10

Sharp, Noel 130, 131–2

Shortt, Peter 61

Sinclair, John 155–6, 254

SIS see also Section V and Section
   IX
   Tim Milne joins 46
   first approaches Kim Philby 50
   officer sent to Soviet Union 135
   at end of Second World War
   155–6
   and Konstantin Volkov 160–161
   possibility of Kim Philby as
   chief of 216
   tries to establish Kim Philby's
   innocence 253–5

Skorzeny, Otto 126

Smith-Cumming, Captain 173

SOE
   Kim Philby works for 53
   Marie Milne works for 64

Solomon, Flora 105

Spain
   Kim Philby as journalist in
   45–50, 202
   Tim Milne travels to 46–7
   demarches sent to 81–3

Stewart, Michael 14, 16, 17, 33

Storm Petrels, The (Brook-Shepherd)
   199

Stuart, Charles 101

Sunday Times viii, xv, 42, 57, 220,
   233, 251

Szegedi-Szűts, György 16
Szegedi-Szűts, István 16

Thomas, Bertram 19
Times, The
    Kim Philby works for 45, 46, 49, 52
Travis, Commander 113
Trevor-Roper, Hugh 100–101, 113, 133, 199, 215, 243, 245–6
Trevor-Wilson, A. G. 102–3, 147
Trinity College, Cambridge
    Kim Philby at 13, 33–4
Trott, Adam von 130
Tucker, Nannie 68, 163, 170, 172
Turkey
    Kim Philby posted to 164–5, 167–8
    Tim Milne visits 166–8, 172–4, 175–6
Twenty-Five European Languages (Lyell) 24

Ustinov, Klop 132

V-weapons 136
Vienna
    Kim Philby moves to 37–9, 223
Vivian, Valentine 137, 140
Volkov, Konstantin 160–162, 184, 224

War Room 145–6
Webster, Tom 113
Wesley, John 59
Westminster School
    Kim Philby at 1–2, 3–11
    Tim Milne at 1–2, 7, 10–11, 58–60
    description of 2–3

White, Dick 98, 225, 254
Wilson, Harold 255
Winnifrith, John 9
Wolff, General 208
WOOD 127
Wyllie, Tom 44

Yogi and the Commissar, The (Koestler) 153
Yugoslavia
    Kim Philby in 20
    Kim Philby and Tim Milne in 23–4, 27–32

Zaehner, Robin 178